T0385601

The Canterbury and York Society

GENERAL EDITOR: PROFESSOR R.L. STOREY

ISSN 0262-995X

DIOCESE OF CARLISLE

CANTERBURY AND YORK SOCIETY VOL. LXXXVIII

The Register of

Gilbert Welton

BISHOP OF CARLISLE

1353-1362

EDITED BY

R.L. STOREY

PROFESSOR EMERITUS
UNIVERSITY OF NOTTINGHAM

The Canterbury and York Society

The Boydell Press
1999

First published 1999
A Canterbury and York Society publication
published by The Boydell Press
an imprint of Boydell & Brewer Ltd
PO Box 9, Woodbridge, Suffolk IP12 3DF, UK
and of Boydell & Brewer Inc.
PO Box 41026, Rochester, NY 14604–4126, USA
website: http://www.boydell.co.uk

ISBN 0 907239 59 5

A catalogue record for this book is available
from the British Library

Details of previous volumes available from Boydell & Brewer Ltd

This publication is printed on acid-free paper

Printed in Great Britain by
St Edmundsbury Press Ltd, Bury St Edmunds, Suffolk

CONTENTS

ACKNOWLEDGMENTS

The Right Reverend Ian Harland, Lord Bishop of Carlisle, has kindly consented to the publication of transcripts of texts in the second volume of the Carlisle Episcopal Registers preserved in the Cumbria Record Office, Carlisle Castle.

I also wish to record my warm appreciation of the staff of the Record Office for their tireless and cheerful assistance in my numerous visits to their search-rooms in Carlisle Castle. Dr Dorothy Owen voluntarily undertook (at a meeting of the Society's Council) the role of general editor in the production of this volume; she inspected — and corrected — both its final draft and its proofs, and we are indebted to her expert care in the discharge of this office. Finally I would like to record my deep obligation to my wife for her unfailing support and advice.

R.L.S.

BIBLIOGRAPHICAL ABBREVIATIONS

Accounts, ed. Lunt	W.E. Lunt, *Accounts rendered by papal collectors in England 1317–1378*, ed. E.B. Graves (Philadelphia, 1968).
BRUO	A.B. Emden, *A Biographical Register of the University of Oxford to A.D. 1500* (Oxford, 1957–9).
CCR	*Calendar of Close Rolls* (HM Stationery Office, 1900–63).
CFR	*Calendar of Fine Rolls* (HMSO, 1911–63).
CIPM	*Calendar of Inquisitions Post Mortem* (HMSO, 1904–).
Complete Peerage	G.E.C., *Complete Peerage of England, Scotland, Ireland, Great Britain and United Kingdom* (1910–59).
Concilia	*Concilia Magnae Britanniae et Hiberniae, A.D. 446–1718*, ed. D. Wilkins (1737).
CPL	*Calendar of Papal Letters* (HMSO, 1894–1960)
CPP	*Calendar of Papal Petitions* (HMSO, 1894).
CPR	*Calendar of Patent Rolls* (HMSO, 1901–).
CWAAS	*Transactions of the Cumberland & Westmorland Antiquarian & Archaeological Society.*
CWAAS	Other publications of the above society.
CYS	Publications of the Canterbury and York Society.
EPNS	*Publications of the English Place-Name Society.*
Fasti	J. Le Neve, *Fasti Ecclesiae Anglicanae 1300–1541* (1962–7).
Foedera	*Foedera, Conventiones, Litterae, etc.*, or *Rymer's Foedera, 1066–1383* (Record Commission,1816–69).
HBC	*Handbook of British Chronology*, 3rd edition, ed. E.B. Fryde, D.E. Greenway, S. Porter and I. Roy (Royal Historical Society, 1986).
Lunt, *Financial Relations*	W.E. Lunt, *Financial Relations of the Papacy with England, 1327–1534* (Cambridge, Mass., 1962).
Nicolson & Burn	J. Nicolson and R. Burn, *The History and Antiquities of the Counties of Westmorland and Cumberland* (1777; reprinted 1976).
PRO	Public Record Office.
Reg. Appleby	Cumbria County Record Office, Carlisle Castle: Register of Thomas Appleby, Bishop of Carlisle (1363–95), DRC/1/2, pp.141–367.
Reg. Halton	*The Register of John de Halton, Bishop of Carlisle*, ed. W.N. Thompson (CYS, 1906–13).
Reg. Kirkby	*The Register of John Kirkby, Bishop of Carlisle*, ed. R.L. Storey (CYS, 1993–5).
Rot. Scot.	*Rotuli Scotiae* (Record Commission, 1814–19).
Summerson	H. Summerson, *Medieval Carlisle* (CWAAS extra ser. 25, 1993).
Test. Karl.	*Testamenta Karleolensia*, ed. R.S. Ferguson (CWAAS extra ser. 9, 1893).
VCH	*Victoria County History.*

INTRODUCTION

The Augustinian canons of Carlisle elected their prior, John Horncastle, as bishop in succession to John Kirkby. He had died outside the diocese and unexpectedly, because he had not made a will, probably at least a week before 3 December 1352, the date of Edward III's licence for the election.[1] It was probably held after Christmas. The king gave his consent to the chapter's choice on 10 January 1353. Approval by the archbishop of York followed, not surprisingly because John Thoresby was the king's chancellor, and on 22 February escheators were ordered to put Horncastle into possession of the see's temporalities.[2]

In this period, it was becoming increasingly rare for English bishoprics to be held by monks elected by their cathedral chapters; the most common exceptions were the smaller, least wealthy sees where the king had no strong interest to impose clerks with a record of reliable service in his government.[3] The meagre, war-torn bishopric of Carlisle made it an unattractive proposition for ambitious 'king's clerks', although its strategic situation in the west march towards Scotland gave cause for some consideration of the role its occupant might have to take in its defence. It was no doubt for this reason that an eminent civil administrator and diplomat, William Airmyn, then keeper of the privy seal, had been elected and promptly confirmed and installed as bishop early in 1325; it is unlikely that so obviously a royal candidate, without local connections, was the free, undirected choice of Carlisle's chapter, in a time known as 'the tyranny of Edward II'.[4] Simultaneously, however, on 13 February 1325, Pope John XXII had conferred the bishopric on John Ross, who was consecrated bishop at Avignon eleven days later. The pope claimed that he had reserved the appointment before Airmyn's election, which he declared to be void; Airmyn consequently resigned. The king had not disputed the papal provision of Ross, apparently because he was anxious to have the pope's good offices in negotiations to end the French occupation of Gascony. Bishop Ross was duly accepted and enthroned.[5] After his death in 1332, the chapter elected Prior Kirkby and Edward III accepted him in remarkable haste. Kirkby petitioned the pope for his confirmation, which was eventually given in December 1333, at the king's request and after Kirkby had incurred expenses at the papal court for which he obtained a loan of £200 from Archbishop Melton.[6]

[1] **525*** (references to entries in the following calendar are shown by their numbers in bold type; the asterisk indicates that there is also a full transcript of this text in the Appendix); *CPR 1350–4*, 366.
[2] Ibid. 408–9; *Fasti*, VI.98. He had been ordained priest 1333 (*Reg. Kirkby*, I.18).
[3] W.A. Pantin, *The English Church in the Fourteenth Century* (Cambridge, 1955), 11–19.
[4] *Fasti*, VI.97; *HBC*, 93; *The Register of William Melton, Archbishop of York* (CYS, 1977–), vol. I, ed. R.M.T. Hill, 81–5.
[5] *CPL*, II.242; *Reg. Melton*, I.85 (no.264); *Fasti*, VI.97.
[6] *Fasti*, VI.97; *Reg. Melton*, I.94–5; *CPL*, II.403; *Reg. Kirkby*, I.32 (nos.181–3).

King Edward's acceptance of Prior Horncastle's election in 1352 may well have been prompted by his appreciation of the services rendered by Bishop Kirkby. Despite his episcopal and monastic orders, the bishop proved himself a brave and enterprising cavalry captain, not only in defence of the border but sometimes well into Scotland. In 1335, he was retained with 40 men-at-arms in Edward's campaign in central Scotland, where he hoped to recover lands granted to Bishop Halton by Edward I.[7] He won the king's commendation for gallantry by relieving the English garrison of Edinburgh castle in 1337, and in 1339 was engaged in an expedition to relieve Perth castle.[8] He was keeper of Carlisle castle from 1339 until he was dismissed in 1345, after his unruly garrison had rioted in the city.[9] In 1346, he was at the battle of Neville's Cross, outside Durham city. As a consequence of the capture there of King David of Scotland, and of Anglo-French truces until 1355, this was presumably Bishop Kirkby's last military engagement: in most of the years between 1335 and 1346, he had been retained for war-service with his followers on wages from the Exchequer; his own rate of pay was 13s.4d. a day.[10] King Edward's continuing confidence in Kirkby was shown in 1348, when he was appointed to escort the king's teenage daughter Joan to Spain.[11]

John Horncastle's tenure of the see of Carlisle was brief (1–5); he continued as prior, until 1376.[12] On 13 February 1353, Pope Innocent VI appointed Gilbert Welton bishop, on the grounds that the previous pope had reserved the see of Carlisle for papal collation.[13] It was now the usual policy of popes when providing their own nominees to English bishoprics to select English clerics expected to be acceptable to the king, sometimes on the basis of the popes' personal knowledge. Thus John Ross, the bishop provided to Carlisle in 1325, was a doctor of civil law who had served cardinals, resided at the papal court, and been an auditor of causes there since 1317.[14] Welton was also an Oxford doctor of civil law, by 1334; it is thus likely that he was born early in the fourteenth century. He had made his career in the service of English bishops, apparently first at Norwich with Bishop Anthony Bek and next at Lincoln with Anthony's brother Thomas; he had received benefices from them in 1333 and 1339 respectively, and was described as a member of the Lincoln household in 1342.[15] In 1343 he exchanged the church of Wistow, in Lincoln diocese, for the prebend of Eaton in Southwell collegiate church and the rectory of Clayworth, both in Nottinghamshire and the diocese of York. He was the chancellor of Archbishop Zouche from 1345, that is the leading members of the archbishop's ecclesiastical household, and was appointed an executor of Zouche's will in

[7] Summerson, I.265; *Reg. Kirkby*, I.41 (no.244).

[8] Ibid., 80, 96 (no.504n.).

[9] Ibid., 83–4, 167 (no.810n.); Summerson, I.275–7.

[10] See also *Dictionary of National Biography* (repr. 1921–2), XI.206–7; *Reg. Kirkby*, I.68 (no.354n.), 78 (no.413), 79 (no.419), 111 (no.550n.), 126–7, 140 (no.690), 158 (no.756).

[11] *Foedera*, III(1).176; *CCR 1346–9*, 570.

[12] *Fasti*, VI.100.

[13] *CPL*, III.482.

[14] *BRUO*, III.1590–1.

[15] *BRUO*, III.2012–13; *CPP*, I.4.

1349; later that year he was promoted to the foremost judicial office of the northern province, that of official of the court of York.[16]

When John Thoresby succeeded as archbishop in 1352, he sent Welton to Avignon to receive his *pallium* from the pope. Although papal letters announcing its grant were dated 5 November, the pall had not been delivered to Welton before Pope Clement VI died on 6 December. Welton had to wait until the next pope, Innocent VI, sent Thoresby letters dated 4 January 1353 stating that Welton would be bringing his pall.[17] He had thus been at the Curia for two months, time enough, seemingly, to become regarded as a suitable candidate for provision to a bishopric; he would have carried letters of credence from the archbishop which would doubtless have commended his distinguished service at York. It is uncertain whether the news of John Kirkby's death had reached Avignon before Welton's departure.[18] The bull for his provision, dated 13 February, must have arrived in England before 5 April, the date of John Horncastle's last recorded act as bishop-elect (5): by then Welton would have been making his second journey to Avignon for his consecration there as bishop of Carlisle on 21 April (15). It may be presumed that he went with the king's approval.[19] It was not the first time Edward had reneged on his consent to a monastic election of a bishop. In the earlier case, the chapter's choice had been put aside in favour of John Thoresby, who now as archbishop of York was disowning his ratification of Horncastle's election.[20] While Thoresby was clearly the king's protégé, however, this cannot be said of Welton.[21] He had risen in entirely ecclesiastical quarters. He was the pope's nominee, and Edward had political reasons for acquiescing to his provision; while Welton's reputation at York would have weighed with the archbishop.

For Welton's return through France, the pope supplied a safe-conduct dated 1 May 1353.[22] While at the Curia, he had presented a number of petitions. One granted on the day before his consecration was for licence to retain his prebends in York and Southwell for a year, or at least until 1 November; the pope agreed to the latter date.[23] Welton's need for this concession was his obligation to pay the pope 1000 florins (about £133) for the service charges due for his provision.[24]

---

[16] *CPL*, IV.209, 217, 218; *Testamenta Eboracensia*, I, ed. J. Raine (Surtees Society, 4, 1836), 55–6. Professor David Smith has kindly supplied many references from the register of Archbishop Zouche showing Welton as chancellor, 1345–9, and official, 1349–Jan. 1352. See also **537n.**

[17] *CPL*, III.469, 487–8. It was conferred by the bishop of Winchester, at Esher (Surrey), on 29 March (*The Register of William Edington, Bishop of Winchester*, ed. S.F. Hockey (Hampshire Record Series, 7, 8, 1986–7), II.69).

[18] The livery of the temporalities of York to Thoresby dated 8 Feb. may indicate when Welton had returned to England and, probably, delivered the pall to Bishop Edington (*Fasti*, VI.3).

[19] This is indicated by the admission of Simon Brisele to the prebend of Osbaldwick on 23 April, after the king's recognition of his title on the 16th (see below, p.xii).

[20] *Fasti*, IV.56.

[21] As suggested by R.G. Davies, 'The Anglo-Papal Concordat of Bruges, 1375', *Archivum Historiae Pontificiae*, 19 (1981), 124–5; cf. A.D.M. Barell, *The Papacy, Scotland and Northern England, 1342–1378* (Cambridge, 1995), 193–4.

[22] *CPL*, III.610.

[23] *CPP*, I.241; *CPL*, III.513.

[24] Lunt, *Financial Relations*, 758; *Cambridge Medieval History* (1911–36), VII.279.

After the king had received his oath of fealty, writs instructed escheators to deliver him the bishopric's temporalities; while Prior Horncastle was ordered to vacate them.[25]

For the next eight months, however, Welton made York his base. His first registered act, on 10 July, was the appointment of the abbot of Holm Cultram as his vicar-general in the diocese (**7***); while M. John Welton was given two commissions which made him, effectively, the bishop's steward and receiver-general of his temporalities in Cumberland, Westmorland and Northumberland (**520–1***). In his absence at Avignon, however, on 23 April, Simon Brisele had been admitted to his canonry of York and prebend of Osbaldwick, which might reasonably have been presumed vacant following his consecration as bishop.[26] Welton clearly intended to fight for the implementation of his papal licence: his first step was to occupy a house in the close at York, probably that attached to the prebend. On 12 July he appointed ten priests and clerks as his proctors to publish his papal graces and, if necessary, defend them by judicial procedures; the party was headed by his former colleague, M. Simon Bekingham, the chancellor of York (**518***).[27] In this period, Welton twice visited the property of his prebend of Southwell at Eaton (**14**, **16**). Archbishop Thoresby would seem to have approved of his suffragan's stay in York: on 11 February 1354, from Westminister, he commissioned Welton to ordain clergy in York minster (**539**). By the time this commission could have reached him, Welton must have planned to conduct his first ordination service in his own diocese.[28] He arrived there at the end of February (**17**). Had he once hoped to repair his financial position while in York, he must have been less sanguine by 30 November, when he directed his vicar-general and John Welton to hold a conference of the prelates and beneficed clergy of the diocese (**14***). They granted a subsidy towards his expenses, the first half to be paid between 13 and 20 April, when the first instalment of the bishop's *servitia* were to be paid to the pope's collector.[29] The clergy's grant was a signal to encourage the bishop into residence.

Welton had recruited a professional entourage. Carlisle diocese was reported to be poorly provided with skilled lawyers in 1329, and Bishop Kirkby had difficulty in securing the regular service of notaries; while one of his officials incurred the wrath of the chapter of York by his alleged contempt of provincial jurisdiction.[30] The quality of legal assistance available to Kirkby, as well as his bellicose temperament, help to explain his embittered relations with the court of York and his harsh treatment of his archdeacon and other subjects. Welton clearly appreciated that his diocese needed an infusion of legal talent. On the day of his consecration, he obtained a papal faculty to choose, examine and

[25] *CPR 1350–4*, 470–1.
[26] *Fasti*, VI.73. It would probably have been the opinion of English common lawyers that Welton could not retain his benefices: that certainly was the view of judges in a similar case in 1409 (R.L. Storey, 'Clergy and common law in the reign of Henry IV', *Medieval Legal Records*, ed. R.F. Hunnisett and J.B. Post (1978), 346).
[27] *BRUO*, I.155–6; *CPL*, IV.217, 218.
[28] On 8 March (**605**). Ordinations in Thoresby's register date from Dec. 1356 (D.M. Smith, *Guide to Bishops' Registers of England and Wales* (Royal Historical Society, 1981), 239).
[29] **32***; Lunt, *Financial Relations*, 758.
[30] *Reg. Melton*, I.93 (no.299); *Reg. Kirkby*, I.116–19, 137 (no.674); also I.144–5.

appoint four notaries.[31] His first official of Carlisle, appointed at Rose on 4 March 1354, was M. Nicholas Whitby, a notary who had been in Archbishop Zouche's household when Welton was his chancellor.[32] M. William Rothbury was already archdeacon of Carlisle. His relations with Welton appear to have been harmonious: they had been contemporaries at Oxford. William was described as a familiar clerk in 1356, witnessed proceedings at Rose, and served on several commissions (**14n.**, **135**).

Another notary, possibly appointed by the bishop, was M. John Welton, who may well have been a kinsman of a younger generation. He had been a student at Oxford, but left without a degree after being involved in a riot there in 1349.[33] Throughout Gilbert's episcopate, John was his most trusted and active household clerk, frequently his proctor, commissary and even deputy, in temporal as well as ecclesiastical business, and finally official of Carlisle.[34] A mark of John's standing is that he had his own seal (**308**). The register makes no mention of one of John's extra-mural operations. The abbot of St. Mary's, York, alleged that the bishop sent men to seize chattels which the abbot had recovered from the bishop's bailiffs of Dalston liberty. The party consisted of Roger Leeds, vicar of Crosby on Eden,[35] John Welton, clerk, John Bridlington,[36] and ten others including John's servant Hugh and Richard Ragarth, clerk.[37] They were said to have attacked the abbot's two servants bringing the chattels from Linstock, one of whom was William Cudge, chaplain.[38] The abbot consequently obtained a commission of oyer and terminer dated 3 June 1356.[39] Such writs are notoriously *ex parte* sources, but this one does suggest that John Welton was a minister in the bishop's secular administration.

Three of the proctors appointed to defend the bishop's graces in July 1353 (**518**), Richard Aslacby, Gerlac de Clave (a German) and John of Peper Harrow, followed him to Carlisle and appear as witnesses at Rose; the first was clearly a particular favourite of the bishop, as was also M. Thomas Salkeld, another notary. The surname of William Ragenhill, the notary who served as registrar throughout Welton's episcopate, suggests he was a native of Ragnall (Notts.), six miles from Eaton. It also deserves notice that at the bishop's first ordination of clergy, in Dalston church, nine had come from York diocese and two from Lincoln (**605**).

THE REGISTER

Welton's register is the first substantial part of the second composite volume of episcopal registers preserved in the Cumbria County Record Office in Carlisle

[31] *CPL*, III.502; *CPP*, I.242.
[32] **23***; *BRUO*, III.2036–7; *CPL*, IV.209, 218. Notaries were entitled *magistri* even if not graduates.
[33] *BRUO*, III.2013.
[34] See Index.
[35] From Sept. 1355 (**565**).
[36] A notary (**103**).
[37] Possibly the clerk purged in May 1356 (**587–8**).
[38] Vicar of Brampton (**405**).
[39] *CPR 1354–8*, 443–4.

Castle (under reference DRC/1/2).[40] It is preceded by a single folio (pp.i-ii) formally entitled as the register of John Horncastle, bishop-elect; this continues only to the verso, where the space remaining has the only known act by Welton's vicar-general (1-6). Next is a table of the contents of Welton's register, faithfully compiled to the extent that it lists every word in the outside margins, not only the descriptive titles of entries but also notes beside wills that executors had accounted (see below, p.xxi) and of omissions from the texts of entries (e.g. 71*); while entries for which marginal titles are wanting have not been listed (477, 600). The list quotes the Roman numerals of folios; these appear to be in the same hand as the main text below as far as Fo.52, and from Fo.53 added, possibly, by the writer of the list of contents. This ends with the letter for the rector of Bowness (Fo.62^v; 604*). There is no mention of the following ordination lists, although they were supplied with folio numbers (63 and 64). At the end of the list (Fo.vii^v) is a reference to the next section of this composite volume written in an early-modern hand,[41] not unlike the hand which paginated the whole volume in arabic numerals from Welton's first folio. The list must have been made after the insertion on Fo.52^v, after the very last of Welton's *acta*, of a copy of royal letters patent dated 14 June 1344, written in a larger, late medieval court hand unlike any other in the register, probably between 1388 and 1400, because the list includes a reference to this copy as if it were another entry in Welton's register.[42]

The register comprises six quires, as follow:

1.	10 folios	(1–10^v; pp.1–20) with entries numbered	1–102 (iii)
2.	8	(11–18^v; pp.21–36)	102 (iv)–183
3.	12	(19–30^v; pp.37–60)	184–282
4.	12	(31–42^v; pp.61–84)	283–422
5.	10	(43–52^v; pp.85–104)	423–517
6.	10	(53–62^v; pp.105–124)	518–604

Finally come two single folios with ordination lists (63–4; pp.125–8).

The register is distinguished by its consistent adherence to professional standards. The parchment is of good quality, every folio being 24 cm wide and 34 cm in depth. Four ruled lines marked the area for writing, 18 cm wide under an upper margin of 1.8 cm, and 27 cm in depth, leaving a bottom margin of 5 cm; the outer side margin is 5 cm wide. The total numbers of lines of text in the marked area are variable, with no spaces between entries; the most frequent total is 59. The same regular hand seems to appear on every page, including the ordination lists. That this was the hand of the registrar, William Ragenhill, is shown by his signature after three entries in 1360 which do not differ from the hand of their preceding and following texts (301, 316, 331). The first entry on Fo.29 is a notarial instrument dated 1359, with Ragenhill's subscription and

---

[40] Described in Smith, *Guide*, 256-7.
[41] The note is *Summa ceremoniarum in ecclesia usitararum et comprehensarum pagina 66*. Actually it is Folio 66, paginated as 139. The text following has been identified as statutes of Robert Chause, bishop of Carlisle 1258–79, and printed in *Councils and Synods, II*, ed. F.M. Powicke and C.R. Cheney (Oxford, 1964), I.626-32; and see I.588-625 for statutes of the diocese of Wells adopted by Bishop Chause.
[42] See 517 and its following note.

sign. The initial *I* is decorated, surmounted with spears, and extends down the margin for the entire length of the main text (**265***). There are other large decorated *I*s for entries made in 1353 (heading the first folio of the quire of 'diverse letters'), 1358 and 1361, differing in scale but not design, save that they have crests of leaves or antlers instead of spears (**518***, **213***, **390**). Ragenhill's notarial subscription, describing himself as the bishop's *scriba*, also appears twice in entries dated 1355, and again in 1360 when he certified letters of institution by John Welton (**97, 103, 308**).

The registrar's task of writing the register appears less onerous when it is observed that the total volume of the bishop's correspondence was slight, with rarely more than five items in a month, and sometimes none at all. Nearly all Welton's registered letters after February 1354 are dated at Rose, and no doubt it was here that the registrar was regularly based and his records stored.[43] He would also have been in active attendance whenever the bishop's court of audience was in session. There were occasions when the bishop sent Ragenhill on commissions of enquiry and to represent him in meetings of convocations at York.[44] He was a proctor of the diocesan clergy in the parliament called to Westminster for 17 April 1357, which the bishop apparently attended as he was at Newark (Notts.) on the 12th and dated letters in London on 3, 12 and 15 May. Their copies in the register are in the usual hand. The third of these letters, appointing the bishop's proctors in convocation, is in the sixth quire 'of diverse letters'. Those of 3 and 15 May, in the main register, are separated by two letters dated at Rose on 30 May.[45] There is a similar disjunction in the record of letters dated 25 April 1354, 21 June and 22–28 July (**35–42**); the first interval coincides with a meeting of parliament. This also indicates that Ragenhill wrote the register from time to time, copying from a collection of letters received, drafts of the bishop's correspondence and other notes, which might have become disordered.

With two exceptions (noticed below), the first five quires present a single, fairly regular chronological sequence of dated entries from beginning to end of Welton's episcopate. A sixteenth-century note at the end of the fifth quire asserts that 'the following twelve pages (*recte* folios) should be inserted earlier in the register because their contents were transactions of Welton's first four years'.[46] This note seemingly inspired a more recent suggestion that there was a binding fault.[47] There is a clear indication, however, that the sixth quire was deliberately created to keep a separate chronological record of particular kinds of business

[43] The bishop's manor of Rose, now Rose Castle, in Dalston parish, is six miles south of Carlisle. Welton obtained a licence for its crenellation in 1355, and its character as a castle probably dates from this time (J. Wilson, *Rose Castle* (Carlisle, 1912), 46, 158, 175; see also *EPNS Cumberland*, I.134–5).

[44] **32*, 324*, 584, 602**. A licence was dated at Rose, 3 June 1356, the day convocation was to meet ; its copy in the register is in the usual hand, but in a paler ink, as is the next entry (dated 26 June), suggesting that both were registered on the same day (**127–8**).

[45] **155** and note, **164–7, 602**. Ragenhill was again a proctor in the parliament of February 1357 which Welton presumably attended: there is a gap of seven weeks in his register from after 25 January (**199n., 208–9**).

[46] See note to heading over **518**.

[47] Historical Manuscripts Commission, *Ninth Report* (1883–4), I.191; cf. Smith, *Guide*, 256.

from July 1353, when the main register was also begun. A writ *dedimus potestatem* dated 26 March 1354 was entered in the first quire, but the full documentation for this business was not completed there because, it was noted, the proceedings were fully registered 'in the quire for diverse letters, etc.' (**27**), as indeed it is in the sixth quire (**530**). Apart from this accident, there is no duplication of entries in the main register of five quires and the sixth quire 'of diverse letters'.

The chronological sequence of 'diverse letters' continues to Fo.62^v. Here there are a writ dated 2 March 1357 sternly reminding the bishop to inform the Exchequer of the name of a collector of a tenth, for which a previous writ was recorded in Fo.15^v of the main register (**149**); an acquittance to the bishop by the receiver of papal nuncios, dated 3 September 1355; the appointment on 12 May 1357 of proctors in a convocation for which the bishop's reply to the archbishop's citation is in the main register (**167**) and finally the discharge of a rector from further proceedings, dated 8 Aug. 1357 (**601–4**). A decision had been made, apparently, to terminate the separate registration of 'diverse letters' after the completion of the quire. This new policy is illustrated by the record of licences for questors. With one exception in 1356 (**143**), all licences of Welton's first four years are in the sixth quire, until 15 March 1357 (**156**), from when they were entered in the main register. The original purpose of the sixth quire seems to have been keeping a separate record of material not strictly concerned with the routine administration of the diocese, as in the main register, but of more personal interest to the bishop himself, the management of his temporalities, and his performance of duties ordered by the king in writs under the great and privy seals, and by commissions from the archbishop of York. In practice, however, the distinction was often forgotten: there are, for instance, three institutions to benefices (**563**, **565–6**), two licences for non-residence (**559–60**) and three letters dimissory to ordinands (**585–6**) among the 'diverse letters'. This irregularity must have been accidental, because both registers would have been at Rose, where nearly all the bishop's letters were dated, some on the same day in both registers (e.g. **8**, **519–21**; **63–6**, **550**; **149**, **593**). Every will, however, and other letters about testamentary business, are in the five quires of the main register.

There are two noticeable departures from the chronological sequence of entries in the first five quires. After recording a mandate from papal nuncios and three documents about their procurations in June and September 1357, the remainder of the recto of Fo.21 (the first folio of the second quire) was left blank for records of payments in later years (**185–194**). The registration of routine entries was continued on the dorse of the folio from October 1357 (**196**). The space remaining after the last procuration was acknowledged was eventually used to record a commission dated 11 May 1359 (**195**). Likewise when the bishop was appointed a warden of the west march in July 1359, Fo.42 was reserved for correspondence arising from this office (**416–422**). This folio appears to be misplaced in the chronological sequence: it is preceded and followed by folios with *acta* in January 1362. The apparent explanation is that Fo.42 is the second half of the opening beginning with Fo.31, which also has entries dated in autumn 1359 (**283–290**): the chronological sequence was broken by making it the outside opening of the fourth quire.

The most numerous category of entries in the register are letters of institution, usually given in full, addressed to newly admitted incumbents of livings following their presentations by the patrons. Unlike his predecessor Kirkby, Welton did not have records made of letters of presentation nor of subsequent letters of the bishop ordering an enquiry into the vacancy, the patron's title to present, and the suitability of his nominee; nor also of the certificates resulting from inquests. That it was to be Welton's normal practice to have such enquiries made, however, is shown in his only commission appointing a vicar-general in 1353 (7*); on later occasions when he delegated institutions, he instructed his commissaries to examine the certificates of inquests (16, 225–6, 307–8). Records of exchanges of benefices in his register were also shorter than Kirkby's, who sometimes quoted the documentation at considerable length, including presentations, certificates giving reasons for exchanges, and appointments of proctors, as well as the commissions of other bishops and the ensuing certificates of execution by the bishop of Carlisle; Welton's record was limited to the two last items.[48] After every record of an institution in his register, including collations to the few benefices in his gift, is a memorandum of a mandate for induction almost always addressed to the archdeacon of Carlisle alone; he did not have an official. Kirkby's registrars were less punctilious in making a similar note; between 1337 and 1342, during his quarrel with the archdeacon, the mandate was recorded as addressed to other commissaries, in flagrant disregard of an inhibition from the court of York.[49]

Welton's register records the issue of 44 licences to rectors to be absent from their churches and excused from personal attendance at synods, mostly for a single year. Of these, ten were for the purpose of study at a university under the terms of Pope Boniface VIII's constitution *Cum ex eo*; five of them were granted to William del Hall, rector of Bowness on Solway, for successive years between 1355 and 1360.[50] M. Henry Sandford, rector of Crosby Garrett, had licences for university in 1353 and 1354, but in five following years licences for his absence were recorded in memoranda not mentioning study; two of these noted that he would be *in loco congruo*, which may have been a university in his case.[51] The same term, however, appears in the note in 1354 of a licence for three years to M. Ralph Ergum, who had been rector of Greystoke from 1316. Kirkby had granted him licences for (unexplained) absence in 1339, 1342 and 1344, but he is not known to have been in Oxford since 1324. He was a canon residentiary of Lincoln from 1335 to 1360, when he died.[52] Six rectors received licences for absence while in the service of local nobles. William de Ebor, of Bolton, had five for a total of eight years, at the request of Ralph Neville of Raby, and Richard Askeby, of Uldale, four for six years in the service of Thomas Lucy of Cockermouth. Walter Loughteburgh was a creditor of William Dacre of Gilsland before the latter presented him to Dacre church in 1359. He failed to

---

[48] E.g. 111–12, 262, 450; cf. *Reg. Kirkby*, I.36–7 (nos.210–225), 158–9 (nos.760–8), 162–3 (nos.784–91).

[49] *Reg. Kirkby*, I. 75 (nos.395, 397), and *passim* to p.146 (no.725).

[50] See both indexes for references for this paragraph.

[51] In the standard full form of a licence under *Cum ex eo*, leave was given to stay 'in loco congruo et honesto ubi viget dinoscitur studium generale' (e.g. Borthwick Institute, York, Register 9 (of Archbishop Melton), fo.331; N.F. 400; dated 12 Jan.1318).

[52] *BRUO*, I.644; *Reg. Kirkby*, I.95 (no.501), 134 (no.661), 158 (no.757); *Fasti*, I.59; K. Edwards, *The English Secular Cathedrals in the Middle Ages* (Manchester, 1949), 339–41.

attend the synod later that year, thus incurring a fine. This was remitted when
he was granted a licence for three years' absence in Dacre's service, for which he
had to pay the bishop £10 in three annual instalments. The only other recorded
proceedings for absenteeism were against M. Henry Heynes, rector of Cliburn,
also in 1359. He was dismissed after producing dispensations under *Cum ex eo*
sealed by previous bishops of Carlisle which were said to have covered the whole
period in question; they should have dated from the time of Bishop Ross, but
only one is recorded in Kirkby's register.[53] That register, however, contains a
mandate of 1339 to order allegedly numerous absentee rectors to return to their
churches.[54] There is no similar general monition in Welton's register. His clergy,
including those with noble patrons, were apparently aware of his vigilance and
his example of residence.[55]

In the tenth year of his episcopate, Kirkby issued an order to all deans and
parochial clergy to prevent the fund-raising operations of unlicensed par-
doners.[56] Welton issued a similar mandate two weeks after beginning his
residence in the diocese (**24**). Kirkby's register shows only one licence to
questors, those for the hospital of Saint-Antoine-de-Viennois, valid for one
year until Michaelmas 1343.[57] There are 32 licences for questors in Welton's
register, all valid for one year. Three groups of questors returned to the bishop
almost annually to have their letters renewed, some with amendments; they
account for a total of 20 licences. These were the quests for building the choir of
Carlisle cathedral, building at Durham cathedral, and the hospital of Saint-
Antoine.[58] A second mandate against unlicensed questors in 1357 named these
three causes and that for San Spirito in Sassia as exempt from the inhibition;
their licences in the year to its date are all recorded (**173**; **142, 593, 599, 156**).
Like the renewed licences for non-resident rectors, they are evidence of the
registrar's conscientious application to detail. He recorded four commissions to
the prior of Carlisle to take the bishop's place in the customary reception of
penitents at the cathedral, twice on Ash Wednesday (**87*, 577**) and twice on
Maundy Thursday (**533, 121**). It was surely a work of supererogation to make a
lasting record of commissions which would have been fully performed two days
after their issue; and if the registrar was so punctilious, it is conceivable that the
bishop made the short journey from Rose personally to admit the penitents in
the years when no similar arrangements were made..

Ordinations of clergy by Bishops Halton and Kirkby had usually been
recorded in their registers, with every service singly for their dates in the same
sequence as those bishops' other *acta*. Welton, however, followed the practice he
knew at York of making ordination lists a separate part of a register. His own is
very similar in design to that of Zouche, drawn up in two columns to a page,

---

[53] **254*** and notes.
[54] *Reg. Kirkby*, I.92 (no.481).
[55] Clerks in the king's service did not require licences for absence (*Reg. Kirkby*, I.146,
no.729). In Welton's time these included Henry Greystoke (**388**, second note), Adam
Hoton (**49**) and John Soulby (**414**).
[56] *Reg. Kirkby*, I.134 (no.663).
[57] Ibid. I.134 (no.707).
[58] In chronological order: Carlisle, **534***; **557, 599, 198, 230, 300, 358, 413**; Durham,
553, 593, 229, 306, 402; S. Antoine, **535, 567, 143, 208, 221, 312, 385**. See Subject
Index for others.

with bold headings for each dated list and of the four major orders.[59] There are only two single folios of Welton's ordination lists, stitched to the last quire along their inner margins (605–622). Although they are not noticed in the table of contents, these folios have been numbered and paginated; there is no question that these lists were not written with the care due to an important record.

THE BISHOP'S AUDIENCE

On 18 January 1358, the official of the court of York wrote asking Welton to supply copies of instruments and other documents in a divorce cause. He replied from Rose on 22 January that a search of his archives found only two records of Thomas Neuton being cited to appear before him in the chapel at Rose on 3 April 1354 and 14 October 1355, giving summaries of the consequent proceedings (206*). There is no other record of this suit in the main register (or 'Diverse letters'). The quotation of precise dates four and three years previously, in so prompt a reply, indicates that the information was readily available. Bishop Halton, in 1315, told the official of York that his judicial records had been destroyed when Scots sacked his manors, which suggests that they had been dispersed.[60] A bishop might hold his court of audience for the exercise of his ordinary jurisdiction wherever he might be in his diocese with his household clerks.[61] As Bishop Welton was almost continually in residence at Rose, his audience was always held there and, for his time, its records had the security of a constant abode. None are known to have survived

The largest category of notices in the register of the bishop acting judicially is of matrimonial causes. This preponderance is not likely to have reflected most of the court's business, which was more probably the prosecution of offenders against the laws of the Church, including those whose absolution was reserved to the bishop in his appointments of penitentiaries (20*, 154, 574–5). The obdurate excommunicates named in Welton's letters to the king invoking the aid of the secular arm doubtless included some offenders adjudged to be contumacious for disregard of his citations to his court or of its sentences.[62] An appeal was made to the court of York by five members of the Oliphant family who alleged that the bishop had excommunicated them without due process and had the sentence published in Westmorland deanery (429*); there is no earlier reference in the bishop's register to this purported case of violence to a clerk by a 'gentry' family.

Beside this *ex officio* jurisdiction, the audience acted in suits at the instance of parties. Disagreements between abbeys and vicars of their appropriated churches could lead to proceedings before the bishop, which he sometimes delegated to commissaries (86, 279, 509). Some of the matrimonial causes heard there were initiated at the suit of wives (130, 206*, 378* and probably 555*). One followed a report to the audience that a marriage had not been

[59] Borthwick Institute, York: Reg. no.10A, ff.1–55[v].
[60] *Reg. Halton*, II.111.
[61] A.H Thompson, *The English Clergy and their Organization in the Later Middle Ages* (Oxford, 1947), 54–7.
[62] See Index of Subjects *s.n.* Excommunication.

consummated (**114***). Another was *ex officio* because a marriage was unlawful; it was soon found that the same woman, Alice Whytefeld, had contracted a second marriage and had children (**320***, **328***). The proceedings in these cases are recorded in the register in the course of letters patent publishing their conclusion with the bishop's sentences that the marriages were null and void; he likewise published and confirmed a similar sentence in the court of the official of Carlisle, the only other court in the diocese (**79***). Letters patent were also issued, and therefore registered, to make it public knowledge that two rectors had been dismissed from further prosecution after answering charges in the bishop's court, for concubinage and unlicensed non-residence; while a third announced that another rector had proved his title to his church (**84***, **254***, **325***).

WILLS

Welton's first recorded act after his arrival in the diocese was his sentence of probate for the will of John de Penreth, vicar of Arthuret. This business was transacted in the chapel of Rose manor on 28 Feb.1354. A copy of the will was made in the register, followed by a record of the sentence (**17**). This was the first will copied into a Carlisle episcopal register, and it became regular practice for all wills proved by the bishop, invariably in the chapel at Rose, to be thus recorded, all in the main section of the bishop's register. Welton's strong interest in testamentary business dated from his experience as chancellor of Archbishop Zouche of York. Indeed, the section of the archbishop's register devoted to testament was begun in 1345, the year when Welton became his chancellor. It is thus possible that he was responsible for the innovation at York, in imitation of practice in Lincoln diocese, where Bishops Burghersh (1320–40) and Bek (1342–47) had testamentary sections in their registers.[63]

It seems to have been usual for bishops of Carlisle to reserve testamentary business to their own care. The only occasion when Halton empowered his official to prove wills and commission executors was in 1311, in his absence at the council of Lyons; on the same day he appointed vicars-general, without mention of testamentary powers.[64] Kirkby's commissions defining the powers of officials made no reference to wills.[65] In 1342, he ordered enquiries to discover who had died in the diocese from two years before his accession as bishop (in 1332) and the names of their executors; he subsequently issued orders for various executors to come before him, or his commissaries, with their accounts and other documents.[66] Welton showed more urgency, charging his registrar to enquire about deaths since 1347, in a commission dated two months after his arrival in the diocese (**34***); but there is no record that he found any evidence of concealments. The wills of two widows of tenants in Dalston barony were proved, at Rose, one by M. John Welton, the second by the registrar (**157**, **294**). The official was charged to appoint a suitable person as administrator for an

[63] Smith, *Guide*, 110–12, 238; *Testamenta Eboracensia*, I.xi, 6–66, *passim*.
[64] *Reg. Halton*, II.37–40.
[65] *Reg. Kirkby*, II.38, 48–9.
[66] *Reg. Kirkby*, I.131–2, 134–5, 138–9, 142.

intestate (**45**), and once to prove a will in Carlisle, that of the sheriff and keeper of the castle (**313**). The substantial will of John Salkeld of Maughonby was proved at his home, some fifteen miles from Carlisle, by John Welton, whose sentence was confirmed by the bishop three days later (**231**). The only general delegation of testamentary business was made for the deanery of Carlisle in the plague-year, 1362 (**478***). Among the other wills, all proved before the bishop, were four which had been proved in the dioceses where the testators had died and which came later to receive the approval of the bishop of Carlisle (**336, 371, 414, 432**).

Until 1360, the note *redd' compotum* appears in the margins beside most of the registered wills proved in the diocese. This note is given most fully beside John Salkeld's will: 'the executors of this testament rendered account on 18 March [1359] and were dismissed' (**231**). With another will it is noted that 'they rendered account and were absolved' (**235**). There is no notice of probate for a former sheriff, Sir William Legh of Isel, whose manor lay on the southern boundary of the diocese; the will may have been proved in York diocese, but a note of account was made in the margin (**91**). Five wills proved before the end of 1359 are said to be nuncupative in the sentence of probate (or margin), as if they had been 'delivered verbally by testators too ill to write or seal'.[67] They are, however, all expressed in the first person (**88, 169, 183, 272**). The lengthy will of the rector of Long Marton was said to have been *nuncupative facti* despite its being in the first person and ending with the statement that he had attached his seal and also that of the official of Carlisle, with his consent (**216**). From December 1359, wills described as nuncupative are expressed in the third person (**280** and later). Another curiosity is the so-called will of William, Lord Dacre, actually a list (in French) of his debts on 29 Sept. 1359; but it ends with the appointment of executors, who were duly admitted when the bishop granted probate in the standard form a month after William's death in 1361 (**388**)

THE BLACK DEATH

The ordinance for a chantry founded in 1361 has the only reference in the register to the Black Death of 1348–9: the lands of an older chantry at Bramery had been made sterile by 'the pestilence which lately afflicted all England, scarcity of tenants and other misfortunes' (**390**). The plague came to Carlisle from the south; 'a sinister coincidence of mortality' among tenants-in-chief of the crown suggests that it was most lethal in Cumberland in September and October 1349. In the city itself, Dr. Summerson calculated from property accounts that the death-toll could have been as high as two-thirds or as low as one seventh of the total population.[68] As Bishop Kirkby's register has not survived for after 1347, a more exact guide to clerical mortality is not available, as it has for other dioceses. In York, it has been estimated that 39% of

---

[67] *The Register of Henry Chichele, Archbishop of Canterbury*, ed. E.F. Jacob (CYS, 1937–47), II.xxi.
[68] Summerson, 279–81.

incumbents died, the lowest figure in nine dioceses for which the estimated average is approximately 45%.[69]

There were 95 parishes in Carlisle diocese,[70] of which about 80 had rectors or vicars instituted by the bishop. The remainder were appropriated to monastic houses without vicarages being established; they were served by canons of those houses or stipendiary chaplains without any known notice of their appointments being made to the bishop.[71] In the thirteen years, 1333–45, Kirkby's register records 56 institutions to rectories and vicarages: sixteen of the vacancies were due to death, twelve by resignation and eight by exchanges from other dioceses. No reasons were given in 20 other cases, and another shortcoming in this record is that examples occur of new incumbents appearing as ordinands although their institutions by Kirkby are not shown in his register.[72] The total number dying in office before 1345 could thus have been considerably more than sixteen; the annual average may have been two, as it was in Welton's first eight years. Only two rectories are known to have been vacant at the time of his accession (**16, 41**).

By the time of his death in 1352, Kirkby would have made institutions to replace casualties of the plague in 1349. Some indication of their number may be estimated from Welton's register when it names incumbents, particularly in institutions giving the causes of death or resignation: in a large proportion of cases it can be shown that different men had held these livings in their last notices in Kirkby's register. Continuous incumbency from his episcopate to Welton's can be demonstrated for up to about 30 of a possible total of 80 parish churches.[73] It is conceivable that clerical mortality in that plague-year was close to the 39% level in York diocese, even after allowance is made for the imperfect record of Kirkby's last years before 1349. Ordinations by Welton of three monks of Holm Cultram in 1354, and seven canons of Carlisle in 1361, may reflect recruitment to replace plague-casualties in those houses (**605, 622**).

The second visitation of the Black Death struck the capital by 10 May 1361.[74] On 5 June, John Soulby, rector of Musgrave, made his will there, where he was employed in the king's service. Although the will was not proved, in London, until 26 November (**414**), his successor was instituted at Rose on 18 July (**386**). John was probably the first Cumbrian victim of the new pestilence. Assemblies

[69] C. Harper-Bill, 'The English Church', *The Black Death in England*, ed. W.M. Ormrod and P.G. Lindley (Stamford, 1996), 86.

[70] A list of *c.* 1328 shows *synodalia* due from 94 churches; it omits Carlisle St. Mary's (*Reg. Kirkby*, II.1–3).

[71] For St. Mary's, see ibid., I.136, 140. See also **97, 253** below; *The Lanercost Cartulary*, ed. J.M. Todd, CWAAS Record Series, 11 (1997), 204–7.

[72] Notes to **50, 289, 443**; also **566** for a vacancy at Newbiggin in 1350.

[73] See footnotes in the calendar to its first references to these benefices. The survivors included Roger Kirkoswald, rector of Bromfield 1344–77 (*Reg. Kirkby*, I.158–9; Reg. Appleby, fo.94; p.295); Thomas Anant, or Anandale, rector of Great Asby 1345–74 (*Reg. Kirkby*, I.165, no.799; *Test. Karl.*, 106); William Arthuret, rector of Great Orton 1337–77 (*Reg. Kirkby*, I.76, nos. 403, 406; Reg. Appleby, fo.92; p.290). They do not occur in Welton's register, nor does the rectory of Dufton where Robert Helton, instituted 1340, was succeeded 'long before' 1361 by William Brampton, who died 1366 (*Reg. Kirkby*, I.111, nos.552–4; *CIPM*, XI.88; *Test. Karl.*, 78).

[74] *CCR 1360–4*, 181–2; *Foedera*, III(2).621.

of diocesan clergy in Carlisle on 2 September and 20 December were not followed by evidence of epidemic disease.[75] There is clear evidence of a serious outbreak in May 1362, with the deaths of William Stapleton and three other parishioners of Edenhall and another of Eamont Bridge.[76] The vicar of Edenhall also died and his successor instituted on 4 June; he too died ten weeks later (**456, 486**). From late June, wills and institutions mark the course of plague down the Eden valley to Carlisle and south-westwards to Wigton. One will was proved in June, for the rector of Scaleby, followed by another for a parishioner of Sebergham on 7 July (**457, 468**). The danger was seemingly not yet sufficiently alarming to persuade the bishop to remain in Rose; unless his journey had a pastoral purpose. He set out after 7 July, and was at Brough under Stainmore on the 18th, in Penrith the following day, and Rose on the 22nd; he visited Carlisle on 25 July.[77] Nine wills were proved in that last week of July. The bishop then commissioned the rector of Beaumont to prove wills in Carlisle deanery (**478**), but Welton continued to receive them, including that of the mayor of Carlisle on 4 August, when he also proved wills of the rector of Kirkby Thore (Westm.) and two of his parishioners (**480, 481, 483**). Next day he proved wills of the vicar of Walton and nine men and women of Thursby, both parishes in Carlisle deanery (**482–3**). There were eight more by 12 September (**485–6, 503, 505–6**). While the pestilence had spent its force in Carlisle deanery by mid-August, the deaths of the rector of Brougham, and the vicars of Bampton, Crosby Ravensworth, Kirkby Stephen, Lowther and Morland show it active in northern Westmorland until early September.[78]

The total number of deaths of beneficed clergy between the first probable plague-victim at Edenhall in May and the last institution in Westmorland in October was fourteen, perhaps close to 20% of the total of incumbents normally instituted by the bishop.[79] Parish priests and other unbeneficed clergy also fell to the plague, but there are no means of assessing their number. That their casualties were considerable was stated by Bishop Appleby in 1363, in a petition for papal licence to ordain 40 priests aged 20 and eighteen more requiring other dispensations.[80] In his first celebration of orders on 16 December 1363, Appleby ordained eight monks of Holm Cultram as acolytes, and five of the seven canons of Carlisle ordained as subdeacons in Welton's last service on 18 December 1361.[81] When Appleby visited Carlisle priory in 1366, he received a list naming the prior and twelve canons; of these, out of a total of fourteen canons ordained

---

[75] **394*, 412***. The rector of Kirkoswald who died in March 1362 was very old and infirm (**431, 441**), as possibly was the rector of Croglin (**445**). The only other incumbent dying earlier in 1362 than June was the rector of Ousby (**434**).
[76] **451–5**. William died on 6 May (*CIPM*, XI.333).
[77] **468, 463, 473, 466**. A commission to negotiate with Scots dated 25 June may be relevant (*Foedera*, III(2).659; *Rot. Scot.*, I.864).
[78] Two deaths at Caldbeck late in October suggest an isolated pocket of plague, but both the rector and (his brother?) the testator were probably quite elderly (**62n., 512, 514**).
[79] Excluding the institution to Ousby on 18 Sept. which followed a vacancy since February (**434, 495**). Thus less than 'the death roll of over 23 per cent' estimated over a longer period, and against a total of 90 benefices, by C.M.L. Bouch, *Prelates and People of the Lake Counties* (Kendal, 1948), 89; see also Summerson, I.299.
[80] *CPP*, I.437.
[81] **622**; Reg. Appleby, fo.78; p.266.

by Kirkby between 1333 and 1342, only Prior Horncastle and his three most senior brethren had survived both plagues of 1349 and 1362.[82]

While the register records wills of incumbents throughout the diocese, lay testators similarly distributed were knights, others who might be described as county gentry, and their wives and widows; also prosperous citizens of Carlisle. Men and women disposing of few goods in short wills, which were often omitted from the register, were generally residents in the Carlisle area, mainly to its south-west. It is likely that most of them were tenants of the bishop's barony of Dalston; they account for the majority of the 40 grants of probate recorded after late July 1362.[83] Inquisitions *post mortem* of more substantial tenants-in-chief of the crown include some for whom no wills are recorded.[84] There are no wills of the vicar of Edenhall who died in May, nor of M. William Salkeld, who was replaced as a rector of Aikton on 7 August and later as master of Carlisle school.[85] What does seem extraordinary is that there is no record of grants of administration of the goods of intestates, of which there had been seven cases between 1354 and 1360.[86] Also absent from the register are notices of institutions to Walton, Edenhall and Bampton, after their incumbents' wills had been proved (**482, 486, 502**). Most other vacancies had been filled with little delay, some before their late parsons' wills had been proved.[87] Rose manor must have been a hive of activity in the summer and early autumn of 1362, frequently visited by clergy being instituted and executors with wills for probate and accounts of their administration. With so much business, it is understandable that some shortcomings can be detected in the register and that for once the registrar apparently had some assistance in keeping it to date.[88]

It has been suggested that the bishop himself may have been a victim of the plague.[89] This is improbable. His death is first reported in the petition for a licence to elect his successor, dated 1 January 1363.[90] The last entry in his register is dated 6 November 1362. It is a memorandum of a licence to William Ragenhill, who had recently been collated to the comparatively wealthy church of Caldbeck, with letters dimissory to all orders. The licence allowed him to be absent to study in a university for the unusually long term of three years (**512, 516**). This was the bishop's reward to the registrar whose services would no longer be required. At his advanced age, and after a harrowing experience in the months of plague, the bishop must have been terminally ill. He lingered until the end of December, his condition of infirmity perhaps like that of incumbents

---

[82] *VCH Cumberland*, II.146.

[83] See Index of Subjects *s.n.* Wills, from **465**.

[84] William Hoton of Ambrose Holm in Wetheral, died 20 June 1362; Roland de Vaux, junior, of Triermain, 20 May; Thomas del Hale of Glassonby, 7 July; William Brounfeld of Grassgarth, in Sebergham, 8 Sept. (*CIPM*, XI.269–70, 341–2, 428–9, 439; see also **509** for Brounfeld).

[85] **484, 513**, and notes.

[86] See Index of Subjects.

[87] As for Kirklinton (**464, 472**); Kirkby Thore (**479, 480**); Kirkby Stephen (**492, 501**).

[88] A will proved on 23 June is in a somewhat larger, heavier hand than Ragenhill's, with its lines more generously spaced (**457**).

[89] Bouch, *Prelates and People*, 90.

[90] *Fasti*, VI.97.

provided with coadjutors (**66, 431**); he is not known to have left a last will and testament. His lasting memorial is that 'sumptuous work', the east front and choir of Carlisle cathedral (**534***).

EDITORIAL METHOD

The calendar shows all persons and places in the manuscript (except the king, in writs). Footnotes giving further details about individuals and benefices are mostly attached to their first reference cited in the index. Placenames are given in their present form; for the first time it occurs, the form in the manuscript is next given in round brackets. Square brackets are used with editorial insertions. As recent scholars have sometimes in their references to Carlisle registers cited folio numbers as 'pages', and *vice versa*, in this volume both folio and page numbers are quoted; also in footnotes referring to the unpublished register of Bishop Appleby.

The Appendix of Texts provides full transcripts of entries of particular interest. The calendar shows which entries are thus printed in the appendix by the addition of asterisks to their serial numbers. The transcripts in the appendix are headed by the same numbers as in the calendar, and appear in numerical order. Cross-references are shown by entry numbers printed in bold figures, with the addition of asterisks when there are also texts in the appendix.

No will has been printed in the appendix because their texts are available in *Testamenta Karleolensia*, pp.1–73. Instead the calendar supplies full details of the contents of wills and their probates; although it does not quote the recurrent notes about accounts (as is noticed in the Introduction, p.xxi). The printed wills have been collated with the manuscript: significant errors and omissions have been corrected in the calendar.

THE REGISTER OF JOHN HORNCASTLE

1 [Common Pleas] writ *admittatis non obstante reclamacione* ordering John, bishop-elect and confirmed, to admit a suitable presentee of Elizabeth, widow of William de Monte Acuto, to a mediety of Kirkbampton (*Magna Bampton*) church because she has recovered the presentation in the king's court at Westminster against John son of Robert de Bampton by default. Tested by John de Stonore, Westminster, 15 Feb. 1353.

2 Presentation to John, bishop-elect and confirmed, by Elizabeth, widow of William de Monte Acuto, of John atte Hurne of Thornton (*Thorneton*), chaplain, to a mediety of Kirkbampton church. London, 13 Feb. 1353.

3 Letters of John, *miseracione divina* bishop-elect and confirmed. (i) Institution of John atte Hurne of Thornton, chaplain, to [the above] mediety, vacant by the death of William de Edenhall, late rector;[1] presented [as above]. (ii) Mandate for his induction to the rector of Great Orton (*Orreton*).Carlisle, 24 Mar. 1353.

4 DEPUTACIO RECEPTORIS. Letters patent of the bishop-elect appointing John de Shupton, rector of a mediety of Linton in Craven (*Lynton*) church, as his proctor to seek, exact and receive tithes, farms, rents and profits, spiritual and temporal, belonging to the bishop. Carlisle, 24 Mar. 1353.

5 (i) Letters of the same instituting Richard de Askeby (dioc. Carlisle) to Uldale (*Ulnedale*) church, vacant;[2] presented by the noble lord, Thomas de Luci. (ii) Note of mandate for his induction to the archdeacon. Carlisle, 5 Apr. 1353.

---

[1] Instituted by 1320 (*Reg. Halton*, II.201, 207); still in 1343, when both medieties then had rectors (*Reg. Kirkby*, I.155, no.744). For the division into medieties, see Nicolson & Burn, II.210.

[2] The previous known rector was Hugh de Roucestr', 1342 (*Reg. Kirkby*, I.132, no.652).

DE TEMPORE DOMINI ABBATIS DE HOLME VICARII GENERALIS.

6   (i) Letters (under the seal of the official of Carlisle) of the abbot of Holm Cultram (*Holmcoltram*),[3] vicar-general of Gilbert, bishop of Carlisle, in his absence, and special commissary for the following business, instituting William de Ebor', clerk, to Bolton church;[4] presented by Alexander de Moubray, kt. (ii) Note of mandate to the archdeacon for his induction. Bolton, 20 Feb, 1354.

---

[3] The previous known abbot was Thomas de Talkane, 1334, 1336 (*Reg. Kirkby*, I.34, no.196; 59, no.306); he had been ordained priest, 1320 (*Reg. Halton*, II.202). The next known abbot was Robert de Suthayk, 1351, who was a (senior) monk in 1333 (*CPP*, I.215; *Reg. Kirkby*, I.21, no.114). He was probably the Abbot Robert until 1365, when Robert de Raubankes was installed (**265, 297, 509**; Reg. Appleby, fo.2; p.144; and see *VCH Cumberland*, II.172).
[4] The last known institution was of John de Whytrigg, 1342 (*Reg. Kirkby*, I.132, no.555).

THE REGISTER OF GILBERT WELTON

[Fo.1; p.1] REGISTRUM VENERABILIS PATRIS DOMINI GILBERTI DE WELTON KARL'
EPISCOPI ANNO CONSECRACIONIS SUE PRIMO.

7* Letters patent appointing the abbot of Holm Cultram vicar-general in
Bishop Gilbert's absence, specifically empowering him to admit presentees to
benefices, make enquiries and arrange their induction; and to appoint and
remove deans and other ministers necessary for the bishop's spiritual jurisdiction. Benefices in the bishop's gift are reserved to his collation. York, 10 July
1353.

8 Note of licence to M. Ralph de Erghom, rector of Greystoke (*Creystok*),[5] to be
absent for one year. York, 12 July 1353.

9 Note of licence to M. Henry de Sandford, rector of Crosby Garrett (*Cross-
bygerard*),[6] to study in England or abroad for one year, in which he is dispensed
not to be ordained priest. York, 11 Sept. 1353.

10 Note of licence to Thomas de Ryppelyngham, rector of Kirkby Thore
(*Kirkebythore*),[7] to be absent for one year, excusing him from attending synods
and chapters, with leave to farm his church, etc. 2 Aug. 1353.

11* [Informal letter to the vicar-general.] When he has confirmation that the
rector of Bolton has entered a religious order, he is to sequestrate the revenues of
the church and provide a chaplain to minister there. York, 4 Sept. [1353].

12* [To the same] Since, according to [the vicar-general's] letters, the rector of
Bolton continues to neglect the cure of souls, the sequestration of the revenues of
the church and appointment of a custodian serving it are to continue until the
rector shows himself ready to undertake it. [The vicar-general] is to continue his
proceedings against possessors of the animals, vessels, implements and other
utensils to which the bishop is entitled. n.d.

[5] Instituted 1316 (*Reg. Halton*, II.115–16); see also Introduction, p.xvii.
[6] The previous rector recorded was 'W.', the bishop's receiver, 1342 (*Reg. Kirkby*, I.125,
no.621). Henry died as rector, 1381 (*Test. Karl.*, 147–8).
[7] Presented by the king, 1352, in an exchange with Ralph de Brantingham, who had
been instituted, 1346 (*CPR 1350–4*, 211; *Reg. Kirkby*, I.169, no.815). Plans for a further
exchange, to Gainford, co. Durham, did not materialise, but Thomas soon resigned
(*CPR 1350–4*, 421, 489; **49** below).

13 Note of a letter to the said abbot [of Holm Cultram] releasing sequestration of the harvested fruits of the said church received by the rector, but not of crops still in the ground. He is also to enquire whether a tenth granted to the king by the clergy of the diocese and other charges on the church have been paid; if not, its revenues are to be sequestrated until they have been paid. 8 Dec. [1353].

14* Commission to the abbot of Holm Cultram and M. John de Welton, clerk skilled in law. The bishop has ordered a conference with the prior and chapter of Carlisle, abbots and priors, the archdeacon of Carlisle,[8] rectors, vicars and other incumbents of the diocese about pressing business concerning him and his church.[9] As he is unable to be present, [the commissaries] are to convoke the above and explain this business in his name, seeking their consent and hearing their deliberations. Eaton (*Eton*),[10] 30 Nov. 1353.

15 Note[11] that Gilbert de Welton was consecrated as bishop of Carlisle by Pope Innocent VI at Avignon. 21 Apr. 1353.

16 [Fo.1^v; p.2] Commission to the [above] vicar-general. Alexander de Moubray, kt., has presented William de Ebor, clerk, to Bolton church.[12] As the bishop is unable to attend to the matter in person, he charges the vicar to enquire how and when the church lawfully became vacant; who has its presentation and last presented; whether the presentee is free and legitimate [by birth], of lawful age, beneficed elsewhere, and if there is any other canonical obstacle to the presenter or presentee; also whether the church is pensionary or apportioned, and what are its assessment and value. If it is found that the church was vacated by the lawful resignation of the last rector, and there is no obstacle, William is to be instituted and inducted. The letters of presentation and of the said resignation are sent for inspection under the seal of the bishop, who wishes them to remain in his archives (*penes registrum nostrum*). Eaton, 4 Feb. 1354.

17 Will[13] of John de Penreth, vicar of Arthuret,[14] dated 3 Feb. 1354 (being healthy in body and mind). Commends soul to God, Blessed Mary and all saints. Burial in chancel or churchyard there, with 5s. for light round his corpse and 5s. for oblations. All vestments and consecrated towels to altar of St. Michael's, Arthuret. A psalter and legend to the church. 10s. for the chancel roof. A mark for bread for the poor on his burial day. His tenements in Carlisle

---

[8] William de Routhbury (see **96**). The date of his institution is not known: see *Fasti*, VI.101–2; *BRUO*, III.1597. In 1372, a clerical jury said he had inducted John de Langholm to Kirkland on 14 Sept. 1350 (Reg. Appleby, fo.58^v; p.251). Earlier that year (11 Apr. 1350), John Mareschal is named as archdeacon in *CCR 1349–54*, 215; *Fasti*, VI.101: he is otherwise unknown. For William's will, 1364, see *Test. Karl.*, 74–6.
[9] See **32, 74**.
[10] See **529**.
[11] In lower margin in a minuscule but possibly contemporary hand .
[12] See **6, 11–13**.
[13] Printed in *Test. Karl.*, 1–3.
[14] Instituted 1333 (*Reg. Kirkby*, I.20, no.104).

to his brother Thomas and his lawful heirs. Two oxen, 2 cows, 2 skeps of flour, 2 of barley, a brass pot, little posnet, little chest given by his father, and suitable bed to his mother. His breviary and other books to John son of Thomas. Each servant 8d. beside his wages, and each page 6d. To Walter de Ormesby, the horses in his keeping except a colt. His kinsman Sir John, canon [of Carlisle], a mare with foal by the tithe of John Armstrang, senior. Thomas de Arthureth, 3 silver spoons. Ellen de Bolton, his wool in Carlisle save for a stone to his mother, 2 cows and a skep of oatmeal. Maud daughter of his kinswoman Alice, 2 heifers of 2 years. Sir John de Wylton, a colt of 2 years and a stirk. Thomas his brother to have all other household utensils of brass and wood except a large brass pot, once Thomas Hogg's, for Richard son of Roger, son of Katherine. The abbey (*abbatie*) of St. Mary, Carlisle, an ox, for his soul. The friars preachers and minor, 4s. The said Richard, a heifer of 2 years. William de Arthureth, bailiff, a mare called 'Fernelan'. John son of Walter de Ormesby, 2 heifers of 2 years and a stirk. John Bone, parish priest of St. Mary's, Carlisle, celebrating for his soul on his burial day, 12d.; the parish clerk there, 3d.; and choir-clerks ringing bells in his memory, 12d. Sir John Baynard, a colt and his best gown. Sir John de Penreth, canon [of Carlisle[15]], a surplice and little mazer cup. Two skeps of oatmeal or a mark to poor parishioners. Residue after payment of debts to his mother and brother Thomas. Executors: Thomas de Penreth, Walter de Ormesby and John de Wylton, priest; with the counsel of Sir John the canon. Witnesses: Sir John de Sebraham, Sir Richard Blese,[16] Robert Byndber, John Aldane and William Taillor.

Sentence that the will was proved before the bishop and administration granted to the executors in accordance with the legatine constitution, in the chapel of Rose, 28 Feb. 1354.

18 Licence (during pleasure) to Margaret, lady of Dacre, for divine services to be celebrated in oratories in her manors or other places in the diocese where she may be, without prejudice to the parish churches. A suitable chaplain of her choice may receive her confessions, enjoin penance and grant absolution, even in cases reserved to the bishop. Rose, 3 Mar. 1354.

[Fo.2; p.3] ANNO QUINQUAGESIMO TERCIO

19 Licence (for one year) to Robert de Kirkeby, chaplain, as confessor to Margaret, lady de Dakre, her familiars and servants, except in cases reserved to the bishop. [Same date?]

20* Licence (until 20 April) to Robert Deyncourt, friar preacher of Carlisle, D.Th.,[17] as confessor and penitentiary to the bishop's parishioners, even in reserved cases excepting violations of liberties of the bishop and his church, opposition of his jurisdiction, rape of nuns; perjury in assises, indictments,

---

[15] Ordained priest 1342 (*Reg. Kirkby*, I.133, no.656).
[16] Ordained deacon 1336 (ibid., I.58).
[17] *BRUO*, III.2170.

matrimonial causes, disinheritance, homicide and mutilation; and also usury. Rose, 3 Mar. 1354.

Note of similar licence to the reader (*lector*) of the Friars Minor, Carlisle. Same date.

21 Commission to the dean of Westmorland, forwarding for inspection letters (to be returned) of Stephen [Aubert], cardinal-priest of SS. John and Paul,[18] on behalf of John de Regle, clerk (dioc. Carlisle). He is to enquire secretly and singly of sworn clergy and laymen whether John is, as said, the son of unmarried parents, and about his life, character and other questions about his suitability [to be dispensed: see **31**]. The report to the bishop by letters patent and close must name the jurors. Rose, 4 Mar. 1354.

22 Note of a similar letter to the same dean on behalf of Richard, clerk, son of William [son of] Richard de Warthecopp. 9 Mar. 1354.

23* Appointment of M. Nicholas de Whiteby, clerk skilled in law,[19] as official of Carlisle, with powers to proceed in causes between subjects and to enquire into and punish offences. Rose, 1 Mar. 1354.

24 Commission to the official of Carlisle. Many unauthorised questors are reported to be travelling round the diocese falsely taking alms from the faithful. All deans, rectors, vicars, parish chaplains and other parishioners are to be publicly ordered not to allow any questors to pursue their business in churches, chapels or other gatherings (*convocacionibus*), nor obey or assist them unless they have letters of approval under the bishop's seal (and none other). Everything belonging to false questors in the hands of subjects are sequestrated pending further orders. Clergy are not to permit questors to remove any money they have collected. Rose, 11 Mar. 1354.

25* Licence to the inhabitants of Kirklinton, whose church is in danger of collapse because of its width: they may remove the outer walls of its aisles and strengthen the interior of the building. Rose, 13 Mar. 1354.

[Fo. 2ᵛ; p.4] HIC INCIPIT ANNUS DOMINI MILLESIMUS CCCᴹᵁˢ QUINQUAGESIMUS QUARTUS.

26 Memorandum that the bishop specially commissioned M. John de Welton as his deputy to cite the vicar of Warcop (*Warthecopp'*) as in other letters to the dean of Westmorland about this matter;[20] also to sequestrate the goods of all dying in Westmorland and to cite their executors or those holding their goods to seek probate of their wills. Rose (in the principal chamber), 26 Mar. 1354.

[18] Pope Innocent VI, 30 Dec. 1352 – 12 Sept. 1362.
[19] See Introduction, xiii.
[20] Possibly **22** (and **21**?).

27 Writ *dedimus potestatem* ordering the bishop to receive the oaths of William de Lye as sheriff of Cumberland, escheator of Cumberland and Westmorland, and keeper of Carlisle castle. Westminster, 4 Mar. 1354.

Memorandum that this writ, the forms of the oaths taken by William and all the proceedings are more fully registered in the quire *de diversis litteris etc.*[21]

28 Will[22] of John, son of Roger de Lancastre, dated 17 Feb. 1354 (being well in mind and memory). Commends soul to its Creator and Redeemer, the Blessed Virgin Mary and all saints. Burial in St. Cuthbert's chapel, Milburn, with 6 pounds of wax and 40d. for oblations. Two cows to provide a candle of one pound for his soul annually before the altar of the Virgin Mary. A chasuble costing 7s. to St. Cuthbert's chapel. A mare with a colt of 2 years for St. Mary's light in Grasmere church. 40s. and a cow to his mother. Two pounds of wax to Ousby church. The same to St. Lawrence's, Kirkland. 6s. 8d. to Thomas de Thorneton, M.Th., Austin friar. A pound of wax to St. Edmund's, Newbiggin. A mare and heifer pastured in *Thorkildale*[23] to William Stodeherd. A horse of his choice to William de Crakynthorp. Twelve marks to a chaplain celebrating for 2 years in Milburn chapel. 2s. to Sir Robert son of Roger de Merton. 71 marks to be equally divided among his wife and 3 legitimate children, but all to his wife if they are not married. Executors: William de Lancastre, William de Crakenthorp and Elizabeth [John's] wife. His seal attached in presence of Robert [de Merton], rector of Newbiggin,[24] William de Denton, rector of Ousby,[25] Sir Robert de Merton, John Wyther.

Sentence of probate, with commission of administration to William de Lancastre and William de Crakenthorp; reserved for Elizabeth. Rose (chapel), 29 Mar. 1354.

29 Licence to William de Ebor', rector of Bolton, at the request of the noble lord, Ralph de Nevill, to be absent in his service for one year; a proctor is to represent him at synods at Carlisle and chapters and provision made for the cure of souls, with a proctor answering for him. Also note of letters dimissory for ordination as deacon and priest. Rose, 29 Mar. 1354.

30 Mandate to the dean of Carlisle. The vicarage of Crosby on Eden (*Crosseby*) is vacant.[26] He is to go there immediately, put all its revenues and goods into safe custody for the [next] vicar, announce that the bishop has sequestrated them, and provide for divine service. He is to report all his actions by letters patent, itemising the goods and their whereabouts, by 6 April. Rose, 29 Mar. 1354.

---

[21] **530**; and see Introduction, xvi.

[22] Printed in *Test. Karl.*, 3–5.

[23] Possibly Thrushgill, in Milburn (*EPNS Westmorland*, II.123).

[24] See **566**.

[25] The last known institution to Ousby was of John de Greyvile, a provisor, 1318 (*Reg. Halton*, II.169; *BRUO*, II.825). William may have been the dispossessed rector of adjacent Kirkland (*Reg. Kirkby*, I.62–3, 73, no.383, 123, no.606).

[26] The previous rector known was Thomas de Dalston, 1338 (ibid., I.84, no.443); and see **562**.

31 [Fo.3; p.5] Dispensation to John de Regle, clerk (dioc. Carlisle), as the son of unmarried parents, to be promoted to all orders and hold a benefice with cure, if he resides; quoting letters of Stephen [Aubert], cardinal-priest of SS. John and Paul, penitentiary of Clement VI, dated Avignon, 1 Sept. 1351. Rose, 29 Mar. 1354.

32* Commission to the dean of Carlisle to collect the subsidy granted to the bishop by the clergy of the diocese to help with his expenses, for its first term, by Easter (13 April) or the following week; an account listing individual payments and non-payments, if any, is to be made by letters patent by 27 April. Rose, 29 Mar. 1354.

   Note of similar letters to the deans of Westmorland, Cumberland and Allerdale. Same date.

33* Mandate of the bishop as executor of a provision by Innocent VI to Robert Thirnbey, a poor priest, to a benefice in the gift of the prior and chapter of Carlisle. The dean of Carlisle is to cite them to appear before the bishop in the chapel of Rose on 21 April if they wish to make any canonical objection. Rose, 29 Mar. 1354.

34* Commission of enquiry to M. William de Ragenhill, the bishop's familiar clerk. Many subjects have for long been keeping goods of intestates and testators without receiving rights of administration. There are many unconsecrated churches and chapels in which services are celebrated daily, about which the bishop wishes to be informed, as about unconsecrated major altars; also about all who have died in the diocese since 1347, testate and intestate, who has their goods and how, and bequests for the repair of the bridge over the Eden near Carlisle; additionally about churches polluted by bloodshed or otherwise. Rose, 25 [Fo.3ᵛ; p.6] April 1354.

35* Admission of William de Tanfeld, monk of St. Mary's, York, to Wetheral (*Wederhale*) priory and the cure of its parishioners, presented by the abbot of St. Mary's; reserving the bishop's rights and all processes etc. in a suit between the abbot and convent and the bishop's predecessors or immediate predecessor, which he intends to maintain.[27] Rose, 21 June 1354.

36 (i) Institution of William del Hall of Bowness (*Bounes*), chaplain, to Bowness [on Solway] church, vacant by the resignation of William;[28] presented by Robert Bruyn, lord of Drumburgh (*Drumbogh*). (ii) Mandate to archdeacon. Rose, 22 July 1354.

37 Letter to Edward III nominating the bishop's clerk, M. William de Ragenhill, for presentation to Arthuret (*Arthureth*) vicarage, now vacant,[29] according to

---

[27] See *Reg. Kirkby* I, nos.420, 458, 475, 490, 497, 623 (for Tanfeld's admission in 1341).
[28] The previous known institution was of William de Kirkebythore, 1342, but he claimed to be vicar of Wigton in 1350 (ibid., I.144, nos.714–15; *CPL*, III.382).
[29] By the death of John de Penreth (**17**).

an ancient agreement with the abbot and convent of Jedburgh (*Jedworth*)[30] and because its temporalities are now in the king's hand. Rose, 25 April 1354.

38 Letters patent of Edward III for the above presentation, in his nomination because the abbot and convent adhere to his Scottish enemies. Westminster, 4 May 1354.[31]

39 (i) Institution of Ragenhill to Arthuret vicarage, nominated [etc., as above]. (ii) Note of mandate for induction to [omitted]. Rose, 23 July 1354.

40 Mandate to the dean of Westmorland to suspend the exaction of a fine (*ab exaccione mulcte*) by the rectors of Brough (*Burgo subtus Staynesmore*)[32] for not attending synods held by the bishop's authority at Michaelmas and Easter last, until Monday before the next synod at Carlisle, releasing any censures; provided that thereafter they wholly answer for these debts. Rose, 24 July 1354.

41 (i) Collation (by lapse of time) to John de Dalston, chaplain, [Fo.4; p.7] of Easton (*Eston*) church, now vacant.[33] (ii) Note of mandate for induction to Richard de Arthureth, chaplain. Rose, 28 July 1354.

42* Letters patent. The certificate about the enquiry into the presentation of William del Hall, priest, to Bowness church questioned whether he was of legitimate age. He appeared before the bishop with witnesses who were examined singly under oath, and so proved his age was legitimate, as the bishop now pronounces. Rose, 22 July 1354.

43 (i) Institution of Robert de Feriby, chaplain, to Barton vicarage, vacant by the resignation of Bro. John de Shirborne;[34] presented by the prior and convent of Warter (*Wartre*). (ii) Mandate for induction to Robert, vicar of Askham (*Ascom*),[35] the archdeacon of Carlisle being *in remotis*. Rose, 5 Aug. 1354.

44 Mandate to the dean of Cumberland to cite John de Langholm, who claims to be rector of Kirkland (*Kirkeland*),[36] to appear before the bishop or his commissaries in the chapel of Rose manor on 25 August to answer for his

---

[30] See *Reg. Halton*, II.61–2, 126; *Reg. Kirkeby*, I.21, no.113.
[31] *CPR 1354–8*, 40; cf. **48** below.
[32] Appropriated to Queen's College, Oxford, 1343 (*Reg. Kirkby*, I.157).
[33] Previous known institution, of unnamed cleric, 1338 (*Reg. Kirkby*, I.84, no.441).
[34] The previous known vicar was John de Fenton, instituted 1345 (ibid., I.166–7).
[35] See **263**. '
[36] Last known rector was John de Skelton, a provisor, in 1347 (*Reg. Kirkby*, I.175). For Langholm's induction in 1350, see **14**, note. Later that year, John de Kirkby, described as rector of Kirkland, obtained a papal licence to hold a second benefice. Apparently forgetting this dispensation, he believed he had forfeited the church by holding Ousby church for a month and more, so prompting Hugh Arlam to seek provision to Kirkland in 1359. Kirkby, however, had already obtained his own provision to that church (*CPP*, I.313, 348; *CPL*, III.394, 603, 608; *Accounts*, ed. Lunt, 158, 206, 373). Langholm died in possession of Kirkland, 1379 (Reg. Appleby, fo.102[v]; p.310), nor can Kirkby's occupation of Ousby be substantiated (cf. **28**, **144**, **255**).

absence, neglect of the cure and removal of goods; certifying by letters patent. Rose, 12 Aug. 1354.

45 Mandate to the official of Carlisle to appoint a suitable rector or vicar as administrator of goods in the diocese which pertain to the bishop's disposal because Lady Joan called FitzWilliam, lady of Soulby (*Suleby*),[37] has died intestate. The administrator is to be sworn to make a faithful inventory of the goods [Fo.4^v; p.8] and of debts, which are to be paid as means allow, and duly render an account. 22 Aug. 1354.

46 Licence to M. Henry de Sandford, rector of Crosby Garrett, to study at a *studium generale* in England or abroad for one year, excusing him from promotion to higher orders; the church must not be neglected and a proctor appointed. Rose, 10 Sept. 1354.

47* Mandate to the dean of Carlisle to command all subjects of the deanery, under pain of excommunication, to pay tithes and especially tithes of sheaves left in their fields, and also those which they have usually carried to the doors of their barns, where tithes were paid; certifying by letters patent before 9 October. Rose, 15 Sept. 1354.

48 (i) Institution of William de Arthureth, chaplain, to Arthuret vicarage, vacant by the resignation of M. William de Ragenhill; presented by Edward III on the bishop's nomination.[38] (ii) Mandate for induction to the archdeacon. Rose, 17 Sept. 1354.

49 (i) Institution of Adam de Hoton, priest, to Kirkby Thore church, vacant by the resignation of Thomas de Riplyngham; presented by Edward III in the minority of Robert de Clifford's heir.[39] (ii) Mandate (as in **48**). Rose, 20 Sept. 1354.

50 Resignation to the bishop of Thomas de Salkeld, rector of Clifton.[40] Rose, 2 Sept. 1354.

51 (i) Note that the bishop collated the said church as shown below. Present: John Welton and Gerlac de Clave[41] [Fo.5; p.9] (ii) COLLACIO ECCLESIE DE CLIFTON

[37] See Nicolson & Burn, I.552–3.
[38] By letters dated 3 Sept. 1354. A previous royal presentation of this William to Arthuret, on 20 Mar., makes no mention of nomination by the bishop (*CPR 1354–8*, 99, 21). Cf. **37–9**.
[39] By letters dated 7 May 1354. Next day, the king presented M. John de Welton, keeper of Newton Reigny chapel, to Kirkby Thore church, in an exchange with its rector, Thomas de Replyngham; but these letters were cancelled on 12 May, on information from Henry de Craystok (*q.v.* under **480**). On 1 Nov., the bishop was pardoned for previously refusing to admit Adam to Kirkby Thore (*CPR 1354–8*, 39, 40, 117–18). Adam was a 'king's clerk' by 1349 (*CCR 1349–54*, 127–8).
[40] Previous known rector was Gregory de Penreth, ordained priest 1346 (*Reg. Kirkby*, I.170).
[41] A familiar clerk, from Speyer diocese, Germany (*Accounts*, ed. Lunt, 246); a notary (**103**).

PLENO JURE VACANTIS. Letters of collation to Thomas de Salkeld, priest. (iii) Note of mandate to archdeacon. Rose, 24 Sept. 1354.

52 Mandate to the dean of Westmorland to collect revenues of Barton vicarage, now vacant, and keep them for the bishop's use until it is clear [to the dean] that a vicar has been instituted and inducted.[42] Rose, 3 Oct. 1354.

53* Monition to the prior of Wetheral not to take corn or hay into Wetheral or Warwick churches and their chapels or others in the diocese belonging to his priory, nor allow any other [persons] to do so, under pain of excommunication for such profanity; certifying by letters patent before Michaelmas. Rose, 13 Sept. 1354.

54 Notes of licences to Richard [de Welwyk], prior of Warter,[43] and Thomas [de Haukesgarth], abbot of Whitby (*Whiteby*),[44] for personal absence from synods at Carlisle. Rose (in the principal chamber), 3 Oct. 1354.

55 Grant to Richard de Hoton of administration of the goods of his wife, Christine, who died intestate, so that he may dispose of them and ordain for the safety of her soul; accounting when required. Rose, 7 Oct. 1354.

56 Letters patent certifying that Richard has accounted [as above] and need not account again. Rose, 20 Oct. 1354.

57* [Fo.5ᵛ; p.10] Commission to the prior of Carlisle to preside at the synod to be celebrated in Carlisle cathedral after St. Luke's [18 Oct.] in place of the bishop, who is engaged on the king's business.[45] Rose, 18 Oct. 1354.

58 (i) Institution of John de Wystowe, chaplain, to Barton vicarage, vacant by the resignation of Robert de Feriby; presented by the prior and convent of Warter. (ii) Mandate to archdeacon. Rose, 18 Oct. 1354.

59* Licence to Richard, prior of Warter, excusing him for as long as he is prior from personal attendance at synods at Carlisle on account of Askham and Barton churches being appropriated to the priory and convent. Rose, 12 Oct. 1354.

60 Note of the like to John, prior of Conishead (*Conyngesheved*), [on account of Orton church]. Rose, 22 Oct. 1354.

[42] Cf. **43**, **58**.
[43] *VCH Yorkshire*, III.238; and see **59**.
[44] See *CPR 1354–8*, 350.
[45] On 5 Oct. 1354, he was appointed to commissions to arrange the release of King David II of Scotland (*Rot. Scot.*, I.769, 771), and was at Berwick upon Tweed making a treaty on 12 November (*Foedera*, III(1).291).

61* Licence to Richard [de Askeby], rector of Uldale, for one year, for services to be celebrated for his parishioners by a chaplain in a chapel in Uldale village, which is distant from the parish church. Rose, 27 Oct. 1354.

62 Licence to Nicholas de Whitrigg', rector of Caldbeck (*Caldebek*),[46] to be absent until next Whitsun [24 May 1355] to visit the Roman court on matters he has explained to the bishop;[47] the church is to be served and a proctor answerable to the bishop appointed. Rose, 30 Oct. 1354.

63 Memorandum that in the principal chamber at Rose William de Arthureth[48] did homage and fealty to Bishop Gilbert for the lands and tenements which he claimed to have, *viz.* half the vill of Cummersdale (*Cumbersdale*) *Magna*[49] in right of his wife Mariota, widow of Thomas de Morpath,[50] for which half she was enfeoffed with Thomas in fee tail; a fourth part of the other half, *viz.* one mediety of it by inheritance from Adam de Crofton, her uncle,[51] and the other by her purchase from Adam de Staffole who held it from the bishop by the same service, in which quarter and another there held by Thomas de Whiterig' is the hamlet of Newby (*Neuby*). William holds these parcels by homage, fealty and cornage. Rose, 30 Nov. 1354.

64 [Fo.6; p.11] Will[52] of Robert de Brounfeld', rector of Melmerby,[53] dated 17 Nov. 1354, in the presence of John Terry, chaplain, Henry de Kyrkbride and Alan de Blennerhasset. Commends soul to God, Blessed Mary and all saints. Burial in the choir of Melmerby church. 40s. for its repair. 20s. for repair of choir. 5 marks for funeral expenses. 20s. for a stone covering his grave. Alan de Blennerhasset, all his tenements in Fisher Street (*Fisshergate*), Carlisle. William Kok', £10. Juliana, William's sister, 5 marks. William, John and Joan, children of [Robert's] brother John, 5 marks. John senior, 10s. John Fairhare, 13s. 4d. Henry de Kirkbride, 5 marks. All his servants, beside wages, 40s. John Shepehird, 6s. 8d. William son of Ranulph, 13s. 4d. Thomas de Salkeld, 40s., a tablecloth, towel and napkin. Richard son of John de Salkeld, 20s. William de Esyngwald, canon of Carlisle, 40s. John de Daker, 13s. 4d. [Robert's] brother William, 40s. to give as arranged. The poor of the town on the burial day, 20s. in bread or money. William de Kirkeby, chaplain, 13s. 4d. William Wendont, 13s. 4d. Thomas Spillgyld, 20s. Adam de Wygton, vicar of Addingham, 5 marks, a little book called 'Porthors', a chalice and a good vestment. [Robert's] brother William, 20 marks unless he has as much by a [previous] assignment. Executors: John de Salkeld, Thomas de Salkeld, rector of Clifton, Adam de Wygton, rector

---

[46] Instituted 1335 (*Reg. Kirkby*, I.45, no.267).
[47] He was appointed a papal chaplain, 22 Apr. 1355 (*CPL*, III.563); he also obtained provision *de novo* to Caldbeck (*Accounts*, ed. Lunt, 90).
[48] Mayor of Carlisle when he died, 1369 (*Test. Karl.*, 89–90).
[49] Tenants there are not named in the rental of 1328 (*Reg. Kirkby*, II.17).
[50] Mayor of Carlisle in 1338 (*CCR 1337–9*, 585).
[51] See Summerson, I.366.
[52] Printed in *Test. Karl.*, 5–6. It omits *Clifton .. rectorem* in the list of executors.
[53] Instituted 1346 (*Reg. Kirkby*, I.173, no.823).

[*sic*] of Addingham,[54] and [Robert's] brother William; they are to have the residue.

Probate by the bishop; administration to the executors named. Rose (chapel), 30 Nov. 1354.

65* Mandate to the dean of Carlisle. The churchyard of St. Mary's cathedral, Carlisle, is under interdict because of recent violence;[55] none of its parishioners have sought its reconciliation. The prior, parish chaplain of St. Cuthbert's, Carlisle, and rectors, vicars and parish chaplains of neighbouring churches, are to be inhibited from admitting to burial any parishioners of St. Mary's without the bishop's licence until the churchyard has been reconciled; names of those violating the inhibition are to be reported to the bishop. Rose, 30 Nov. 1354.

66* Mandate to the official of Carlisle to investigate a report that John [de Gilcrouce], vicar of Dearham (*Derham*),[56] is aged, impotent and almost speechless, and if he needs a curator. Rose, 30 Nov. 1354.

67 Note of licence to Richard [de Askeby], rector of Uldale, to be absent for one year while in the service of the noble lord Thomas de Lucy. 12 Dec. 1354.

68 Note of letter to the dean of Allerdale to inhibit the vicar and parishioners of Torpenhow from any burials in its churchyard until it is reconciled. 11 Dec. 1354.

69 [Fo.6^v; p.12] (i) Sentence confirming the election of Thomas de Hextildesham, canon of Lanercost, OSA, priest,[57] of lawful age and legitimate birth, as prior of Lanercost, vacant by the resignation of John de Bothecastre.[58] The election was held in the chapter house at Lanercost, 2 Dec. 1354. The bishop supplements any defects in form, etc., and commits cure and administration to Thomas. (ii) Oath of obedience by the prior-elect.[59] (iii) Mandate to the subprior and convent to obey Thomas as prior. (iv) Mandate for his installation to the archdeacon. Lanercost, 2 Dec. 1354.[60]

70 (i) Letters patent certifying that the bishop confirmed the election in the chapel at Rose, 7 Dec. 1354.
(ii)* Memorandum that on this day, in the principal chamber at Rose, Prior Thomas swore to observe the following injunctions by the bishop: he would foster charity and be gentle to everyone in the house; act only with the convent's

---

[54] The previous known *vicar* of Addingham was Bro. Thomas de Kyrkoswald, recalled to Carlisle priory in (?)1342 (ibid., I.138, no.677); for Thomas Salkeld, see **50–1**.
[55] See **543**.
[56] Previous known vicar was John de Bridekyrk, 1342 (*Reg. Kirkby*, I.132, no.652); and see **80**.
[57] Ordained subdeacon, 1341 (*Reg. Kirkby*, I.115).
[58] Elected 1338 (ibid., I.87, nos.459–62).
[59] Printed in Nicolson & Burn, II.500; translated in *VCH Cumberland*, II.154.
[60] The last two items are only 'dated as above', but **71** shows that the bishop was at Lanercost for the election.

consent in important business; have the common seal kept by three or two canons; keep few if any dogs; take no part in common hunts; allow neither canons or laymen of the priory to keep dogs; and observe the bishop's ordinance for the previous prior.

71* Letters patent. When the bishop lately went to Lanercost priory, John de Bothecastre, the prior, with all the canons, appeared before him in the chapter house. [Fo.7; p.13]. Asserting that he was too old[61] and feeble to continue in office, John besought the bishop to accept his resignation, which he did. With the canons' consent, the bishop then ordained a portion for John's necessities, *viz.* buildings in the precinct; two canons' daily allowances of food and drink; annually two pairs of new boots and shoes and 46s. 8d. for woollen and linen clothing and other needs (13s. 4d. at Christmas, 20s. at Whitsun and 13s. 4d. at Michaelmas); fuel and candles at need. He is to have an attendant, who is to have the same daily allowance as free servants (*viz.* 'yeomen') have in the priory, and similar wages and clothes yearly or 6s. 8d. *in lieu* of clothing, like other servants there, at St. Nicholas' [6 Dec.]. Monition to the prior, subprior, cellarer, sacristan and other canons to observe the above under pain of excommunication. Lanercost chapter house, 2 Dec. 1354.

72 Confirmation of this ordinance by Thomas de Hextildesham, prior, and the convent. Lanercost chapter house, 10 Dec. 1354.

73 (i) Institution of Henry de Wakefeld, clerk,[62] to Melmerby (*Melmorby*) church, vacant by the death of Robert de Brounefeld; presented by Adam Parvyng'. (ii) Mandate to archdeacon. Rose, 15 Dec. 1354.

74 Commission to the dean of Carlisle to collect the second instalment of the subsidy granted to the bishop by his clergy [as in **32**] by Christmas, under pain of suspension, excommunication and interdict; accounting [Fo.7ᵛ; p.14] by 16 February. Rose, 15 Dec. 1354.
   Note of similar letters to the deans of Allerdale, Westmorland and Cumberland. Same date.

75 Note of licence to William, rector of Kirkbride,[63] to be absent for one year. 16 Aug. 1354.

76 Memorandum that in the principal chamber at Rose, Robert Grout' of Carlisle did homage and fealty to the bishop for the lands and tenements he claims to hold, with the same services, etc. 16 Jan. 1355.

---

[61] He was ordained subdeacon and deacon in 1310, and priest in 1315 (*Reg. Halton,* II.25, 30, 111).
[62] 'A typical civil servant'; bishop of Worcester 1375–95 (*A Calendar of the Register of Henry Wakefield,* ed. W.P. Marett, Worcestershire Historical Society, n.s. 7, 1972, xxxiii, xxxv).
[63] The previous known rector was John de Misterton, 1347 (*Reg. Kirkby,* I.171, no.820).

77* Appointment of John de Shupton, rector of a mediety of Linton in Craven (dioc. York), and M. William de Ragenhill, the bishop's familiar clerks, as commissaries general for all causes in his audience. Rose, 15 Jan. 1355.

78 Memorandum of dispensation for bastardy of Richard son of William [son of] Richard de Warthecopp, clerk, by authority of Stephen [Aubert], bishop of Ostia and Velletri, penitentiary of Clement VI; he has a testimonial letter. Dalston parish church, 20 Dec. 1354.

79* Letters patent inspecting an instrument by the official of Carlisle and M. William de Fenton, notary, publishing the sentence in a divorce cause between Elizabeth daughter of Peter de Tylliol, kt., deceased, plaintiff, and Thomas son of Thomas de Rokeby, kt., junior. Elizabeth's proctor claimed that the marriage with Thomas was invalid because at the time it was contracted he was under the age of puberty. She was unwillingly forced to make the contract but never freely consented and now sought its annulment. Thomas accepted her case. Her witnesses were examined, both parties questioned, and a date agreed for hearing the definitive sentence. This was pronounced by the official: Elizabeth had proved her case and the marriage was declared void [Fo.8; p.15] in St. Cuthbert's church, Carlisle, 24 May 1354. Witnesses: Masters Adam de Caldebek' and Walter de Helton, skilled in law, William de Ragenhill, notary, of York and Carlisle dioceses, and others [unnamed]. Subscription by William de Fenton, clerk (dioc. Carlisle), notary by papal authority; he was present at the sentence by M. Nicholas de Whiteby, official of Carlisle. Confirmation under the bishop's seal, dated Rose, 10 Dec. 1354.

80 (i) Institution of John de Derham, priest, to Dearham vicarage, vacant by the resignation into the bishop's hands of John de Gilcrouce; presented by the prior and convent of Guisbourgh (*Gyseburn*). (ii) Mandate to archdeacon. Rose, 31 Jan. 1355.

81 Mandate to the dean of Carlisle. It is rumoured that unknown evildoers attacked Joan daughter of Isabel, widow of John de Brounfeld, in Sebergham (*Seburgham*) churchyard. The dean is personally to enquire there about whose hand had struck her, whether it was a churchyard, and other circumstances, reporting by letters patent. Rose, 27 Jan. 1355.

82 Memorandum[64] of probate of the nuncupative will [not quoted] of John Wright of Sebergham and grant of administration of his goods to William Walker and William Lothen of Sebergham. Rose, 3 Feb. 1355.

83 Licence to William [del Hall], rector of Bowness, to study in a *studium generale* until 7 July; the church is to be served by a chaplain and a responsible proctor appointed. Rose, 5 Feb. 1355.

---

[64] Printed in *Test. Karl.*, 7, with mispelt surnames.

84* Letters patent. John de Boghes, vicar of Kirkby Stephen,[65] was charged by the bishop *ex officio* for incontinence with Margaret Wyvill and others, and for publicly keeping her as his concubine, contrary to a legatine constitution.[66] After examining him, the bishop decided he had not incurred the constitution's penalty and had already been sufficiently corrected for incontinence. He is discharged from further impeachment [Fo.8ᵛ; p.16] and dispensed if any dispensation is required. Rose, 5 Feb. 1355.

85 Letters patent. John, vicar of Kirkby Stephen, priest, had been cited to show the bishop his title as incumbent and letters of orders. He appeared with many letters and public instruments, and sought confirmation of his possession. After inspecting them and other evidence, the bishop pronounced his title canonical and sufficient and confirmed the legality of his holy orders, absolving him from further impeachmant. Dated as above.

86 Commission to Masters Nicholas de Whiteby and John de Welton, the bishop's familiar clerks skilled in law (or one of them), to hear and determine a suit pending or likely before the bishop between the abbot and convent of Fountains (*Fontibus*) as appropriators of Crosthwaite (*Crosthwayt*) church, and Thomas Inne, its vicar,[67] about their claim to an annual pension of ten marks and oath of fealty to the abbot; certifying the bishop after the conclusion. Rose, 5 Feb. 1355.

87* Commission to the prior of Carlisle to deputise for the bishop (who is detained on business) on Ash Wednesday [18 Feb.], when it is customary for penitents to come to the cathedral. Rose, 16 Feb. 1355.

88 Probate[68] of the nuncupative will of Robert son of Adam son of Walter de Forneby, as follows:
  Commends soul to God. Burial in churchyard of St. Andrew's, Aikton, with best beast as mortuary, and a skep of oatmeal and an ox for the poor. Parish chaplain, 12d. Gilbert de Forneby, 12d. Friars minor, Carlisle, 3s. Friars minor of the same,[69] 3s. Eden bridge, 3s. Fabric of St. Mary's, Carlisle, 3s. Reasonable funeral expenses. Residue, if any, to a chaplain celebrating for his soul. Executor: William Brownyng, his brother.
  Grant of administration to William Brounyng. Rose (chapel), 10 Mar. 1355.[70]

---

[65] Instituted 1336 (*Reg. Kirkby*, I.63, no.335); ordained subdeacon 1321 (*Reg. Halton*, II.207
[66] See *Councils and Synods*, II (cited xiv, n.41), I.252–3, II.756–7.
[67] Or *June*? – misread as *Lune* in Nicolson & Burn, II.87. The previous known institution was of Richard de Graystok, in 1313; perhaps the same named Richard (only) in 1331 and 1338 (*Reg. Halton*, II.79; *Reg. Kirkby*, I.8, no.61, 88, no.467). Inne's immediate predecessor is named as Richard de Esyngwald in **195**. See also **319n**.
[68] Printed in *Test. Karl.*, 7–8.
[69] *Sic*. In error for 'preachers' in either bequest?
[70] Margin: *Reddidit compotum et dimissus est*.

89 Appointment of M. Adam de Caldbek, clerk skilled in law, as official of Carlisle. Rose, 10 Mar. 1355.

Note that he swore on the Gospels that he would faithfully execute the office.

90 [Fo.9; p.17] Memorandum that on 13 Mar. 1355, John de Blenkansopp', John Maresshall and Richard Halden of Carlisle appeared before the bishop in the principal chamber at Rose. They sought absolution from their excommunication for obstructing him and his ministers in Carlisle.[71] This the bishop did after they had sworn to obey the church, do penance (to be decided) and not repeat the offence.

On 15 March, John Wyrshipp', William de Ebor', Thomas Strang', Thomas Sadler, Robert del Strayt', Luke Taillour, Adam Blissedblode, Adam Derman, William de Carlton and Alan Skynner of Carlisle made a similar plea in the chapel at Rose and were absolved after taking the same oath. Their penance was specified in a mandate to the dean of Carlisle (of that date), which states that they had drawn arms on the highroad in Carlisle to prevent the bishop's servants buying victuals. On the three Sundays before Easter (from that day) each one was to walk, bare-headed and clad only in shirts and breeches, from Caldew Gate carrying a candle, to say prayers at the high altars of the cathedral, St. Cuthbert's and the church of the Friars Minor, where the candles were to be left. The dean was to supervise, and explain in English to people in those churches the reason for this penance.

John Wyrshipp' failed to complete his penance. He returned to the bishop for absolution, which was granted at the request of Thomas de Lucy.

On 2 April, at the instance of Matthew de Redemane,[72] the bishop commissioned the prior and subprior of Carlisle, and the parish chaplains of St. Mary's and St. Cuthbert's, to absolve all concerned, save for leading citizens whose absolution was reserved to the bishop.

91 Will[73] of William de Lygh, kt., dated 17 Nov. 1354. Commends soul to God. Burial in churchyard of St. Michael's, Isel, with best horse as customary. Bequests of silver coin to his children: Richard, £10; William, 10 marks; Edmund, 10 marks; Thomas, 5 marks; Peter, 5 marks; Margaret, £10; Mariot, £10. William de Toft and his wife, 6 bullocks and 6 heifers. John the [C]lerk, Richard le Spenser and Cecily de Baggeleygh, one cow each. John Wright and his brother Roger, two beasts worth 20s. Residue to his wife Margaret. Executors: Margaret and William de Toft. Witnesses: Robert Leycestre and William Hobsone. Sealed.

---

[71] This incident is discussed in Summerson, I.352. Dr. Summerson will print this text in a volume to be published by the Surtees Society.

[72] Probably the Matthew Redman who was lieutenant to Thomas Lucy as keeper of Carlisle castle in 1356 (J.L. Kirby, 'The keeping of Carlisle castle before 1381', *CWAAS*, 2nd ser. 54 (1955), 137–8).

[73] Printed in *Test. Karl.*, 8–9. There is no notice of probate but in the margin is the usual note, *Redd' compotum*. See **551** for William's illness.

92 [Fo.9ᵛ; p.18] Signification to the king that Nicholas, servant (*famulo*) of Robert Roos, has been excommunicate for 40 days at the instance of the bishop's office. Rose, 20 Apr. 1355.

93* Mandate to the dean of Carlisle. Many rectors and vicars named in a schedule owe various sums to the archdeacon of Carlisle for procurations in his visitations, despite being warned, as he has complained. They are to be told to pay him within 15 days under pains of suspension and excommunication for persons and interdict for their churches, which are to be published daily. The dean is to report when required by the archdeacon, by letters patent naming non-payers. n.d.

94 Note of licence to Robert [de Boyvill], rector of Thursby (*Thoresby*),[74] to be absent for two years, farming the church, with a proctor, etc. 20 June 1355.

95 Mandate to the official of Carlisle quoting letters of Edward III (dated 9 (*sic*) June 1355) ordering prayers and processions for the safety of the king and his army in France.[75] There are to be processions on the fourth and sixth days of every week in St. Mary's. Carlisle, and all parish and conventual churches in the diocese, and daily celebration of seven penitential psalms and the litany; [Fo.10; p.19] with an indulgence of 40 days for those participating. Rose, 26 June 1355.

96 Mandate of the bishop as executor of a papal grace to John de Praye, a poor clerk (dioc. Carlisle), to M. William de Routhbury, archdeacon of Carlisle, forwarding papal letters to be inspected.[76] Enquiry is to be made about John's life and associations; if he is found to be honest, etc, and unbeneficed, and there is no canonical obstacle, he is to be provided, instituted and inducted (in person or by proxy) to a benefice in the gift of the abbot and convent of St. Mary's, York, if there is one in the diocese now or soon to be vacant. Rose, 11 June 1355.

97 Notarial instrument. When the bishop recently visited the prior and chapter of Carlisle, he learned that they hold as appropriated the parish churches of St. Mary, Carlisle; St. Cuthbert, Carlisle, with Sebergham chapel; Hayton, with Cumrew (*Comrewe*) and Cumwhitton (*Comquntyngton*) chapels; Crosscanonby (*Crosseby in Allerdale*); Camerton (*Camberton*); Ireby (*Irby*); Bassenthwaite (*Beghokirk*); Castle Sowerby (*Soureby*); Rockcliffe (*Routhecliff*); Edenhall (*Edenhale*) with Langwathby chapel; and Addingham (*Adyngham*) with [Little] Salkeld chapel. With the exceptions of Sowerby and Edenhall, none of these churches have vicars but are served by stipendiary chaplains.

They also have pensions from the following churches: Lowther (*Louthre*), 26s.

---

[74] Instituted 1316 (*Reg. Halton*, II.124; see also Nicolson & Burn, II.205–6).

[75] Dated 1 June in *Foedera*, III(1).303; *CCR 1349–56*, 210.

[76] In a petition to the pope (granted 19 Dec. 1354), John claimed to have accepted St. Lawrence's, Appleby (in St. Mary's gift: *CPP*, I.290). The previous known vicar was John de Carleton, in 1336, the next William Colyn, in 1359 (*Reg. Kirkby*, I.60, no.308; **268** below). John Pray became vicar of Helmsley, Yorks. (in Kirkham's gift), until he exchanged to Morland,1368 (Reg. Appleby, fo.22, p.181; Nicolson & Burn, I.444, where his name is misread as Bray).

8d.; Kirkland, 26s.; Ousby (*Ulnesby*), 6s. 8d.; Hutton in the Forest (*Hoton*), 2s.; Castle Carrock (*Castelkairok'*), 2s.; Kirkcambeck (*Cambok'*), 2s.; Bewcastle (*Bothecastre*), 6s. 8d.; Upmanby (*Ukmanby*), 2s. 6d.; the abbot and convent of Holm Cultram, £6.

The bishop cited the prior and chapter to show their title. Their proctor produced instruments etc. and witnesses. After all were considered, etc., the bishop pronounced that the prior and chapter's title to these churches and pensions was proved and dismissed them from further impeachment.

Recorded as an instrument by M. William de Ragenhill, clerk and notary, the bishop's registrar (*scriba*), with his sign and subscription, and the bishop's seal. Rose, 27 June 1355.

Witnesses: M. William de Routhbury, archdeacon of Carlisle; Nicholas de Whiterig, rector [Fo.10ᵛ; p.20] of Caldbeck; and M. Thomas de Salkeld, rector of Clifton, notary by papal authority.

98 Note of licence to M. Ralph de Erghom, rector of Greystoke (*Craystok'*) to be absent for three years in a suitable place, excused from attending synods and chapters, etc. Rose, 12 July 1355.

99 Mandate to the parish chaplain of Crosscanonby. Inhabitants of Allerby (*Crosseby Aylward*) are failing in their duty to their parish church of Aspatria (*Aspatrik'*), not going there on Sundays and feastdays to hear divine service. When asked by the vicar of Aspatria, the chaplain is to order them to attend or compel their obedience by canonical censures. n.d.

100 Mandate to the vicars of Irthington and Brampton in Gilsland (*Gilles-land*).[77] With the death of Prior Thomas [de Hextildesham], Lanercost priory is vacant, its care now resting with the subprior. The vicars, under pain of excommunication for negligence, are to go there on 22 and 23 July and order all present and absent (under the same pain) not to oppose the subprior in the vacancy so that he and the officers he has appointed may do their duties; certifying by 1 August. Rose, 18 July 1355.

101 To the subprior of Lanercost. The bishop has received and been asked to confirm the postulation by the subprior and canons of Richard de Ridale, canon of Carlisle,[78] to be their prior. Some canons of the house, however, have elected their fellow canon, John de Nonyngton. The bishop wishes that canonical statutes will be observed with regard to the postulation and election. Next Saturday and Sunday [25 and 26 July], it is to be proclaimed in the conventual church that Bro. John and any objectors to the postulation or election are to appear before the bishop in the chapel at Rose on 27 July, to provide reasons, if any, why he should not confirm the postulation or election; he intends to proceed whether they come or not. The time has been set to avoid a long

---

[77] No vicar of Irthington is named in this register (see also **266**, **446**); the last known as instituted was Laurence de Caudre, 1337 (*Reg. Kirkby*, I.76, no.405). For Brampton, see **405** below.
[78] Ordained deacon, 1339 (*Reg. Kirkby*, I.98).

vacancy. The subprior and all canons are cited to come, and certify execution by letters under their common seal. 20 July 1355.

102 (i) Sentence confirming the postulation of Richard de Ridale, canon of Carlisle, professed Augustinian and priest, of lawful age and birth, to the priory of Lanercost vacant by the death of Thomas de Hextildesham; celebrated in the chapter house, 15 July 1355. The bishop has supplied defects in form. With the consent of the prior of Carlisle, where Richard was professed. (ii) Oath of obedience by Prior Richard to Bishop Gilbert, his successors and ministers.[79] (iii) Mandate to the subprior and canons to obey him. [Fo.11; p.21] (iv) Note of mandate to the archdeacon to do his part (*quod incumbit*). [Rose, 27 July 1355.]

103 TRANSUMPCIO EXEMPLIFICATIO ET AUCTORIZACIO QUORUMDAM INSTRUMEN-TORUM ET LITTERARUM CONCERNENCIUM APPROPRIACIONEM ECCLESIE DE WYGGE-TON. Notarial instrument. The abbot and convent of Holm Cultram appeared before the bishop. They have letters and instruments concerning their appro-priation of Wigton church, save for a portion for its vicarage. They need to show them to various judges, both in the Roman court and in England, to defend their rights. They dare not take them from place to place because of Scottish attacks and dangers of the road in England, at sea and abroad. The bishop has agreed to their requests that copies be made by notaries and declared authentic. The documents are as follow:

'Johannes etc.' as is clearly written in the register of John de Kirkeby, late bishop of Carlisle. Bishop [Welton] has examined them and declares them free of any defects. There are four documents: two sealed with the seal of Bishop John in red wax; another with the common seal of the chapter of Carlisle in green wax; and the other with the seals of two commissaries in white wax.[80] The copies are full, correct and may be trusted throughout the world (*ubilibet per orbem terrarum*), as the bishop certifies by his authority as ordinary in the presence of notaries and others. [Rose,] 21 Sept. 1355.

Subscription by William de Ragenhill, clerk (dioc.York), notary and registrar (*scriba*) of Bishop Gilbert, again describing the seals of the above four documents, adding that three of them were instruments with the signs and subscriptions of M. John de Hakthorp, notary; all were faithfully copied by the bishop's order. Dated at Rose as above, in the third year of Pope Innocent VI. Witnesses: Masters William de Routhbury, archdeacon of Carlisle, and John de Bridelyngton and Gerlac called de Clave, clerks and notaries.

104 Sentence. In his visitation of the diocese, the bishop learned that the abbot and convent of Holm Cultram had long held Wigton parish church as appropriated for their use; they were cited to show their title. [Fo.11ᵛ; p.22] They appeared before the bishop for judgment as appointed, and in a written article stated that they had for a long time peacefully held the church and its revenues, save for a vicar's portion. A date was set, when they produced documents and witnesses, which were examined and judicially published without any objector appearing. A date was set to conclude the business

---

[79] Printed in *VCH Cumberland*, II.154.
[80] See *Reg. Kirkby*, I.34–5, no.196.

when, with expert counsel, the bishop declared that the appropriation was canonical, and the monks and their monastery dismissed from further impeachment. Rose, 1 Oct. 1355.

105 Memorandum that the bishop appointed John, vicar of Penrith (*Penreth*), as his dean of Cumberland. 10 Oct. 1355.

106 Memorandum that the prior and convent of Watton were given letters under the bishop's seal allowing their appropriation of Ravenstonedale (*Ravenstandale*) church. Also that the prior was given a licence excusing him from attendance at synods during the bishop's episcopate, with proviso for a proctor, etc. Rose, 2 May 1355.

107 Letters patent confirming the appropriation of Wigton church to Holm Cultram [mostly repeating **103**: adding that a proctor appeared for the convent at the first session, who claimed that its occupation had been *per tempora non modica* and not opposed by previous bishops of Carlisle, and produced many documents and many witnesses; objectors were summoned for the next session, but none came]. Rose, 17 Oct. 1355.

108 [Fo.12; p.23] Presentation by the bishop to John [Gynwell], bishop of Lincoln, of his dear clerk, Richard de Aslacby, to Moorby (*Moreby*) church (dioc. Lincoln), now vacant. Rose, 1 Jan. 1356.

109 Note of grant to Robert de Thirneby, clerk with first tonsure, of letters dimissory to all orders. 8 Jan. 1356.

110 Presentation by the bishop to Thomas [Hatfield], bishop of Durham, of Richard de Thirneby, clerk, to Newburn (*Neuborne*) vicarage (dioc. Durham), now vacant. Rose, 17 Jan. 1356.

111 Commission of Thomas [Hatfield], bishop of Durham, for an exchange of benefices between M. John [son of] Thomas de Appelby,[81] rector of St. Nicholas', Durham city, and Robert de Appelby, rector of Newbiggin (*Neubiggyng*).[82] Auckland (*Aukeland*) manor, 14 Dec. 1355.

112 (i) Collation to Robert de Appelby, clerk, of St. Nicholas', Durham, in the bishop of Durham's gift, in the person of Thomas son of John Tailor (*Cissoris*) of Appleby (*Appelby*), chaplain, his proctor; vacant by the resignation, in person, of M. John Thome in this exchange. (ii) Certificate to the bishop of Durham. [Fo.12ᵛ; p.24]
(iii) Institution of M. John Thome, clerk, to Newbiggin church, vacant by the resignation of Robert by the above proctor; presented by William de Crakanthorp.
(iv) Note of mandate to the archdeacon. Rose, 25 Jan. 1356.

---

[81] See *BRUO*, I.40–1.
[82] Instituted 20 Sept. 1355 (**566**).

113 Note of licence to Richard [de Askeby], rector of Uldale, to be absent for one year while in the service of the noble lord Thomas de Lucy. 12 Feb. 1356.

114* Letters patent.[83] It was delated to the bishop's audience that William del Park and Ellen Bogher, both of Carlisle, contracted matrimony *per verba de presenti* but did not solemnise it. They were cited to show their reason why they should not be compelled. On appearing in the audience, they confessed that William's frigidity was such that he could not have intercourse with any woman, even though he and Ellen had been left together in bed. Another date was appointed, when they brought many witnesses, whose testimony convinced the bishop that the alleged impediment was true. He therefore annulled the contracted marriage. Rose, 27 Feb. 1356.

115* Mandate to Thomas [del Close], rector of Brougham,[84] and John de Dokwra, chaplain. Unknown parishioners of the bishop's peculiar church of Penrith broke up a path of stone and earth in its churchyard, made to give its ministers decent access to the church and choir. They did this on a feast day during the celebration of mass. They threw stones at the adjacent buildings of the manse, damaging its roof, walls and doors. From next Sunday [30 Jan.] Thomas and/or John are to announce in Penrith church that the perpetrators must recompense the church and bishop within ten days or incur sentence of major excommunication, which is to be published until they have sought absolution; enquiry is to be made for their names. [Fo.13; p.25] Rose, 28 Jan. 1356.

116* Memorandum that John de Wilton, John Taverner, Robert de Thresk' and other parishioners of Penrith came before the bishop in the chapel at Rose and confessed that they, with many others, had broken and removed the path. They humbly sought absolution from excommunication. The bishop, moved by their entreaties and in regard to Roger de Salkeld,[85] who came with them, absolved those who were present. He appointed the vicar [of Penrith], also present, as his deputy to absolve all involved. The penance for offenders, absent as well as present, was that they should collectively offer a wax candle of 3 pounds in Penrith church before the image of the Virgin Mary on Sunday next [20 Feb.]. Rose, 14 Feb. 1356.

117 Letters patent appointing Agnes, widow of Adam Houlotsone of Triermain (*Trevermane*), who died intestate, administrator of his goods in the bishop's jurisdiction. Rose, 10 Mar. 1356.[86]

---

[83] Quoted in Summerson, I.363.
[84] See **166**, **262**. A Thomas was rector in 1336 (*Reg. Kirkby*, I.60, no.308), and before him Thomas de Warthecop in 1316 (*Reg. Halton*, II.136). The father of Thomas del Close, however, was alive when he died, 1362 (**488**).
[85] Perhaps the bishop's auditor in 1347 (*Reg. Kirkby*, I.173, no. 824).
[86] Partly printed in *Test. Karl.*, 9 (with *deodatis* for *decedentis*).

118   Note of probate of the will [not quoted] of Thomas Houlotsone and grant of administration to Alan Notshagh and Christine, widow of Thomas, executors named in the will. Same date.[87]

HIC INCIPIT ANNUS DOMINI MILLESIMUS TRECENTESIMUS QUINQUAGESIMUS SEXTUS.

119   Note of licence to John de Walworth, prior of Hexham (*Hextildesham*), excusing him for as long as he is prior from personal attendance at synods at Carlisle on account of Isel (*Isale*) and Renwick (*Ravenwyk*) churches being appropriated, provided that he appears by proxy. Rose, 6 Apr. 1356.

120   Mandate to the dean of Carlisle to order abbots, priors, rectors, vicars, other clergy and people to appear at the visitation of M. William de Routhbury, archdeacon of Carlisle, on the dates and places named in a schedule; certifying the bishop or archdeacon before the first date it gives, with names of those cited. Rose, 16 Apr. 1356.
    Note of similar mandates to the other deans.

121   Note of commission to the prior of Carlisle to lead (*introducendum*) penitents into Carlisle cathedral and reconcile them, as is customary. 19 Apr. 1356.[88]

122   Letters patent. While visiting the church and diocese, the bishop found that the prioress and convent of Rosedale (*Rosdale*; dioc. York) hold the parish church of Torpenhow (*Torpenhowe*) as appropriated. They claimed, when cited, that their occupation was ancient, and produced charters and documents of previous bishops of Carlisle and patrons, with confirmation by Carlisle cathedral chapter. The bishop finds their possession canonical and dismisses them from further impeachment. Rose, 4 May 1356.

123   Letters patent [in French] Request for safe conduct for the bearer, Adam Godeloke of Kirkandrews (*Kirkandres*), purveyor of corn and ale (*briez?*) for the bishop's household, until Michaelmas next. Rose, 16 May 1356.

124   [Fo.13ᵛ; p.26] Note of licence to William de Ebor', rector of Bolton, to be absent for one year while serving Lady Alice de Nevill. 6 May 1356.

125*   Mandate of John [Thoresby], archbishop of York. He had agreed with prelates attending the recent parliament at Westminster[89] that provincial councils should be held in Canterbury and York to devise a remedy in grave matters concerning both the condition and liberty of the English church and

---

[87]   Printed ibid., 9. There is no marginal note of account.
[88]   For Maundy Thursday, i.e. 21 April (cf. **87**, **533**).
[89]   23–30 Nov. 1355 (*HBC*, 562). For Welton's absence, see **571**.

clergy and the defence of the realm.[90] Citation of the bishop[91] and, through him, of abbots, priors, deans and provosts of collegiate churches, and archdeacons, to appear in person, chapters and colleges by one proctor, and clergy of the diocese by two proctors, to a council in York cathedral commencing 3 June; they are to take part in its business and accept its ordinances. Absentees will be prosecuted. The bishop is to announce that those with grievances in matters pertaining to the council's correction will have audience, and to certify by letters patent naming those cited. Westminster, 12 March 1356.

126 Mandate to the prior and convent of Lanercost. The bishop will visit them on Thursday 26 May. All are to appear in the chapter house to receive his corrections and injunctions. Absent brothers and *conversi* are to be recalled. Inhibition against any attempt to prejudice the visitation. Letters patent certifying compliance are to be delivered by that day, naming all brothers, absent as well as present. Rose, 6 May 1356.

127 Licence to Robert de Kirkeby, rector of a mediety of Aikton (*Ayketon*),[92] at the request of Margaret de Dacre, lady of Gilsland (*Gillesland*), for absence for one year while in her service; excused from personal attendance at synods in Carlisle and chapters, with the church being served by proxy, etc. Rose, 3 June 1356.

128 [Fo.14; p.27] Licence to William de Ebor, rector of Bolton (*Boulton*), at the request of the noble lord, Ralph[93] de Nevill, kt., to farm the church for one year, provided he leaves a responsible proctor. Rose, 26 June 1356.

129 Note that William [del Hall], rector of Bowness, was licensed to study (*standi in scolis*) for one year and be absent from synods. Rose, 1 Aug. 1356.

130 CASSACIO CONTRACTUS MATRIMONIALIS INTER JOHANNEM DE DISTYNGTON ET CHRISTIANAM SPICER. Letters patent. Christine called Spicer of Carlisle requested the bishop to divorce and dissolve her marriage with John de Distyngton (*quondam de facto contractum celebratum divorciare dissolvere et irritare*) on the grounds of John's previous carnal knowledge of her daughter Agnes. Wishing to be just to both parties, the bishop called them to his audience. He appointed commissaries, who found that Christine had proved her case and, after deliberation, annulled the marriage *sentencialiter vice nostra*, as the bishop now announces to all concerned. Rose, 30 June 1356.

131 Note of licence to William de Burton, abbot of Whitby,[94] excusing him for as long as he is abbot from attendance at synods at Carlisle, visitations and other

---

[90] For this crisis, see R.L. Storey, 'Simon Islip, Archbishop of Canterbury (1349–66): Church, Crown and Parliament', *Ecclesia Militans*, ed. W. Brandmüller, H. Immenkötter and E. Iserloh, 2 vols., Paderborn (1988), I.145–6. See also **149**.
[91] See **584**.
[92] The last known rector of this mediety was Thomas le Spenser, in 1339 (*Reg. Kirkby*, I.96, no.507; cf. **154** below).
[93] MS. John: cf. **29**, **164**; *Complete Peerage*, IX.499–501.
[94] Elected April 1356 (*CPR 1354–8*, 365); cf. **54**.

meetings (*convocacionibus*) of clergy on account of Crosby Ravensworth (*Crossebyravenswath*) church being appropriated. 9 Sept. 1356.

132 (i) Institution of Henry de Whitebergh, chaplain, to Stapleton (*Stapelton*) church, vacant by the resignation of Henry Martyn;[95] presented by John de Stapelton. (ii) Archdeacon to induct. [Rose,] 11 Sept. 1356.

133 (i) Institution of M. Robert de Suthayk, clerk, to Stapleton church, vacant by the resignation (by his proctor, M. Adam de Caldebek) of Henry de Whytebergh, chaplain, in exchange for Bewcastle (*Bothecastre*) church;[96] presented by John de Stapelton. (ii) Institution of Henry to Bewcastle, vacant by Robert's resignation; presented by the prior and chapter of Carlisle. (iii) Note of mandate to the archdeacon to induct both rectors or their proctors. Rose, 16 Sept. 1356.

134 (i) Collation to Richard de Aslakby, chaplain, of Dalston vicarage, vacant by the death of Henry Hund'.[97] (ii) Archdeacon to induct. Rose, 7 Nov. 1356.

135* Commission to the prior of Carlisle, M. William de Routhbury, archdeacon of Carlisle, M. John de Welton, the bishop's familiar clerks, and the official of Carlisle. According to the canons, there should not be services or burials in undedicated places. The bishop has learnt that in the church or chapel [Fo.14ᵛ; p.28] of St. Alban in Carlisle city services are celebrated and burials made in it and its churchyard.[98] The bishop does not known whether it has been dedicated and commonly reputed a sacred place, or even if it has been a parish church or chapel from ancient times. The commissaries (or two of them) are to enquire into the truth with clerks and laymen of the city and surrounding places, reporting after the inquest. Rose, 20 Oct. 1356.

136 Commission to Thomas de Salkeld, rector of Clifton, following a complaint by the archdeacon of Carlisle, to order rectors and vicars who have not paid procurations due for his visitations, despite frequent requests, to pay him within 15 days, or compel them strictly (*arcius*) by sentences of suspension, excommunication and interdict. Rose, 21 Oct. 1356.

137 (i) Collation to Henry Martyn, chaplain, of Scaleby church, vacant by the death of Walter de Swetehopp'.[99] (ii) Archdeacon to induct. Rose, 26 Oct. 1356.

138 Mandate to the parish chaplains of St. Mary's and St. Cuthbert's, Carlisle, to forbid their parishioners from celebrating or hearing services in St. Alban's

---

[95] The previous known institution was of John de Kirkeby in 1338 (*Reg. Kirkeby*, I.84, no.439).

[96] Robert was instituted to Bewcastle in 1306 (*Reg. Halton*, I.251–2, II.30). He often occurs, as official of Carlisle, in *Reg. Kirkby*.

[97] Only occurs previously as 'H. H.' in 1342 (*Reg. Kirkby*, I.138, no.679).

[98] See R.L. Storey, 'The Chantries of Cumberland and Westmorland. Part I', *CWAAS*, 2nd ser. 60 (1960), 69–71; see also **138, 142.**

[99] The previous known institution was of Roger Cromwell in 1345 (*Reg. Kirkby*, I.162, no.786). See also **559.**

chapel as the enquiry (135) has found that it is not consecrated, under pains of suspension for celebrants and excommunication for hearers. Rose, 12 Nov. 1356.

139 Will[100] of Matthew de Redmane, dated at Carlisle, 2 Nov. 1356. Commends soul to God, Blessed Mary and all saints. Burial in churchyard of [friars] preachers, Carlisle, with best beast to parish church as mortuary. Friars preachers, Carlisle, 20s. Friars minor there, 20s. Bro. Robert Deyncourt,[101] 6s. 8d. Simon the clerk, 6s. 8d. A pound of wax to burn round his corpse. For a wake (*in convocacione vicinorum*), 20s. A pilgrim to St. James, 40s. His burgage in Fisher Street to his wife Emmot; also 29 marks owed by Sir William de Craystok'[102] for a horse and other animals; and the residue to pay his debts, if any. Executors: Gilbert de Hothwayt and Emmot.

Probate by the bishop, with grant of administration to Emmot. Gilbert de Hothwayt', in person, refused to act. Rose (chapel), 14 Nov. 1356.

140 (i) Institution of Robert de Bolton, chaplain, to Stapleton church, vacant by the resignation of M. Robert de Suthayk'; presented by John de Stapelton. (ii) Archdeacon to induct. Rose, 16 Nov. 1356.

141 Note of licence to M. Henry de Sandford, rector of Crosby Garrett, to be absent for one year in a suitable place and not attend synods; and that in an oratory of his father, Robert de Sandeford at Sandford, he may have a chaplain once or twice a month [Fo.15; p.29] to celebrate during that year. Rose, 21 Nov. 1356.

142 Will[103] of John Caldesmyth, chaplain, of Carlisle,[104] dated 12 October 1356. Commends soul to God, Blessed Mary and all saints. Burial in St. Mary's churchyard, Carlisle; 3s. 4d. in wax. Friars preachers, 10s. [Friars] minor, 6s. 8d. Eden bridge, 3s. 4d. Each chaplain celebrating in Carlisle city, 6d. in equal portions. The convent, 10s. for a pittance. St. Mary's fabric, 6s. 8d. Lights of Blessed Mary in the choir and outside in the parish church, 3s. 4d. Ellen daughter of John de Seyntdynis, 3s. 4d. Workmen and the poor on his burial day, 6s. 8d. St. Alban's fabric, 6s. 8d. All his vestments with ornaments to St. Alban's altar there in perpetuity. His breviary to Robert son of John de Sancto Dionisio when he comes of age and enters ecclesiastical service, but the book is to be sold for distribution among the poor if he does not take holy orders. John Boon, the parish chaplain, 6s. 8d. Agnes servant of Robert Powetsone, 12d. The parish clerk, 12d. Peter son of Ellen Bogher, 7s. which her husband owes. John Brounfeld, 12d. Residue to his sister Mariot for distribution among the poor as the executors ordain. Executors: Sir John Boon and Robert Powetsone. Witnesses: John Halden, Thomas the clerk and Mariot.

---

[100] Printed in *Test. Karl.*, 9–10
[101] OP (see 20).
[102] Probably Baron Greystoke (see 265).
[103] Printed in *Test. Karl.*, 10–11. It is in error with the date, Wed. before St. Michael in Monte Tumba.
[104] Probably employed in St. Alban's chapel.

Probate by the bishop; administration granted to named executors. Rose (chapel), 20 Nov. 1356.

143 Licence addressed to abbots, priors, rectors, vicars, parish chaplains and others celebrating in churches and chapels of the diocese. They are to admit questors of the hospital of Saint-Antoine-de-Viennois (*sancti Antonii Vienn' diocesis*) bearing these letters and allow them to take collections from their parishioners, notwithstanding the bishop's inhibition (see **24**); valid for one year. Rose, 24 Nov. 1356.

144 Will[105] of Lady Agnes, wife of Sir Richard de Denton, dated at Ousby, 2 Sept. 1356 (being *compos mentis*). Commends soul to God and Blessed Mary. Burial in Thursby church before Blessed Mary's altar, with best beast as mortuary, and the second beast to Denton church as mortuary; 3 stones of wax to burn round her body, a mark for oblations and 30s. in doles for the poor. The friars minor, Carlisle, 10s. The friars preachers, Carlisle, 10s. The Austin friars of Penrith and Appleby,[106] to share 6s. 8d. The nuns of Armathwaite, 10s. John de Kirkbride, 2 oxen, 2 cows and 2 heifers. Lady Cecily de Hermythwayt, 2 cows. Christine, [Agnes'] kinswoman, 2 cows. Robert Lynok', 2 cows. Robert Lynok', 2s. John Fauconer, 2s. John del Hall, 2s. Thomas his brother, 2s. John son of Robert, 2s. Adam his brother, 12d. Lady Cecily, the best brass pot, and Christine, a brass pot. A chaplain celebrating for her soul in Thursby church, 6 marks. Residue to her lord Sir Richard de Denton. Executors: Richard de Denton, John his brother and William de Denton, rector of Ousby.
    Note of probate and grant of administration to executors named. Rose (chapel), 2 Dec. 1356.

145 Letters patent testifying that Robert de Briscawe is free from any matrimonial contract and there is no canonical obstacle to his marriage. Rose, 14 Dec. 1356.

146 Signification to the king that Gilbert Raket, priest,[107] and Richard de Ranull' [Fo.15ᵛ; p.30] have been excommunicate for 40 days at the instance of the bishop's office. Rose, 19 Dec. 1356.

147 Note of similar letters against Thomas Paulyn, Walter Shepehird of Newton Reigny (*Neuton*),[108] William Gunsone and William Casse. Rose, 16 Dec. 1356.

148 Appointment of William Gerard of Carleton (*Carlton*), chaplain, as administrator of the goods of Agnes, widow of William de Barneby of Carleton, who died intestate. Rose, 21 December 1356.

---

[105] Printed in *Test. Karl.*, 12–13. There is no note about account.
[106] Carmelites.
[107] See **162**.
[108] Possibly an associate of Gilbert Raket (**146**, **162–3**).

149 Commission to the prior of Carlisle, quoting a writ of Edward III (dated Westminster, 21 Nov. 1356), ordering the bishop to appoint a collector in Carlisle diocese of the first part of a tenth granted to the king by the clergy of York province in their last council or convocation in St. Peter's, York; to be paid on 2 February and 1 August [1357], the second part subject to certain conditions, as was certified by John [Thoresby], archbishop of York.[109] The prior is appointed collector. Rose, 20 Dec. 1356.

150 Note of licence, for one year, to William de Lancastre for services in an oratory in his house at Howgill (*Holgill*). Rose, 29 Dec. 1356.

151 Licence to Richard de [Askeby, rector of] Uldale, at the request of Thomas de Lucy, lord of Cockermouth (*Cokirmutht*), to be absent in his service for two years; a proctor may represent him at synods at Carlisle [etc.]. Rose, 12 Feb. 1357.

152 Note of grant to John de Clibborne, acolyte, of letters dimissory to all orders. Same date.

153 Note of grant to Thomas de Penreth, subdeacon, of letters dimissory for the diaconate. 25 Feb. 1357.

154 [Fo.16; p.31] Licence (for one year) to M. William de Salkeld, rector of a mediety of Aikton (*Ayketon*),[110] as confessor and penitentiary to the bishop's parishioners, even in reserved cases excepting poachers in Rose park and other places or liberties of the bishop and his church; violators of those liberties, removal of fugitives seeking sanctuary in churches, chapels or churchyards; rape of nuns [etc. as in 20]. Rose, 1 Mar. 1357.

155 Mandate to the official of Carlisle quoting the king's writ of summons to a parliament at Westminster on 17 April (dated Westminster, 15 Feb. 1357).[111] The official is to give notice (*premuniatis*) to the prior and archdeacon of Carlisle to attend in person, Carlisle chapter by a proctor, and clergy of the diocese by two proctors;[112] certifying the bishop by 2 April. Rose, 15 Mar. 1357.

156 Note of licence for one year to Hugh de Jarum, questor for the hospital of San Spirito in Sassia (*Sanctus Spiritus in Saxia*), Rome. Same date.

157 Memorandum[113] of probate before M. John de Welton of the will [not quoted] of Christine, wife of William Taillor of Unthank, with grant of administration to Thomas Blome and Maurice Scot, her executors. Rose (in the chapel), 20 Mar. 1357.

---

[109] As in *CFR*, VII.16. See also **125, 200, 601**.
[110] Instituted 1339 (*Reg. Kirkby*, I.96, nos.505–7).
[111] As in *CCR 1354–60*, 398. For Welton's attendance, see Introduction, xv.
[112] The clergy's proctors were Masters John de Welton and William de Ragenhill, clerks (PRO, S.C.10 (Parliamentary Proxies), file 27, no.1319).
[113] Printed in *Test. Karl.*, 13.

158 Memorandum that there is a letter about the oath of obedience to the bishop of Carlisle by the master of the order of Sempringham (*Sempyngham*), on account of Ravenstonedale church being appropriated to the prior and convent of Watton, towards the end of the fifth folio of the register of John de Rosse, former bishop.

159 Mandate to the dean of Carlisle to order the clergy and people of his deanery to appear at the visitation of M. William de Routhbury, archdeacon of Carlisle.[114]
Note of similar mandates to the other deans. Rose, 28 Mar. 1357.

160 Memorandum of a letter to the king against Robert del Wolhous and Reginald Feror of Sowerby Wood (*Sourbywode*) who have been excommunicate for 40 days. 3 Apr. 1357.

161* [Fo.16ᵛ; p.32] Commission to M. Adam de Caldebek', official of Carlisle, and Thomas de Salkeld, rector of Clifton, the bishop's familiar clerk. The prior and chapter of Carlisle, abbots, priors, rectors, vicars and other beneficed persons of the diocese lately granted the bishop a subsidy of 200 marks (payable in equal portions on 9 April and 24 June next), for reasons explained to them for the bishop and spontaneously accepted, agreeing that they could be compelled to pay by ecclesiastical censures. The commissaries are to collect the whole sum due for the first term, giving acquittances if necessary, and to compel payment by sentences of suspension, excommunication and interdict, with both or one of them giving the bishop an account of receipts when required. They are to report by letters patent in due course, giving the names of defaulters, if any. Rose, 2 Apr. 1357.

162 Memorandum that Gilbert Raket resigned custody of the chantry of Newton Reigny (*Neuton*) chapel. The bishop immediately appointed him keeper of the chapel until Whitsun, excusing him from accounting for any revenues to the chantry in the meantime. Rose (chapel), 5 Apr. 1357.

163 Memorandum that Hugh de Louthre, junior, appeared before the bishop and confessed that he had prevented the imprisonment of Thomas Paulyn and Walter Shepehird of Newton Reigny, against whom royal writs had issued at the bishop's request;[115] he humbly sought absolution from excommunication for this violation of ecclesiastical liberty, to which the bishop graciously admitted him, enjoining salutary penance. Same date.

164 Note of licence to William de Ebor', rector of Bolton in Allerdale, to be absent for two years in the service of Sir Ralph de Nevill; with a proctor at synods and farming the church's revenues. London, 3 May 1357.

---

[114] The only difference of substance between this mandate and **120** is the list of those cited; but the marginal title has been struck through, as are the name of the archdeacon and two other references to his office; while *vacat* is in the left hand margin.
[115] See **147**. Hugh was the son and heir of Hugh Lowther III, kt., sheriff 1351–4 (*CFR*, VI.307, 408; H. Owen, *The Lowther Family* (1990), 25–7).

165   (i) Collation to Roger de Ledes, chaplain, of Aspatria (*Aspatrik'*) vicarage, vacant by the death of Adam Deyncourt.[116] (ii) Note of mandate for induction [to whom omitted]. Rose, 30 May 1357.

166   Note of licence to Thomas del Cloos, rector of Brougham, to be absent while in the service of Lord [Roger] de Clifford; excused from synods. Rose, 30 May 1357.

167   To John [Thoresby], archbishop of York. The bishop received his letters at Newark (*Newerk'*) on 12 April [as quoted]. The archbishop intends to celebrate a provincial council in York cathedral on 19 May about matters concerning the condition and liberty of his church, diocese and province, as well as the defence of the realm, on which King Edward has expressed his will (*nobis velle suum exposuit*),[117] trusting to devise a remedy with the counsel of the bishop and other prelates. Citation of the bishop [etc., similar in form to **125**, continuing to Fo.17; p.33, where the date of the archbishop's mandate is omitted[118]].

Certificate that the bishop has cited those concerned; their names are in a schedule. The bishop's inn, London, 15 May 1357.

168   To M. Hugh Pelegrini, treasurer of Lichfield (*Lych'*), papal nuncio in England. The bishop received his letters [quoted; dated London, 28 April] at Rose on 1 June, asking (for the papal chamber) what churches, monasteries, chapters, colleges and convents are immediately subject to the papal court, or exempt from visitation or ordinary jurisdiction by papal authority. The bishop is to examine his registers and report within a month, naming the orders of exempt houses.

After examination of his registers, the bishop reports that the only houses exempt from ordinary jurisdiction in respect of visitation are the abbey and convent of Holm Cultram (Cistercian) and the abbey and convent of Shap (Premonstratensian). Rose, 3 June 1357.

169   Probate[119] of the nuncupative [*sic*] will of John Corour of Bothel (*Bothill*), as follows:

Dated 7 May 1357. Commends soul to God. Burial in churchyard of St. Michael's, Torpenhow, with best beast and cloth as mortuary, and 2d. for oblations and lights. A chaplain celebrating for his soul for half a year, 40s. Thomas de Kirkland, parish chaplain [of Torpenhow], 3s. Joan his daughter, 4 marks sterling, which he wishes to remain in the custody of Peter de Morland, vicar [of Torpenhow],[120] until she marries. Emma his wife, 4 marks. Residue to

---

[116] The previous known collation was of Robert Bully, 1334 (*Reg. Kirkby*, I.31, no.173).
[117] Royal letters of 22 Feb. 1357 asked both archbishops to hold convocations on 24 April (*CCR 1354–60*, 398). See also Storey, 'Simon Islip' (cited under **125**), 148–9, correcting its note 85: these letters are not indexed in *CCR*.
[118] *viz.* Cawood, 31 Mar. 1357 (*Concilia*, ed. Wilkins, III.41); and see **602**.
[119] Printed in *Test. Karl.*, 14. There is no note about account.
[120] Instituted 1355 (**561**, **563**).

be equally divided between Emma, John and his other children. Executors: Peter son of Reginald and Richard del Heynyng' of Bothel.

Grant of administration to Peter; reserved for Richard. Rose (chapel), 6 June 1357.

170 (i) Collation to John de Bramwra, chaplain, of the chapel or chantry of Newton Reigny, vacant by the free resignation of Gilbert Raket before the bishop. [Fo.17^v; p.34] (ii) Note for induction by archdeacon. Rose, 9 June 1357.

171 (i) Collation to John de Grandon, clerk in holy orders, of Crosby on Eden (*Crosseby juxta Eden*) vicarage, vacant by the resignation of Roger de Ledes; he has taken the [usual] oath to reside in accordance with legatine constitutions.[121] (ii) Note for induction [by whom omitted]. Rose, 9 June 1357.

172 Probate[122] of the will of Adam Deyncourt, vicar of Aspatria, as follows: Dated 20 April 1357. Commends soul to God. Burial in choir. His sisters are to keep the cloths, beds, vessels and other goods he has given them. Residue, after payment of debts, is to remain with his kinsman Adam de Crosseby, chaplain, until he disposes of them; appointing him executor.

Grant of administration to Adam. Rose (chapel), 5 June 1357.

173 To the dean of Carlisle. Despite the bishop's inhibition to all parochial clergy, unlicensed questors have been admitted to churches and chapels, seducing the people with fabricated letters. All clergy are to be ordered, under pain of excommunication, not to allow questors in churches, chapels or other gatherings unless they have letters sealed by the bishop and none other; excepting proctors for the fabric of the cathedrals of St. Mary, Carlisle, and St. Cuthbert, Durham, Saint Antoine [de Viennois] and San Spirito [in Sassia, Rome], named in letters sealed by the bishop. Enquiry is to be made about all acting as questors in the deanery, and a report made by 3 July. Rose, 10 June 1357.

174 Mandate to the dean of Carlisle, referring to the subsidy [as in **161** – censures]. [Fo.18; p.35]. Henry Martyn, rector of Scaleby, Robert de Bolton, rector of Stapleton, Adam de Foresta, rector of Kirkcambeck (*Cambok'*),[123] John de Kerby, vicar of Burgh by Sands (*Burgo super Sabulones*),[124] and Thomas de Rotheland, vicar of Farlam (*Farlham*),[125] although often warned, have not paid for the first term. They are to be warned to pay within eight days, under pain of

---

[121] See **30**, *n.*, **562**, **565**; and cf. **180**.

[122] Printed in *Test. Karl.*, 15.

[123] No rector known since Simon de Tyrer's institution, 1306, and ordination as deacon, 1308; the church was destroyed by 1319 (*Reg. Halton*, I.248, 306; II.184–5). An unnamed rector occurs 1332 (*Reg. Kirkby*, I.21, no.113).

[124] The previous known institution was of Hugh de Hayton, 1338 (ibid., I.84, nos.435–6).

[125] No vicar known since William de Ricardby's institution, 1316; the church was destroyed by 1319 (*Reg. Halton*, II.126, 184). An unnamed vicar occurs 1332 (*Reg. Kirkby*, I.21, no.113, 26, no.137). See also **367**.

censures on themselves and their benefices. The dean is to report by 7 July.
Rose, 12 June 1357.

175 Licence (as in **143**) to admit the bearers, Thomas de Cokerton and John
de Yhedyngham, questors of the house of St. Mary of Bethlehem (*Bethleem*).
Rose, 14 June 1357.

176 (i) Institution of Robert de Merton, chaplain, to Newbiggin church,
vacant by the resignation of Thomas de Salkeld, clerk, as proctor of M. John
[son of] Thomas de Appelby, the last rector; presented by William de
Crakanthorp. (ii) Note of mandate to the archdeacon. Rose, 17 June 1357.

177 Commission to M. William de Routhbury, archdeacon of Carlisle. He has
complained to the bishop that, despite his monitions, some rectors and vicars
have failed to pay him procurations due for his visitations. He is empowered, for
one year, to enforce payment by sentences of suspension, excommunication and
interdict. Rose, 1 Aug. 1357.

178 Note of licence to William [del Hall], rector of Bowness, to study at a
studium generale in England for one year; farming revenues and excused from
synods. Rose, 1 Aug. 1357.

179 Note of licence to John de Langholme [rector of Kirkland][126] to be absent
for one year in a suitable place in England; excused from synods. Rose, 18 Sept.
1357.

180 [Fo.18ᵛ; p.36] (i) Collation to John de Grandon, deacon, of Crosby on
Eden vicarage, now vacant.[127] (ii) Note for induction [by whom omitted]. Rose,
17 Oct. 1357.

181 (i) Will[128] of Robert del Shelde of Carlisle, dated 5 Oct. 1357. Commends
soul to God, Blessed Mary and all saints. Burial with friars minor, Carlisle. Half
a stone of wax to make four candles, two for the friars minor and two for his
parish church. The same friars 40s., if possible, and a mazer cup priced 14s. To
John Boon, his small mazer, iron stove with a sword, and a dinner table with
embroideries for an ecclesiastical vestment. The parish clerk, 12d. Four
chaplains at the funeral, 4d. each. Nicholas Topcliff, servant, a tabard with
hood. Richard Fobour, his silver plated knife. Residue to his wife Agnes
(appointed executrix). Witnesses: Richard Fobour, Nicholas Topcliff, servant
of John Boon, chaplain.
    (ii) Note of probate and grant of administration to Agnes. Carlisle, 19 Oct.
1357.

182 Memorandum that Thomas de Belthorp appeared before the bishop and
read a letter [fully quoted] of M. Ralph de Erghom, rector of Greystoke,

---

[126] Supplied from margin. Cf. **44**.
[127] In form for collation to a rectory; cf. **171**.
[128] Printed in *Test. Karl.*, 15–16.

appointing him and Richard, parish chaplain of Greystoke, as Ralph's proctors to resign the church and be instituted, etc., to Fulstow (*Foulstowe*) church, dioc. Lincoln; as Ralph's seal is not well known, he uses that of the dean of Christianity of Lincoln, whose assent is recorded; dated Lincoln, 18 Sept. 1357.

The bishop accepted the resignation after its declaration by Thomas, reserving his dues in the vacancy. Custody of the vacant church was committed to Richard de Brampton, chaplain, who took an oath to collect its revenues for the bishop. A commission about this was sent to Richard and the dean of Cumberland. Rose (the principal chamber), 12 Oct. 1357.

183 Probate[129] of the nuncupative [*sic*] will of William Wryght of Irthington (*Irthyngton*), as follows:
Dated 6 Oct. 1357. Commends soul to God, Blessed Mary and all saints. All goods, after payment of debts, to his wife Juliana and children. Executor: Thomas Lowry.
Administration granted to Thomas. Rose, 25 Oct. 1357.

184 [Fo.19; p.37] Talleyrand[130] [de Périgord, cardinal] bishop of Albano, nuncio of the Holy See, to the bishop of Carlisle or his vicar or vicars general. Pope Innocent VI has sent him and Nicholas [Capocci], cardinal priest of S. Vitale, to England and granted them letters for procurations to help pay their expenses, at the same rates as other cardinals sent to England as legates; both letters are quoted (dated Villeneuve lès Avignon, 8 April 1356). As they have incurred great expenses, procurations are required for the present year from 21 June, which the bishop is appointed to collect for both cardinals from all prelates and clergy [Fo.19ᵛ; p.38] in his diocese, and also similar procurations for this first year for their proctors as if a legate were in England; with faculty to excommunicate those disobedient, etc., [Fo.20; p.39] their absolution being reserved to the legates. The original letters were published in the church of Chartres. Dated in the monastery of St. Jean-en-Vallée, Chartres (*in valleya Carnoten'*). Present: Roger, archbishop of Palermo (*Parnornittan'*), Bishops Bertrand of Nevers (*Nivernen'*), Peter of Sarlat (*Sarlacen'*), Archambaud of Lavaur (*Vauren'*), Bertrand of Sénez (*Senecen'*) and Guy of *Massanen'*; Bertrand Folcam, auditor of causes in the papal palace, and Luke Rodulphi, archdeacon of *Cammen'*, DCnL. Subscription by Elias de Lascoutz' of Puy-Saint-Front, Périgueux (*villa Podii sancti Frontonis Petragoricen'*), notary by papal and imperial authority. 21 July 1356.

185 Commission to the prior of Carlisle to act for the bishop in this matter, sending the cardinal's letters. He should act with such diligence lest by his negligence any of the censures or pains should fall on the bishop or himself, *quod absit*. He is to report by 1 August, sending names of payers and non-payers, and these letters. Rose, 23 June 1357.

---

[129] Printed in *Test. Karl.*, 16–17.
[130] The initial *T* is 2 cm square and decorated. For this mission see Lunt, *Financial Relations*, 651–5.

186* Certificate to Cardinal Talleyrand.[131] The bishop received his letters on 23 June and notified all concerned in his diocese. From his records [described] and particularly from acquittances of the cardinals last in England and France and their proctors for procurations for one year, [it appears that they were paid] at the rate of 4d. in the mark of the assessed valuation of benefices including the bishop's *mensa*; the total was 43 marks, 5s. 9d.,[132] as appears in the acquittances of two cardinals which [Talleyrand] may see. Benefices in the city [Fo.20ᵛ; p.40] and diocese in the march towards Scotland have been impoverished by destructive invasions by Scots in the past and often recently. The same sum has been levied, with difficulty, in order to avoid censure. The benefices taxed are listed in attached rolls, which the bearer will deliver. Carlisle, 12 Sept. 1357.

187 Appointment by Cardinal Talleyrand of M. Pontius de Vereriis, rector of Walpole (dioc. Norwich), as his proctor to receive from Bishop Gilbert by the hands of Thomas de Salkeld, rector of Clifton, £14 9s. 6½d. for his portion of the procurations due for the first year of his nunciature. London, 28 Sept. 1357.

188 Letters patent of Cardinal Nicholas acknowledging receipt from Bishop Gilbert of the [unspecified] procurations collected from his clergy for his first year. London, 26 Nov. 1357.

189 Commission of Cardinals Talleyrand and Nicholas to the bishop of Carlisle or his vicar or vicars general to absolve abbots and other clergy liable to pay procurations and incurring excommunication or other pains for non-payment. London, 23 Nov. 1357.

190 Certificate to the cardinals. The bishop received their letter on 28 October [1357], quoting it 'from word to word, as in the last mandate', for procurations in the second year of their nunciature. This mandate is with letters of cardinals, acquittances and other memoranda about these procurations in the bishop's archives. Note that this letter was fully certified by the bishop's order, with the date changed to 23 Jan. 1358. This certificate was delivered in London to M. Luke de Tholomeis, chamberlain of Cardinal Nicholas.

191 [Fo.21; p.41] Letters patent of Cardinal Nicholas (similar to **188**) for procurations in his second year; he is fully satisfied. London, 20 Feb. 1359.

192 Letters patent of Hugh Pelegrini, treasurer of Lichfield, papal nuncio in England, as proctor of Cardinal Talleyrand, acknowledging receipt from Bishop Gilbert by the hands of M. John de Welton of £14 9s. 6½d. for procurations due for the second year; except for any money for these procurations still in Carlisle diocese. London, 25 Nov. 1357.[133]

---

[131] The opening initial *R* is also 2 cm square and decorated.
[132] I.e. £28 19s. 1d., the same sum as in the only acquittances for two cardinals in 1338, when the charge was not based on the new assessment (*Reg. Kirkby*, I.82–4, nos.429 and note, 432, 443–4). Nos.**187–8**, **191–2** below show that both cardinals twice received halves of this sum in 1357–8.
[133] Probably in error for 25 Feb. 1358 (Lunt, *Financial Relations*, 653).

193 Memorandum that a commission (dated London, 19 Feb. 1358) was granted to the bishop or his vicar general to absolve all defaulters in his diocese in the same terms 'as written in the preceding folio' (i.e. **189**).

194 Memorandum. The cardinals were certified for their third year in the same form, under another date [not given]. They were satisfied, and made an acquittance preserved in the bishop's archives with the acquittances for the first and second years.

195 Commission[134] to Adam de Alneburgh,[135] dean of Allerdale, Alan rector of Plumbland (*Plumland*),[136] and Thomas de Suthayk, William called Thomasson of Penrith and Henry Clerk of Crosthwaite, chaplains, quoting letters of Innocent VI dated Avignon, 1 Oct. 1358:

The pope received a petition of John Henrey of Broughton (*Borughton*)[137] claiming to be vicar of Crosthwaite. On its vacancy by the death of Richard de Esyngwald, possession had been disputed by Thomas Inne[138] and William de Celario of Adlingfleet (*Athelyngflete*), priests, of Carlisle and York dioceses. William was provided canonically and took possession, excluding Thomas, who claimed lawful provision as vicar and appealed to the court of Clement VI. After many proceedings at William's instance before M. Aymerico Colneti, canon of Chartres (*Carnot'*), and William de Gunello, canon of Narbonne (*Narbonen'*), papal chaplains and auditors, Innocent, on becoming pope,[139] committed the case for completion to all auditors. William (de Celario) then died, and the pope conferred all his rights in the vicarage on John.[140] The provision of Thomas to the vicarage was therefore rash and unjust; it was revoked and orders made for his removal and John's induction, recovery of receipts by Thomas, and payment of his expenses. Thomas had appealed against this sentence. John had consequently petitioned that as he had never enjoyed peaceful possession of the vicarage and the definitive sentence was in his favour, the vicarage should be sequestrated in accordance with a constitution of Clement VI. Pope Innocent, in agreement, orders the bishop or others to sequestrate the vicarage and support the vicar (*illi qui finalem in causa victoriam obtinebat*) in his duties; opponents are to be censured.

The commissaries (or two of them, including the dean) are to execute these papal letters, reporting before 9 June. Rose, 11 May 1359.

---

[134] Later inserted in the space 14.3 cm deep under **194**; there are 41 lines of writing (cf. 28 lines in the 12 cm of **191–4** above); and see Introduction, xvi.

[135] Ordained priest 1333 (*Reg. Kirkby*, I.18, no.97).

[136] Previous known rector was Thomas de Dayncourt, 1342 (*Reg. Kirkby*, I.132, no.652). Alan recurs in 1360 (**371**).

[137] Priest of Worcester dioc. in his provision to a church in the gift of St. Mary's, York, 1351 (*CPL*, III.445). Crosthwaite was appropriated to Fountains abbey, while the vicarage was in the bishop's gift (Nicolson & Burn, II.87).

[138] See **86**.

[139] 30 Dec. 1352.

[140] On 12 Jan. 1357, in *Accounts*, ed. Lunt, 103, 132, 158, 182. The last notice, in the account for 1363–4, states that John Henry never had possession of the church because the benefice was a vicarage; and see **318** and note.

196 [Fo.21ᵛ; p.42] (i) Institution of Richard de Hoton Roef, clerk, to Greystoke church, vacant by the resignation of M. Ralph de Ergom; presented by the noble lord, William de Craystok', kt. (ii) Archdeacon to induct. Brough, 30 Oct. 1357.

197 Note of dispensation of William Gray, clerk, son of unmarried parents, by authority of letters of Francis [de Aptis], cardinal-priest of St. Mark, penitentiary of the pope. 21 Dec. 1357.

198 Note of renewal for one year of letters to make a collection (*questum*) for the fabric of Carlisle cathedral, in the same terms as the last letters save that no proctor or nuncio is named, 'as appears'.[141] 7 Jan. 1358.

199 Mandate to the official of Carlisle quoting the king's writ of summons to a parliament at Westminster on 5 Feb. (dated Westminster, 15 Dec. 1357),[142] for execution [as in **155**], reporting by 22 Jan. Rose, 7 Jan. 1358.

200 Commission to the prior of Carlisle, quoting a writ (dated Westminster, 12 Dec. 1357): in several writs, the king ordered the bishop to appoint collectors of the first half of a tenth due on 2 Feb. [1357] and also of its second half due on 1 August which, at its last meeting in York, the council of the prelates and clergy granted without conditions (*simpliciter et absque condicione aliqua*), as Archbishop [Thoresby] certified.[143] The bishop has not yet reported the names of collectors to the Exchequer; if he has not deputed the collector of the first half to collect the second, he should appoint other suitable diocesan clergy who are to answer at the Exchequer for all the money on 2 Feb. [1358], when the bishop should have certified their names. [Fo.22; p.43] The prior is to collect the second half for 2 Feb. Rose, 8 Jan. 1358.

201 Mandate to the official of Carlisle. There have been many reports of mendicant friars interrupting services in churches and chapels, not preaching but offering indulgences with empty words, seeking money and not souls, with open books in their hands, as if they were questors, contrary to the canons, observances of their orders and ancient custom.[144] The official is to order all deans and parochial clergy, under pain of excommunication, not to admit any mendicant friar or any other questor, particularly during services, unless they show the bishop's licence; reporting by 22 Jan. Rose, 8 Jan. 1358.

---

[141] Cf. **599** in 'diverse letters' section.
[142] As in *CCR 1354–60*, 433. The clergy's proctors were again John Welton and William Ragenhill; the latter and Peter de Morland, vicar of Torpenhow, were the archdeacon's proctors (Parl. Proxies, file 28, nos.1356, 1359; cf. **155**, note). For the bishop's attendance, see Introduction, xv.
[143] This meeting of convocation, which withdrew the conditions (see **149**, **167**), met on 19 May 1357 (*HBC*, 596; *Concilia*, ed. Wilkins, III.41). Writs to collect the second half tenth issued on 15 June (*CFR*, VII.40–1), apparently escaping Welton's notice. See also **601**.
[144] More fully translated to here in *VCH Cumberland*, II.198.

202 Note of dispensation of Nicholas de Bounesse, clerk, son of unmarried parents, by commission of Francis, cardinal-priest of St. Mark, papal penitentiary. 22 Jan. 1358.

203* Mandate to the dean of Carlisle. The bishop has learnt that Adam, rector of Castle Carrock[145] is afflicted with leprosy, so that because of his deformity and his parishioners' horror he cannot minister the sacraments. He is to be cited to appear before the bishop in the chapel at Rose on 11 Jan., if he can, or otherwise by an informed and empowered proctor, to give cause why the bishop should not assign him a coadjutor. Rose, 31 Dec. 1357.

204 Commission to the official of Carlisle. The bishop recently enquired into defects of the chancel, books and other ornaments of Greystoke church dating from the time M. Ralph de Erghom was rector, as shown in the attached certificate. As the bishop is too busy to deal with the matter immediately, he empowers the official to proceed, citing persons concerned, reporting afterwards. Rose, 22 Jan. 1358.

205 DIMISSIO PRIORIS ET CONVENTUS DE WATTON SUPER USURPACIONE PROBACIONIS TESTAMENTORUM ETC. Letters patent. The prior and convent of Watton were impeached before the bishop to defend their claim to grant probate of wills of parishioners of their appropriated church of Ravenstonedale; they proved their title and were dismissed.[146] Rose, 24 Sept. 1357.

206* Certificate to the official of the court of York[147] quoting his letter (dated York, 18 Jan. 1358). He is hearing a case of divorce between Thomas de Neuton and his wife Alice. She has claimed that there are many [Fo.22ᵛ; p.44] instruments and documents supporting her case in the bishop's archives, of which he is asked to send transcripts under his seal, in haste.

The bishop has found in his archives that on Alice's suit Thomas was called before him on 3 April 1354, when he appeared in the chapel at Rose. Asked why he had removed her from conjugal cohabitation and not supplied her with necessities, Thomas admitted that he had not lived with her and, because of his debts, been unable to support her. After some argument, he promised on oath to resume cohabitation within eight days, treat her with conjugal affection and support her as his means allowed. The bishop then ordered him to fulfil these undertakings under pain of excommunication.

Thomas again appeared there before the bishop on Alice's suit on 14 Oct. 1355. Charged that he had not yet readmitted or supported her as he had sworn and so committed perjury and incurred excommunication, he confessed his failure but said that he was making an agreement with Sir William Dacre for a portion to be paid annually to Alice for her keep; and he asked for a stay in

---

[145] An Adam, rector there, was licensed to study, 1341; but John de Beghokyrk was presented, although not recorded as instituted, 1347 (*Reg. Kirkby*, I.126, no.628, I.175, no.837).

[146] The lord of the manor still had this jurisdiction in modern times (Nicolson & Burn, I.521).

[147] Identified by Professor David Smith as M. Thomas de Bucton (see *BRUO*, I.300).

proceedings until the outcome of this negotiation with Lady Dacre and Sir William, which the bishop granted. Since then the bishop has done no more in this business, nor has he found any other instruments or documents about it in his archives. Rose, 22 Jan. 1358.

207* Letter missive to [the official of York] asking him to favour Alice in this business; the bishop has learnt that she has not been fairly treated. Rose, 22 Jan. [1358].

208 Note of licence for one year at the request of Hugh de Jarum as questor of the hospital of Saint-Antoine-de-Viennois. Rose, 25 Jan. 1358.

209 Mandate to the prior and chapter of Carlisle. The bishop has received papal letters (sent for inspection by them and all interested) ordering him, under pains and censures, to visit his clergy and people. In compliance, he intends to come to their chapter house on 9 April and cites all to appear before him or his commissaries, to accept his visitation, commands and corrections. Absent canons and *conversi* should be recalled. Prejudicial acts are forbidden. A certificate listing present and absent canons is to be delivered by that day. Rose, 13 Mar. 1358.

210 Note of similar mandate to the prior and convent of Lanercost for visitation in their chapter house on 11 April. [Rose, 13 Mar. 1358.]

211 Mandate to the prior and his fellow monks of Wetheral. The bishop has received papal letters [as in **209**] and therefore intends to come to their chapter house[148] on 10 April [Fo.23; p.45] to visit them and Wetheral church [continuing as in **209**, but omitting *conversi*]. Rose, 13 Mar. 1358.

212 Mandate to the dean of Carlisle. The bishop has received papal letters [as before] and is thus bound to visit his diocese and receive customary procurations in coin. Order to cite all rectors, vicars and priests of parochial churches and chapels in the city and deanery; also other chaplains and clerks in churches, chapels and oratories; religious and other ecclesiastics claiming appropriated churches or partial tithes, portions or pensions in alien parishes or churches contrary to *jus commune*; and keepers of perpetual chantries, chapels or oratories. From every parish, according to its size, four or six trustworthy men of good repute are to be called to answer customary articles, on days and at places listed in a schedule. Rectors and vicars are to show letters of institution and, like chaplains, letters of orders. Claimants of appropriated churches, pensions, etc., chantries, celebrants in oratories, are to show their titles. A certificate is to list names of churches etc. and persons cited. Rose, 16 Mar. 1358.

Note of similar letters to the other deans for the visitation by papal authority.

---

[148] MS. 'in your chapter house of Lanercost'; the last word is underdotted.

213* Pope Innocent [VI][149] to the bishop of Carlisle, his vicar-general and the official of Carlisle. Although all archbishops and bishops are required by the canons to carry out the office of visitation for the nourishment and correction of their clergy and people, many are forced to be absent from their churches or fear to leave their cities because of wars or other just impediments. The pope considers it appropriate that archbishops and bishops unable by themselves to discharge their responsibilities should appoint capable men to perform this duty of visitation. With the counsel of cardinals and prelates at the papal see, he orders the bishop (or in his absence his vicar-general and/or official) to appoint one or more Godfearing men to visit non-exempt churches, monasteries, other ecclesiastical places, chapters, colleges and convents of the city and diocese of Carlisle [Fo.23ᵛ; p.46] once only immediately after receipt of this letter or in the year following, receiving from them in coin the procurations due to a bishop visiting them in person, according to the constitution of Pope Benedict XII. To save time, the pope empowers [such commissaries] to visit up to three or more churches, monasteries [etc.] in one day, receiving procurations [as above], save from those excused from visitation; not withstanding constitutions of Gregory X, Innocent IV, Benedict XII and other popes, nor any papal privileges and indulgences. The pope hopes that faithful, diligent performance of this work will be richly rewarded. He has no wish, however, that poor [places] should be compelled to pay beyond their means, if at all. Villeneuve-lès-Avignon, 23 Aug. 1355.

214 COMMISSIO AD VISITANDUM CIVITATEM ET DIOCESIM KARL' AUCTORITATE APOSTOLICA PREDICTA. Commission to Masters William de Routhbury, archdeacon of Carlisle, Adam de Caldebek, official of Carlisle, and John de Welton, the bishop's familiar clerk skilled in law. The bishop is obliged by papal mandate (sent herewith) to visit his city and diocese personally or by commissaries and receive procurations in coin; being prevented by business from exercising the office of visitation and collection of procurations, he appoints them in his stead during pleasure. Rose, 8 Apr. 1358.

215 (i) Institution (in the person of Sir John de Merton, his proctor) of William de Loundres, priest, to [Long] Marton (*Merton*) church, vacant by the death of John de Morland;[150] presented by Thomas de Musgrave, kt., by reason of the dower of Isabel, widow of Robert de Clifford. (ii) Archdeacon to induct. Rose, 20 Apr. 1358.

---

[149] With a large, decorated initial *I*, 5.5 cm high. This mandate was directed to all archbishops and bishops in the pope's obedience, not only in the British Isles, as implied by *CPL*, III.617. A first version, dated 1 Sept. 1354, is printed in *Innocent VI: lettres secrètes et curiales*, ed. P. Gasnault and others, Bibliothèque des Écoles Françaises d'Athènes et de Rome, Paris and Rome, 1959–, II.146–51; it is also noticed in *CPL*, III.615–16. Some variants in the revised version of 23 Aug. 1355 are given in *Innocent VI: lettres . . .*, III.153–60. Bishop Welton seemingly received his copy of the mandate on 19 June 1357 (**291**). See also Lunt, *Financial Relations*, 713–16, which shows that the pope expected a large share of the procurations thus collected..

[150] Instituted 1334 (*Reg. Kirkby*, I.34, no.195).

216 Probate[151] of the nuncupative [*sic*] will of John de Morland, rector of Long Marton, as follows:

Dated at Marton, 20 March 1358. Commends soul to God, Blessed Mary and all saints. Burial in the choir of St. Margaret's, Marton, with 2 pounds of wax for light, 18d. for oblations and $1\frac{1}{2}$ skeps of oatmeal, a salted beef, 2 porks and 6 muttons for the poor. His larger mazer and larger copper pot to the Carmelite friars, Appleby. His smaller mazer to Lady Isabel de Clifford, consort of Sir Thomas de Musgrave. To the friars preachers and minor of Carlisle, Austin of Penrith and Carmelite of Appleby, 40d. each. To the prior and convent of St. Mary's, Carlisle, 100s. for a pittance; and 40s. for its fabric. To celebrate for his soul, the souls of his parents, John de Halghton, once bishop of Carlisle, Sir Robert de Clifford, Robert Clifford junior,[152] Sybil [John's] sister, Robert his brother and Robert de [Fo.24; p.47] Mebourne, chaplain; also for the good estate of Isabel de Clifford, consort of Sir Thomas de Musgrave, and for her soul after death, 12 marks. To the 4 bridges over the Eden at Appleby and [Temple] Sowerby (*Sourby*), and over Trout Beck (*Trutbek*') at Kirkby [Thore] and Marton, 2s. each. To John de Sourby, his robe of the prior of Carlisle's livery (*secta*). To John de Merton, another good robe. To Sir Richard de Brampton, his new tunic with hood. The bed in which he is lying to Alice de Apedale. A truckle bed and stone of wool to John Peny. Another bed and robe to Robert de Stelyngton'. The three daughters of his brother Robert living in Reagill (*Revegill*), a cow and stone of wool each. John del Hill, Adam Smith (*Fabro*) and [the testator's] nephew John living in Maulds Meaburn (*Mebournemauld*'), a bullock each. Robert de Stelyngton', a copper pot and a pan. Alice de Apedale, a cauldron. Robert de Thesdale, 2s. John brother of Alice de Apedale, a cow other than the cow and bullock which are his. John Aspir, a stone of wool and 2s. Little Nicholas de Caldebek, 2s. and a stone of wool. The fabric of Marton church and its bell-tower, 40d. William de Apedale, his better iron-shod wagon with its harness and two good bullocks. Each woman servant, a cow. Another iron-shod wagon to his nephew John at Brampton. Residue to Thomas de Salkeld, rector of Clifton, Thomas de Slegill and Richard del Hale, without any dispute, his executors. Under his seal and the seal of of the officiality of Carlisle, at [John's] request and with the official's consent.

Administration granted to the above-named executors. Rose (chapel), 15 Apr. 1358.

217 Note of licence to John de Derwentwater, kt., for one or more chaplains to celebrate in oratories in his manors of Derwent Water and Bolton,[153] without prejudice to their parish churches. 23 Apr. 1358.

218 Note[154] of probate of the nuncupative will [not quoted] of Thomas Jonson of Sowerby (*Sourby*), with grant of administration to William Whytehed and Henry son of Mariota, the executors named. Rose (chapel), 10 May 1358.

[151] Printed in *Test. Karl.*, 17–19, which omits the penultimate sentence, *Et nos officialis Karl' ad rogatum specialem dicti domini Johannis huic testamento sigillum nostrum apposuimus in testimonium premissorum.*
[152] Died 1344 and 1345 respectively (*Complete Peerage*, III.291–2).
[153] See Nicolson & Burn, II.78, for a chapel at Bolton, Westm.
[154] Printed in *Test. Karl.*, 19.

219* Commission to M. John de Welton, the bishop's familiar clerk skilled in law, to correct etc. all defects and crimes found by the commissaries in the papally authorised visitation of the city and diocese and proceed judicially in all articles and matters arising, with powers of coercion; the bishop wishes to reform them sharply, as ordered by the pope, but is too busy to act himself. Rose, 13 May 1358.

220 (i) Collation to Richard de Aslacby, priest, of Stanwix (*Staynwygges*) vicarage, vacant by the death of Richard de Caldebek.[155] (ii) Note of mandate for induction to M. William de Salkeld, rector of a mediety of Aikton, and John Boon, chaplain, because the archdeacon is *in remotis*. Rose, 19 May 1358.

221 Note of renewal for one year of the letters for the questors of the hospital of Saint-Antoine-de-Viennois, giving them preference over all other questors save those for the fabric of Carlisle cathedral. Rose, 11 Feb. 1359.

222 [Fo.24ᵛ; p.48] Letters patent. While visiting the diocese, the bishop learned that the abbot and convent of Shap (*Heppa*) hold as appropriated the parish churches of Shap, Bampton and Warcop. They were cited before the bishop to show their title, which they did by proctor, proving their rights and unbroken possession by many instruments, privileges and documents, and further with witnesses who were sworn and examined; opponents were cited but none came. At the proctor's request, the bishop pronounced that Shap's appropriations were proved and lawful, dismissing it from further impeachment and confirming the appropriations. Rose, 20 Aug. 1358.

223 (i) Collation to Adam de Alenburgh, chaplain, of Aspatria vicarage, vacant by the resignation of Roger de Ledes. (ii) Archdeacon to induct. Rose, 28 Aug. 1358.

224 (i) Collation to Roger de Ledes, chaplain, of Dalston vicarage, now vacant.[156] (ii) Archdeacon to induct. Rose, 28 Aug. 1358.

225 [Fo.25; p.49] Commission to M. William de Routhbury, archdeacon of Carlisle, to examine the certificate of an inquest into the presentation of John de Morland, chaplain, to the vacant vicarage of Bampton by the abbot and convent of Shap, its patrons, the bishop being too busy for this business; and if there is no obstacle, to admit and institute him in accordance with the relevant legatine constitution, and have him or his proctor inducted. Rose, 19 Oct. 1358.

226 [Letter of institution] by the archdeacon, quoting the above commission, to John de Morland. He has examined the matter of his presentation to Bampton vicarage by the abbot and convent of Shap, its patrons, and the inquest ordered by the bishop, and finding no obstacles instituted him; the

---

[155] The last known vicar was Thomas Hogge, collated 1316; a commissary in 1338 (*Reg. Halton*, II.127; *Reg. Kirkby*, I.89, no.472n.); perhaps mentioned in **17**.
[156] Presumably by resignation of Richard de Aslacby (see **134**, **220**).

vicarage was vacant by the resignation of John de Hauville[157] by Robert de Hepp', chaplain, his proctor. Rose, 19 Oct. 1358.

227 Note of letters to the deans in customary form for the archdeacon's visitation. 12 Oct. 1358.

228 Note of commission to the archdeacon to proceed against non-payers of his procurations, valid for one year, in same form as was accustomed, under the bishop's seal. Rose, 2 Nov. 1358.

229 Note of renewal until Michaelmas following of letter of licence to questors for the fabric of the cathedral of St. Cuthbert, Durham.[158] Rose, 22 Dec. 1358.

230 Note of renewal for one year of letter of licence to questors for the fabric of Carlisle cathedral, with the names of John Boon and Thomas Hogge inserted; they may admit others deputed by the prior and chapter. Rose, 16 Jan. 1359.

231 Will[159] of John de Salkeld of Maughonby dated 1 Jan. 1359. Commends soul to God, Blessed Mary and all saints. Burial in churchyard of St. Michael's, Addingham; best beast for mortuary; 20s. for wax; $\frac{1}{2}$ mark for oblations. His cockle-shell to the prior and convent of Carlisle. 100s. to the fabric of the church of Carlisle abbey. 40s. to making a new window in its chancel. 100s. to the cellarer(?)[160] of Carlisle. 100s. to the prior and convent of the same. 20 marks in equal portions to the friars minor, Austin, preachers and Carmelite of Carlisle, Penrith and Appleby. 100s. to the fabric of Eden bridge by Salkeld. $\frac{1}{2}$ mark to Eden bridge by Kirkoswald. 40s. to the little bridge in [Inglewood] forest by *Wodemouth*. The rector of Kirkland, 20s. The sons and daughters of John de Salkeld junior, 40s. John [the testator's] bastard son, 10 marks. Adam vicar of Addingham,[161] 20s. Richard [the testator's] bastard son, 40s. The prioress of Armathwaite and her sisters, 40s. Thomas his chaplain, 20s. beside his salary. Remigius the chaplain, $\frac{1}{2}$ mark. Henry rector of Hutton in the Forest,[162] 20s. Various chaplains praying and celebrating for his soul, 40s. at his executors'

---

[157] Hauville claimed to have become vicar in an exchange authorised by the pope, as provisions, on 21 Nov. 1357; Robert de 'Hempp', the previous vicar, was to succeed Hauville as vicar of Shalford, Surrey (*CPP*, I.303; *Accounts*, ed. Lunt, 158, 206, where the name of the church is misread as Brampton). 'Hempp' is probably a misreading of 'Hepp' (i.e. Shap). A Robert de Hepp was ordained priest, with title from Shap abbey, 1341 (*Reg. Kirkby*, I.115). There is no record, however, of Hauville being vicar of Shalford, nor of Robert de Hepp (*Register of William Edington* (cited in Introduction, xi, *n*.17), I.167 (no.111), 176 (no.1176), and indexes).

[158] *Dunelm'* interlined and *Karli'* struck through: *Dunelm'* in margin.

[159] Printed in *Test. Karl.*, 20–2. Marginal note: ' + *executores istius testamenti reddiderunt compotum xviii° die Marcii etc. Lix° et dimissi sunt.*'

[160] MS. *celerarion'*; but possibly *orlerarion'*.

[161] See **64** and note.

[162] Presumably the Henry de Staynwigges named as rector in 1356 in a licence to grant the manor of Hutton to Thomas de Hoton (*CPR 1354–8*, 383). Henry was ordained priest, 1341 (*Reg. Kirkby*, I.115). Previous known rector was Robert Parvyng, instituted 1310; a commissary, 1337 (*Reg. Halton*. II.13; *Reg. Kirkby*, I.75, no.396).

discretion. John del Brigge of Penrith, because he is a pauper, ½ mark. Thomas del Paneteri, 40d. Henry de Kirkbride, if he is alive, 40s. John son of Christine Sporier, 13s. 4d. Holm Cultram abbey, 13s. 4d. for a pittance. Lanercost abbey [*sic*], 10s. for its pittance. John de Benyngton, 5s. Various chaplains celebrating for his soul, as far as can suffice, 20 marks. William Dandeson, 10s. Henry his brother, 40s. Robert his servant, 40d. William de Swyndale and his children, 20s. William Addyson, 10s. John Bisshopp, ½ mark. William le Reede's wife, 40d. Joan[163] Wasseson' *wyf*, 12d. Tyok, 12d. John son of Simon, 5s. 8d. The vicar of Edenhall, 40s. Agnes Purdelok, 12d. Beatrice Wyndow, 12d. William de Waberthwayt, 13s. 4d. At the disposition of Adam vicar of Addingham, 20s. Dom Thomas de Kirkoswold,[164] 13s. 4d. Joan Mauchall, 40d. [Fo.25ᵛ; p.50] and half a stone of wool. Hugh Louson, 5s. Walter de Cestre, 40d. John Brown, ½ mark. Emmota daughter of John Armestrang junior, 5 marks. Margaret daughter of William Nelson, 13s. 4d. Maud daughter of William de Cletre, 20s. Sir Hugh de Louthre, 13s. 4d. William de Kirkeby, chaplain of Melmerby, 13s. 4d. Thomas del Bek, 10s. John Hunter, 10s. Richard Vaus, the burgage in Carlisle which [the testator] has by his gift, to him and the legitimate heirs of his body, with reversion to Richard's father Roland, his heirs and assigns. Mariota daughter of Adam Emson of Lazonby, 13s. 4d. John de Wylton, for his labour, 20s. Residue to his brother Richard de Salkeld, [the testator's] wife Margaret, and Adam de Wygton, vicar of Addingham, his executors.

Letters patent. The attached will was proved at Maughonby (*Merghanby*) on 22 Jan. 1359 before M. John de Welton, clerk, the bishop's commissary *ad hoc*, and administration granted to the executors named. Confirmed by the bishop. Rose, 25 Jan. 1359.

232 (i) Institution of Robert Parvynk', clerk, to Skelton church, vacant by the resignation of John Parvynk';[165] presented by Adam Parvynk', kt.[166] (ii) Archdeacon to induct. Rose, 25 Jan. 1359.

233 Will[167] of Adam de Bastenthwayt dated 15 Dec. 1358 (being sane in mind and belief but terminally ill, expecting to take rather than escape the way of all flesh). Commends soul to God, Blessed Mary and all saints. Burial in the cloister of Holm Cultram monastery next to his father and mother, if the abbot and convent consent, with his best horse saving the right of the parish church of St. Bega, Bassenthwaite (*Bastenthwayt*) from which his body is taken; with 12 stones of wax for light, 20 marks for the poor, 1 mark for oblations, 12d. and victuals for 12 widows for daily vigil round his body and praying for his soul until his burial, and 100s. for expenses on that day. Chaplains celebrating for his soul for one

---

[163] MS. *Johe'*
[164] Canon of Carlisle, once vicar of Addingham (see **64**, note).
[165] John Parvyng, king's clerk, was ratified as rector, 1352 (*CPR 1350–4*, 355; *BRUO*, III.1431). Before him Richard de Aston was rector in 1346 and 1349, in licences for plurality (*CPL*, III.220, 291); still in 1350 (*CCR 1349–54*, 203). The last known institution was the collation, by lapse, to John de Kirkby, 1343 (*Reg. Kirkby*, I.155, no.741).
[166] He had bought a mediety of the advowson in 1353 (*CPR 1350–4*, 473).
[167] Printed in *Test. Karl.*, 22–4.

year, 42 marks, *viz.* two priests at Bassenthwaite (*Beghokirk*),[168] one [each] at Plumbland, Torpenhow, Bolton, Crosthwaite and Uldale. The abbot of Holm Cultram, 40s., and each monk there, 2s., so that they pray for his soul. The prior of Carlisle, 40s., the cathedral fabric, 100s. for forgotten tithes, and each canon there, 2s., for their prayers. The friars preacher, Carlisle, 20s. The friars minor there, a mark. The Austin friars, Penrith, 20s. The Carmelite friars, Appleby, ½ mark. A man making pilgrimage to St. James, 4 marks. The rector of Plumbland, 40s. to celebrate for the soul of Thomas de Plumland; if he refuses, he is to choose a suitable priest. St. Cuthbert's chapel[169] and his (*or its*) image, and to make glazed windows for the chapel, 6 marks. Joan his daughter, 20 marks. Agnes his daughter for her apparel and adornment, 10 marks. Ellen his daughter and her children, 5 marks. Isabel wife of Thomas de Haryngton, 5 marks. For his soul, 12 paupers are to be dressed in woollen cloth, each having 4 ells and a pair of shoes. Remainder to John de Derwentwater, kt., Robert Brunne, Richard de Hoton, rector of Greystoke, and William de Mulcaster. Isabel daughter of John de Bastenthwayt, 20s. Executors [the above] Sir John, Robert, William and Richard, appointed in the presence of many trustworthy [people]. Sealed with his seal by his own hands. Through unwonted forgetfulness, bequeathes 40s. to his daughter Agnes.

Probate before the bishop and grant of administration to Robert Bruyne, Richard de Hoton and William de Mulcastre; reserved for John de Derwentwater. Rose (chapel), 31 Jan. 1359.

Later, on 4 Feb. 1359, administration was committed to John de Derwentwater at Bassenthwaite by the dean of Allerdale, commissary *ad hoc*.

234 [Fo.26; p.51] Letters patent. In the commissaries' visitation by papal authority, it was found that the abbot and convent of Calder (dioc. York, Cistercian order) hold the parish church of Gilcrux (*Gilcrouce*) to their use. Cited before the commissaries to show their title, they appeared by proxy. Various letters and documents by previous bishops of Carlisle and from the Holy See in confirmation were shown; witnesses were also brought, sworn and examined. After full consideration with experts, the bishop finds that the monks had held the church from time out of mind and canonically taken its fruits, confirming their possession and dismissing them from further impeachment. Rose, 12 Oct. 1358.

235 Probate[170] of the nuncupative [*sic*] will of William son of Christine de Aynstapellyth, as follows:

Dated 7 May 1358. Commends soul to God, Blessed Mary and all saints.

---

[168] *Beghokirk* is shown as a form of the name of St. Bees, but not for Bassenthwaite, in *EPNS Cumberland*, II.263, 430. St. Bees, however, was in the barony of Copeland, later named the ward of Allerdale above Derwent, which was then in the archdeaconry of Richmond and York diocese. As this will shows, Bassenthwaite church was dedicated to St. Bega, and notices of *Beghokirk in Allerdale* in Carlisle episcopal registers show it as a church in this diocese, appropriated to Carlisle priory (*Reg. Halton* (whose editor gave this identification), I.196, II.185, 193; *Reg. Kirkby*, I.88, no.469, II.2).

[169] The dedication of Plumbland church to St. Cuthbert is noted in *Test. Karl.*, 23.

[170] Printed in *Test. Karl.*, 24. Margin: *reddiderunt compotum et absoluti sunt.*

Burial in churchyard of St. Michael's, Ainstable (*Aynstapellyth*), with best beast for mortuary. 2s. to be given to chaplains to celebrate for his soul. Residue to his wife Isabel and his little ones (*parvis*) so that she pays his debts as far as his share of those goods allows. Executors: Isabel and Thomas son of Robert de Aynstapellyth.

Administration granted to the executors named. Rose (chapel), 4 Feb. 1359.

236 Note of licence to William [del Hall], rector of Bowness, to stay *in scolis* for one year, as in the constitution *Cum ex eo*; excused from synods and farming revenues. Rose, 2 Sept. 1358.

237 (i) Institution of John Parvynk', priest, to Skelton church, vacant by the resignation of Robert Parvynk';[171] presented by Adam Parvynk', kt. (ii) Archdeacon to induct. Rose, 18 Feb. 1359.

238 Note of licence to William de Denton, rector of Ousby, to be absent in a suitable place until Michaelmas; at the request of William de Lancastre. 17 Feb. 1359.

239 Note of licence to Richard [de Askeby], rector of Uldale, at the request of Agnes, lady de Lucy, to be absent in her service for two years; excused from synods and chapters. Rose, 11 Feb. 1359.

240 Letters patent. In the commissaries' visitation by papal authority, it was found that the prior and convent of Watton (order of Sempringham, dioc. York) hold the parish church of Ravenstonedale [continuing as in 234 without citing the origin of the documents produced. Fo.26ᵛ; p.52] Confirmation of the appropriation, etc. Rose, 18 Feb. 1359.

241 Licence for one year to Richard de Salkeld for a chaplain to celebrate in an oratory in his manor of Corby (*Corkeby*), without prejudice to his parish church. Rose, 18 Mar. 1359.

242 (i) Institution of John de Seburgham, chaplain, to Walton vicarage, vacant by the resignation of John de Silvirside;[172] presented by the prior and convent of Lanercost. (ii) Archdeacon to induct. Rose, 13 Mar. 1359.

243 Note of licence for one year to Thomas de Shirburn as questor for Holy Trinity, *Mersill*. 7 Mar. 1359.

244 Note of letters dimissory to [further] orders to Stephen de Meborn, subdeacon. 7 Mar. 1359.

245 Note of grant of indulgence of 40 days for the soul of Thomas de Canounby, buried in Bolton (*Boulton*) church. Same date.

---

[171] See **232**.
[172] Previous known presentation was of Robert de Staynewygges, 1340. Silverside was ordained priest, 1342 (*Reg. Kirkby*, I.108,133, nos.535–6, 656).

246   Note of licence for one year to William Lengleys, kt., for divine services in an oratory in his castle of Highhead (*Heyheved*) and another newly built near the castle.[173] 18 Mar. 1359.

247*   Mandate to the prior and subprior of Carlisle, archdeacon, official, priors of Lanercost and Wetheral, and all deans, rectors and vicars, to denounce as excommunicate everyone party to an attack on William Caudryman, apparitor of Carlisle deanery. He had gone on duty to Brampton on a market day[174] as many would be there. Some who had planned to prevent him from discharging his office, assaulted and wounded him, crying 'As you have had some of us called before the bishop's ministers, take them these gifts'. This wicked injury to the church's jurisdiction [etc.] must not be left unpunished. Rose, 28 Apr. 1359.

248   [Fo.27; p.53] Mandate to the dean of Westmorland, sending letters of Francis [de Aptis], bishop of Florence (*Florentin'*), papal penitentiary in the absence of Giles [Albornoz, cardinal] bishop of Sabina, senior penitentiary, on behalf of John son of John de Wakthwayt, clerk (dioc. Carlisle). The dean is to enquire through trustworthy clerks and laymen, on oath, whether John is the son of unmarried parents, himself continent, of good repute and otherwise suitable; reporting by letters patent and close. Rose, 24 Apr. 1359.

249   Note of licence to William de Loundres, rector of Long Marton, to be absent for one year while serving Sir Thomas de Musgrave (at his request); excused from synods. 17 May 1359.

250   Letters patent. While visiting his diocese, the bishop learned that the prior and convent of Hexham hold the parish churches of Isel and Renwick as appropriated. Appearing before the bishop by proxy, they claimed immemorial possession with episcopal approval, not contradicted, and produced instruments, records and witnesses; after their examination, the bishop judicially pronounced his confirmation, with dismissal from further proceedings. Rose, 5 Apr. 1359.

251   Licence to William de Kendale, prior of Hexham, at the entreaty of Gilbert de Hothwayt', excusing him for three years from personal attendance at synods at Carlisle on account of Isel and Renwick churches being appropriated, provided that he appears by proxy.[175] Rose, 5 Apr. 1359.

252   Mandate to the parish chaplain of Sebergham. The vicar of [Castle] Sowerby (*Sourby*) has complained that many of his parishioners have been attending services and receiving sacraments in Sebergham chapel. They are to be ordered, [Fo.27ᵛ; p.54] under pains of interdict and excommunication, to

---

[173] Lengleys, chief forester of Inglewood, received licence to crenellate Highhead in 1342 (*CPR 1340–3*, 536).
[174] Tuesday (Nicolson & Burn, II.491).
[175] Cf. **119**: William was elected prior in 1358 (*The Priory of Hexham*, ed. J. Raine, Surtees Society 44, 46 (1864–6), I.clxvii) The above licence is printed ibid., II.142–3.

attend their parish church. The chaplain is not to admit any of them to sacraments or services without the vicar's licence; reporting by Ascension [30 May]. Rose, 8 May 1359.

253 Letters patent. In the commissaries' visitation by papal authority, it was found that the prior and convent of Guisborough hold the parish churches of Bridekirk and Dearham [continuing as in **234**]. Rose, 2 May 1359.

254* Letters patent. While visiting the diocese, the bishop learned that M. Henry called Heynes of Ross, rector of Cliburn, had frequently been absent in distant places from the time of his induction, neglecting his cure and parishioners and spending the revenues; nor had he been ordained priest within a year of his induction, despite having peaceful possession.[176] He was therefore cited before the bishop, when he showed letters dispensing him to study in accordance with the chapter *Cum ex eo*, and also licences for non-residence, all sealed by previous bishops.[177] The bishop observed that these dispensations required Henry to be only a subdeacon and that they fully covered him. After deliberation, he was dismissed from further impeachment. Rose, 1 May 1359.

255 (i) Collation to M. John de Welton, clerk, of Ousby church, vacant by the death of William de Denton. (ii) Note of mandate for induction to the dean of Cumberland, the archdeacon being *in remotis*. Rose, 14 May 1359.

256 Will[178] of William Bowet, rector of Dacre,[179] dated 24 May 1359 (being sane in mind and memory). Commends soul to God, Blessed Mary and all saints. Burial in choir of St. Andrew's, Dacre. For light round his body, 9s. For expenses at his funeral, 40s., and 10s. for the poor. £4 to celebrate masses for his soul. 13s. 4d. to be divided equally among the four orders of friars. John Snoddyng, his kinsman, 20s. William Spenser, 13s. 4d. John Bowet', 13s. 4d. Thomas de Burgh, 13s. 4d. William son of Thomas Bowet, 13s. 4d. Alice Bowet, 13s. 4d. Richard de Laton, 6s. 8d. Gilbert Bowet, chaplain,[180] 40s. and a *Porthors*. Remainder to Thomas Bowet', his kinsman. All these legacies are to be paid from the tithes of his sheaves of corn now growing when they can best be raised. Executors: Thomas Bowet' and Gilbert Bowet', chaplain. Witnesses: Richard de Laton, John Snoddyng, John Dewy, Henry Palfrayman.
    Probate, with administration to both executors. Rose (chapel), 1 June 1359.

257 [Fo.28; p.55] To John Bell of Appleby, clerk, quoting letters of Francis, bishop of Florence [etc. as in **248**; dated Avignon, 7 Mar. 1356] to the bishop of

---

[176] He had been collated by 1331, doubtless by his uncle(?), Bishop Ross; ordained deacon, 1333 (*Reg. Kirkby*, I.3,24, nos.16,123); died 1367 (Reg. Appleby, fo.9ᵛ; p.158).

[177] Only one, of 1342, is registered (*Reg. Kirkby*, I.142, no.705).

[178] Printed in *Test. Karl.*, 25.

[179] *Alias* William de Burgh (see **260**), rector in 1328 (Nicolson & Burn, II.381). There had been Bowets in Brough since the 12th century (ibid., I.566).

[180] Ordained priest, 1340 (*Reg. Kirkby*, I.112, no.555).

Carlisle or his vicar-general. John son of John de Wacthwayt, clerk (dioc. Carlisle),[181] had sued to be dispensed for his natal defect as the son of unmarried parents, so that he may be ordained and hold a benefice, even with cure of souls; he was unable to visit the papal see in person because of wars and dangers on the roads. The bishop was charged to enquire about John's character, etc., and to absolve and dispense him. Having now received laudable testimony by due enquiry, the bishop dispenses John from the above defect so that he may hold a benefice, even with cure, provided he resides. Rose, 27 May 1359.

258   Note of licence to Thomas de Bampton, rector of a mediety of Kirkbampton,[182] to be absent for one year in a suitable place; excused from personal attendance at synods and chapters. 7 June 1359.

259   Note of grant of similar licence to Thomas [del Close], rector of Brougham. Penrith, 21 July 1359.

260   Letters of William de Routhbury, archdeacon, and Adam de Caldebek, official, to Walter de Loutheburgh, chaplain, quoting the bishop's commission (dated Penrith, 19 June 1359). Sir William de Dacre had presented Walter, clerk, to Dacre church, vacant by the death of William de Burgh.[183] They were to receive this presentation, make enquiry about Walter's character and usual articles about the vacancy, and institute and induct him if the enquiry is favourable. Having held the enquiry, they now institute him, ordering his induction by the archdeacon, saving the rights etc. of the bishop. Penrith, 25 June 1359.

261   Letters patent of Bishop Gilbert, Prior John [de Horncastre] and the chapter of Carlisle, as appropriators of the parish church of St. Nicholas, Newcastle upon Tyne (Durham dioc.), appointing M. John de Welton, skilled in law, Robert de Welton, clerk, and John de Dalston, as their proctors to collect tithes of coppice-wood and mined 'sea' and other coal (*silve cedue et fodinorum carbonum maritinorum vulgariter nuncupatorum ac aliorum fodinorum quorumcumque*) due to them in the parish. Carlisle, 1 August 1359.

262   [Fo.28ᵛ; p.56] (i) Commission of John [Gynwell], bishop of Lincoln, for an exchange of benefices between Henry de Wakefeld, rector of Melmerby, and William de Pulhowe, rector of Sharnford (Lincoln dioc.), sending the report of an enquiry by the archdeacon of Leicester's official. Old Temple, London, 4 July 1359. (ii) Institution of Henry, priest, to Sharnford, following his resignation of Melmerby to Bishop Gilbert by his proctor, Thomas del Close, rector of Brougham (who also acted as proctor in the institution); presented by the king.[184] (iii) Certificate to the bishop of Lincoln. (iv) Institution of William, priest, to Melmerby (with Thomas del Close also his proctor); presented by

---

[181] Note change of surname: 'Wacthwaite' not traced as placename near Appleby.
[182] Presumably the Bampton family mediety (cf. **3** and note), to which the last registered institution was of William de Appelby, 1343 (*Reg. Kirkby*, I.155, nos.740,744).
[183] See **256** and its second note.
[184] By letters dated 3 July 1359 (*CPR 1358–61*, 234).

Adam Parvynk', kt. (v) Mandate to the archdeacon to induct William. Rose, 2 Aug. 1359.

263 (i) Institution of John de Wyntryngham, canon of Warter, to Askham vicarage, vacant by the resignation of Bro. Robert de Balne;[185] presented by the prior and convent of Warter. (ii) Archdeacon to induct. Rose, 2 Aug. 1359.

264 Chancery writ *dedimus potestatem* to receive a recognisance by Nicholas de Skelton, which he wishes to make before the bishop, who is to establish whether Nicholas has been satisfied for £100 in which William de Dacre is bound in a recognisance made in Chancery; and whether Nicholas sues for the cancellation of this recognisance on the rolls of Chancery. After receiving Nicholas' recognisance, the bishop is to certify Chancery under his seal, returning this writ. Westminster, 20 Feb.1359.
[Return] Nicholas came before the bishop and made a recognisance; he is satisfied for the £100 and wishes the recognisance about them to be cancelled.[186]

265* [Fo.29; p.57] Notarial instrument about oblations at the funeral of William, Baron Greystoke, in Greystoke church on 8 August 1359.[187] The bishop celebrated mass and therefore received the oblations at the offertory, *viz.* helms, swords, shields, lances, armoured horses and men in the baron's arms (two of each, one for peace, the other for war), as is customary, and money from the lords, knights and others in the congregation. After he had completed the office of burial, the bishop called these nobles, prelates and others before him and in their presence gave Joan, Sir William's widow, all the oblations (which were his due), save for the money which was reserved for the clerks of his chapel. Witnesses: the noble lords Ralph de Nevill, Thomas de Lucy, lord of Cockermouth, Roger lord de Clifford, Henry Lescropp, Thomas de Musgrave senior, knights; Brothers John, prior of Carlisle, Robert, abbot of Holm Cultram, and Lambert, abbot of Shap; and Masters William de Routhbury, archdeacon of Carlisle, and Thomas de Salkeld, rector of Clifton, notary; Richard de Aslakby, vicar of Stanwix, the notary [below] and a copious multitude.
     Sign and subscription by William de Ragenhill, clerk (dioc. York), notary by papal authority.[188]

266 Memorandum of mandate to the prior of Lanercost, vicars of Brampton, Irthington and Walton, and John Boon, parish chaplain of St. Mary's, Carlisle, to publish the excommunication of all who attacked William Caudryman,

---

[185] Recently elected prior of Warter (**281**). Bro. Robert de Dalum, instituted 1346, was possibly the same (*Reg. Kirkby*, I.173–4; see also **43**).
[186] See *CCR 1354–60*, 502.
[187] He died at Brancepeth, 10 July (*Complete Peerage*, VI.194–5). His plan to create a college in Greystoke church, approved by the bishop in 1358, was thus not effected until 1382 (*VCH Cumberland*, II.205).
[188] The notary's sign (6 cm in diameter) and subscription follow, with a space 5 cm deep beneath struck through by cancellations. The entry begins with a decorated *I* extending down its entire length (9 cm).

apparitor in the deanery of Carlisle, as in the second folio above (247); they were ordered on their obedience and under pain of excommunication for neglect, and to certify by 8 September. 16 Aug. 1359.

267   Note of commission to M. William de Salkeld, rector of a mediety of Aikton, and John Boon and John Marshall, chaplains,[189] to claim and receive clerks accused before the king's justices of gaol delivery in Carlisle. 18 Aug. 1359.

268   Note of similar commission to William Colyn, vicar of St. Lawrence's, Appleby, and John Toke, vicar of St. Michael's, Appleby,[190] for gaol delivery at Appleby. Same date.

269   Note of letters dimissory to all orders to Thomas Eday, clerk with first tonsure. Same date.

270   [Fo.29ᵛ; p.58] To John de Derwendwatre, clerk (dioc. Carlisle), quoting letters of Francis, bishop of Florence, papal penitentiary in the absence of Giles [Albornoz, cardinal] bishop of Sabina (dated Avignon, 26 July 1356); John had sued to be dispensed as the son of unmarried parents. After enquiry, the bishop dispenses him to be ordained and hold a benefice with cure, provided he resides. Rose, 29 Sept. 1359.

271   (i) Collation to Thomas de Cullerdoune, priest, of Stanwix vicarage, vacant by the resignation of Richard de Aslacby, its last rector [sic], in an exchange for Wigton vicarage, which Thomas has resigned.[191] (ii) Collation to Richard of Wigton vicarage in this exchange. (iii) Archdeacon to induct both vicars. Rose, 16 Oct. 1359.

272   Probate[192] of the nuncupative [sic] will of Simon de Haythwayt, as follows: Dated 31 July 1359. Commends soul to God, Blessed Mary and all saints. Burial in churchyard of St. Michael's, Dalston, with best beast (*averio*) for mortuary, 12d. for oblations and 6d. for lights. John son of Nicholas Parker, an ox. Thomas son of Nicholas Parker, a heifer. The children (*parvis*) of William son of Magota, a cow. [Simon's] wife [Fo.30; p.59], 7 sheep and his share of a horse. The high altar of Dalston [church], half a skep of oats. The chapel of Blessed Mary, Dalston, 6d. His executors, 2 skeps of oats. William de Haythwayt, a skep of oats. Residue to his wife to arrange for the safety of his soul. Executors: Henry Mariotson and William son of Simon.
      Administration to the executors named. Rose (chapel), 22 Sept. 1359.

---

[189] These chaplains appear in similar commissions (326, 542, 579). As Boon was the parish chaplain of St. Mary's, Carlisle (e.g. 266), it is likely that Marshall was the chaplain of St. Cuthbert's, Carlisle's other parish church.

[190] Confirmed as vicar, 1344 (*Reg. Kirkby*, I.161, no.777).

[191] Presented to Wigton by the king in the vacancy of the see, 1352 (*CPR 1350–4*, 384); see also note to 36.

[192] Printed in *Test. Karl.*, 26.

273 Note of letters dimissory to all orders to Henry Scarlet of Penrith, literate; at the request of Sir Thomas de Salkeld. 27 Oct. 1359.

274 Mandate to the prior and official of Carlisle quoting letters of John [Thoresby], archbishop of York (dated Cawood, 24 Oct. 1359), ordering the bishop to comply with the king's writ (received on 22 Oct.; quoted) asking for prayers and processions for his expedition to France, dated Westminster, 12 Aug. 1359.[193] Order for processions in Carlisle cathedral and all churches of the diocese, with prayers for the safety of the king, his army and allies, and for their victory to the honour of God, [Fo.30ᵛ; p.60] salvation of the kingdom and benefit of the English church; with an indulgence of 40 days for all taking part. Rose, 4 Nov. 1359.

275 Note of renewal for one year of letters to questors for the fabric of the collegiate church of St. John, Beverley; at the suit of Thomas de Cokerton, its proctor. Rose, 7 Nov. 1359.

276 Note of a release from proceedings (*dimissionem*) against the abbot and convent of Whitby about their appropriation of Crosby Ravensworth (*Crossebyravenswart*) church. 1 Nov. 1359.

277 Letters patent. In the commissaries' visitation by papal authority, it was found that the prior and convent of Conishead (dioc. York) hold the parish church of Wharton (*Ouerton*[194]) [continuing as in **240**]. Confirmation of the appropriation, etc. Rose, 18 Nov. 1359.

278 Note of licence to M. Henry de Sandford, rector of Crosby Garrett, to be absent for one year; excused from synods and chapters. Rose, 18 Nov. 1359.

279 Letters patent. Bro. Nicholas de Preston, vicar of Warcop,[195] was under sentence of excommunication for non-payment of sums due to the bishop for a pension and to the abbot and convent of Shap according to a composition between them and Nicholas. He is now absolved, with a penance, after information that he has fully paid these debts. Rose, 25 Nov. 1359.

280 Probate[196] of the nuncupative will of John Lowry, as follows:
Dated 19 Nov. 1359. Commended soul to God, Blessed Mary and all saints. Burial in churchyard of St. Michael's, Arthuret, with best beast for mortuary and 10s. for oblations and lights. Lights of Blessed Mary in Arthuret church, 20s. As a pittance for the image of Holy Cross there, a skep of barley and a skep of oats. For a candle to burn before it, a half skep of rye. The fabric of St. Mary's,

---

[193] Printed *Foedera*, III(1).442; *CCR 1354–60*, 645.
[194] Recte *Querton* (*EPNS Westmorland*, II.26).
[195] Canon of Shap, ordained deacon, 1342 (*Reg. Kirkby*, I.133–4). Last recorded institution to Wharton, on Shap's presentation, was of Bro. Hugh de Hoveden, in 1320 (*Reg. Halton*, II.200–1). See also **544**.
[196] Printed *Test. Karl.*, 26–7, which omits date of will.

Carlisle, 13s. 4d. Lights there, 10s. Eden bridge, 10s. and a skep of barley. The friars preachers, Carlisle, a skep of barley and a skep of oats. The friars minor, Carlisle, a skep of barley and a skep of oats. William de Arthureth, his term and title in *Le Blamyre* in Scotland, to find a chaplain celebrating for his soul and all souls for three years. Residue to his wife Emma and their children. Executors: Emma and Adam Hyneson. Witnesses: William [de Arthureth], vicar of Arthuret, Richard the chaplain,[197] and William de Arthureth.

Administration to named executors. Rose (chapel), 2 Dec. 1359.

281 Licence to Robert de Balne, prior of Warter, excusing him for as long as he is prior from personal attendance at synods at Carlisle on account of Askham and Barton churches [as in **59***]. Rose, 1 Oct. 1359.

282 Note of letters dimissory to sacred orders to Adam de Wygton, vicar of Addingham. n.d.

283* [Fo.31; p.61] Letters patent. During the bishop's visitation by diocesan authority, the prior and convent of St. James, Warter (dioc. York), were summoned to show their title to hold the churches of Askham and Barton, a pension of a mark in Clifton church, partial tithes in Sockbridge and Tirril, also in High and Low Winder in Barton parish. They appeared by proxy, firstly about Askham, the pension and partial tithes, showing lawful documents by bishops of Carlisle and others of the faithful; they had enjoyed undisturbed occupation from time immemorial. About Barton church, they produced a [deed of] appropriation by John [Halton], bishop of Carlisle,[198] and its confirmation by Carlisle priory, which gave causes for the appropriation. Although [Bishop Welton] should accept [Halton's] assertion, he has taken the testimony of many witnesses and documents, and pronounces the priory and convent are fully entitled to their possession of both churches, the pension and tithes, dismissing them as absolved for all time. Rose, 1 Sept. 1359.

284* Mandate to the vicar of Penrith. It was decreed by the holy fathers that anyone who robs the buildings of ecclesiastics would incur sentence of greater excommunication. After last Michaelmas, however, persons unknown stole a black ox of the bishop's from places and pastures of the bishopric in Penrith parish. They and their accomplices are to be denounced as excommunicate in Penrith church on All Saints day and the following Sundays and festivals when most people are there, with bells rung, candles lit, etc., until further notice. [The vicar] is to enquire for their names and report by 20 November. Rose, 28 Oct. 1359.

285 Note that the vicar of Penrith was ordered, under the bishop's seal, to suspend execution of the above mandate until further orders. Rose, 7 Dec. 1359.

[197] Possibly Richard Blese, witness at Arthuret in **17**; and/or Richard de Arthureth (**41**).
[198] Dated 1318 in *Reg. Halton*, II.177–8.

286 Note of letters dimissory to all orders to William del Lynehous of Uldale (*Ulfdale*), clerk with first tonsure. 9 Dec. 1359.

287 Letters patent (in French) asking for free passage and safe conduct for the bearer, John Senyer of Dufton, who is the appointed purveyor of corn for the bishop's household; to be valid until Easter next. Rose, 1 Nov. 1359.

288 Presentation by Edward III of John de Soulby, clerk, to [Great] Musgrave church, now vacant, in the king's gift because the bishopric was lately vacant. Westminster, 16 June 1359.[199]

289 Three Common Pleas writs *admittatis non obstante reclamacione* ordering the bishop to admit the king's presentee to [Great] Musgrave church because he has recovered his presentation against (i) Robert Kerrol, chaplain,[200] by judgment of the court; (ii) William de Ellerton, chaplain, by default; (iii) the bishop, by default. [All] tested by Robert de Thorpe, Westminster, 12, 28 and 28 Nov., 1359.

290 Memorandum that on the feast of St. Stephen, after the ninth hour, in the principal chamber, the above John de Soulby, clerk, presented these writs and presentation to the bishop, who immediately ordered the official to enquire about the vacancy and other usual articles.[201] Rose, 26 Dec. 1359.

291* [Fo.31ᵛ; p.62] From the bishop as papal delegate to the official of York, his commissary general or deputies, and any others concerned. On 19 June 1357 he received papal letters as follow: 'Innocencius . . . . visitacionis officium etc.' as in the ninth folio preceding [i.e. **213***]. By their authority, the bishop visited the diocese by deputy. Many religious claiming to hold benefices, tithes and pensions were cited to show their titles, among them the abbot and convent of St. Mary's, York, holding the churches of Kirkby Stephen, Morland, Bromfield, St. Michael's and St. Lawrence's, Appleby, Wetheral and Warwick, and partial tithes and pensions in the diocese. Their proctor, Adam de Burton, came before the deputy and said they had many letters, instruments and documents of popes, bishops of Carlisle, the chapter of Carlisle and various temporal lords, which he showed, together with a written proposition. Wishing to examine them for sufficiency and admissibility, the deputy cited the abbot

---

[199] Dated 16 June 1359 in *CPR 1358–61*, 226.
[200] As Kerrot, provided 1357, after claiming the church's reservation to the pope because the previous rector, John de Stoketon, had died after visiting Rome for the jubilee in 1350 (*CPP*, I.294; *CPL*. III,582; *Accounts*, ed. Lunt, 158, 206; see also Barrell, *Papacy, Scotland and Northern England* (cited in Introduction, xi, n.21), 53). John is known as rector 1341–3 (*Reg. Kirkby*, I.115 (ordained deacon), 145 no.721). It was reported to Chancery in 1364 that after John's death, Bishop Kirkby collated William de Sandford, who was followed by William de Ellerton, whose patron was not named in the same register, with John Soulby being the last known rector (Reg. Appleby, fo.1ᵛ; p.142). Ellerton, however, was presented by the king in letters of 10 May 1358 (*CPR 1358–61*, 39).
[201] See **307–8**.

and convent to appear before the bishop or his deputies, as he certified the bishop. They did not come or send a proctor, despite repeated summons, and were warned that they would be deemed contumacious, although [the bishop] was willing to receive them at another date. He therefore gives notice of these particulars to the official (and others addressed) and by papal authority orders them not to take any action to impede this visitation and process prejudicial to the holy see, to which [the bishop] appeals in this document.[202] Rose, 4 Jan. 1360.

292   Writ *dedimus potestatem* for the bishop to receive the oath of Matthew de Redemane as sheriff of Cumberland and keeper of Carlisle castle, to which he has been appointed (during pleasure) by letters patent. Westminster, 6 Oct. 1359.[203]

Form of oath (in French). He will faithfully serve the king as sheriff of Cumberland, guard his and the crown's rights nor allow their concealment, telling the king or his councillors if he cannot; nor respite for gifts or favour any debts which can be levied without harm to the king's debtors. He will treat the people of his bailiwick, rich and poor, faithfully and lawfully, nor harm any for gift, promise, favour or hatred. He will serve writs faithfully. He will appoint only loyal bailiffs, under oath, for whom he is prepared to answer.[204]

Return. The bishop received Matthew's oath on 8 January 1360 and delivered him the above-mentioned letters patent.[205]

293   Memorandum that in the prior's chamber in Carlisle priory William de Lancastre was granted a licence, for one year, for divine service to be celebrated in an oratory in Howgill (*Holgill*) manor. Carlisle, 8 Jan. 1360.

294   Memorandum of probate of the nuncupative will [not given] of Emma wife of Thomas Potter of Hawksdale (*Haukesdale*) before William de Ragenhill and grant of administration to the said Thomas and Thomas son of John Smyth, her brother, the executors named. Rose (chapel), 16 Jan. 1360.

295   Licence, for two years, to Margaret, widow of William de Lygh kt., because her manor of Isel is distant from the parish church, [Fo.32; p.63] for a chaplain to celebrate in an oratory in the manor; without prejudice, etc. Rose, 16 Jan. 1360.

296   Mandate to the prior and official of Carlisle. On 18 January, the bishop received letters of John [Thoresby], archbishop of York, which quote a writ of Edward III: in view of a threatened Scottish invasion and enemy activity outside the realm, the archbishop is asked to call the bishops and clergy of his province soon, and treat with them for a suitable remedy for the defence of the church

---

[202] **304** shows the bishop at St. Mary's soon afterwards.
[203] See *CFR*, VII.102.
[204] In same form as for sheriff of Rutland, 1388, save that the latter has an additional clause about the under-sheriff (*Royal Writs addressed to John Buckingham, Bishop of Lincoln*, ed. A.K. McHardy, CYS (1997), 114).
[205] See **313**.

and realm (tested by Thomas the king's son, keeper of England, at Woodstock, 18 Nov. 1359).[206] The archbishop therefore summons a provincial council to meet in York on 12 February (Cawood, 8 Jan. 1360).[207] [The prior and official] are to cite abbots, priors and the archdeacon of Carlisle to attend in person, the chapter of Carlisle and other convents with single and diocesan clergy with two proctors; and also announce that anyone with pertinent grievances should appear in the council; certifying the bishop by 2 February. Rose, 19 Jan. 1360.

297 Certificate to the archbishop that his mandate [said to be quoted] has been published. Those cited are named in a schedule. Rose, 6 Feb. 1360.

John, prior of Carlisle; its chapter
Robert, abbot of Holm Cultram; its convent
Lambert, abbot of Shap; its convent
Richard, prior of Lanercost; its convent
William, prior of Wetheral; his fellow-monks
William de Routhbury, archdeacon of Carlisle
Masters Adam de Caldebek and Thomas de Salkeld, proctors of the clergy.

298 Note of mandate to the dean of Westmorland to sequestrate the revenues of [Great] Musgrave church, said to be vacant, warning that violators will be excommunicated; arrange services during the vacancy; and certify by 23 February. 7 Feb. 1360.

299 Memorandum of probate of the nuncupative will [not given] of Thomas Walker of Sebergham; his goods were granted to Sibbota, his widow, to pay his debts, and administration to her and Thomas Saunderson, named executors. 7 Jan. 1360.

300 [Fo.32ᵛ; p.64] Licence[208] for John Boon, chaplain, Thomas Hogge, and other proctors of the prior and chapter of Carlisle to collect alms for rebuilding the cathedral choir; with an indulgence for 40 days, valid for one year. Rose, 20 Jan. 1360.

301* Declaration by the bishop that he has been in lawful possession of his see for a long time, peacefully, of good repute and free of any canonical sentence. He now has cause to believe that his status may be challenged and disturbed. He therefore, in this statement, appeals to the papal see and, for tuition, to the court of York, putting himself under their protection.

[206] See *CCR 1354–60*, 599; *Foedera*, III(1).458.
[207] The archbishop's mandate for this council to Bishop Hatfield of Durham is printed in *Records of the Northern Convocation*, ed. G.W. Kitchin, Surtees Society 113 (1907), 91–4. It begins by stating that for reasons given in a royal writ, and other causes, the archbishop had decreed a provincial council to be held in York Minster on 27 Jan. 1360; but for causes newly arisen, which would be explained to Hatfield, he had decided to hold the council on 12 February. The above writ is then quoted and the mandate then continues in the same form as in the above mandate to Welton (also in terms similar to **125***). For the bishop's attendance, see date of **304**.
[208] As in **534***, the earliest of these licences for Carlisle, with amendments (shown in Appendix) in 1357 (**599**) and **300** above.

Memorandum that the bishop read this statement while walking before the door of the chapel at Rose, in the presence of Peter de Morland, vicar of Torpenhow, Richard de Aslacby, vicar of Wigton, Adam de Foresta, rector of Kirkcambeck, and William de Ragenhill, notary [with his signature]. 27 Jan. 1360.

302 Note of licence to Walter de Loutheburgh, rector of Dacre, to be absent for three years from 23 June while serving Sir William de Dacre; excused from synods, etc. and given a letter.

The bishop remitted his fine (*mulcta*) for absence from the synod at Carlisle after Michaelmas 1359 as a favour to Clement de Skelton,[209] who came with [Walter]. Memorandum that he is to pay the bishop £10 as alms to the bishop for this licence, *viz*. 5 marks each year from 24 June next, for which he was bound judicially under pain of excommunication; in the presence of Clement de Skelton. Rose, 31 Jan. 1360.

[margin] He paid 5 marks on 23 August 1360 for the first term, and 5 marks on 2 July 1361 for the second; he owes 5 marks.

303 (i) Collation to Thomas de Salkeld, chaplain, of Torpenhow vicarage,[210] vacant by the resignation of Peter de Morland in an exchange. (ii) Collation to Peter de Morland, priest, of Clifton church, resigned by Thomas in this exchange. (iii) Archdeacon to induct to both churches. Rose, 7 Mar. 1360.

304 Note that in the grounds (*septa*) of St. Mary's monastery, York, the bishop, by apostolic authority, dispensed John de Burton, clerk (dioc. Carlisle), the son of unmarried parents, to be ordained to all orders and hold a benefice with cure of souls, provided he resides; also granting letters dimissory to all orders. York, 16 Feb. 1360.

305 [Fo.33; p.65] (i) Collation to Peter de Morland, priest, of Torpenhow vicarage, vacant by the resignation of Thomas de Salkeld in an exchange. (ii) Collation of Thomas, priest, of Clifton church vacant by Peter's resignation. (iii) Mandate to the archdeacon to induct both parsons. Rose, 21 Mar. 1360.[211]

306 Licence for Robert Jardyn, proctor of the prior and convent of St. Cuthbert's cathedral, Durham, to make a collection for its fabric; valid until 12 March [1361]. Rose, 31 Mar. 1360.

307 Commission to M. John de Welton, clerk skilled in law, to examine the certificate of an inquest into the presentation of John de Soulby, clerk, to [Great] Musgrave church by Edward III,[212] the bishop being too busy to attend to the matter in person; and if there is no obstacle, to admit him [etc., as in **225**]. Rose, 2 Apr. 1360.

---

[209] See probate in **388**.
[210] See **561** and note; also **305**.
[211] See **303**.
[212] See **290**.

308 Letters patent of John de Welton, clerk, as the bishop's commissary [said to quote the above commission]. The inquest found that the church was vacant, the king its patron because of the late vacancy of the see, and there were no canonical obstacles to the presentee; he was instituted and the archdeacon ordered to induct him after his obedience was received; saving the rights of the bishop and his church. Under [the commissary's] seal, dated as above.

Subscription of William de Ragenhell, clerk (dioc. York), notary, at the commissary's request made in the principal chamber, Rose, 2 Apr. 1360, in the presence of M. Thomas de Salkeld, clerk, notary. [Fo.33ᵛ; p.66] The commissary carried out this process in the chapel at Rose, on the same day, in the presence of the notary [William], the said M. Thomas, and Peter de Morland, Richard de Aslacby and John de Grandon, [vicars] of Torpenhow, Wigton and Crosby on Eden

309 Writ *dedimus potestatem* for the bishop to receive the oath of Christopher de Moriceby, appointed sheriff of the county of Carlisle during pleasure. Tested by Thomas the king's son, keeper of England, Westminster, 24 Mar. 1360.[213] Return. The bishop received the oath on 3 Apr. 1360.

310 Signification to the king that Thomas Thwaytesman, Ellen daughter of John Gardyner of Melmerby, Patrick de Man and Alice wife of Richard de Grenehowe of Denton have been excommunicate for 40 days at the instance of the bishop's office. Rose, 8 Apr. 1360.

311 Mandate to the official of Carlisle quoting the king's writ of summons to a parliament at Westminster on 15 May, with *premunientes* clause (tested by Thomas, keeper of England, Westminster, 3 Apr. 1360),[214] for execution [as in **155**], reporting by 3 May. Rose, 17 Apr. 1360.

312 Licence for one year to Hugh de Jarum, questor for the hospital of Saint-Antoine-de-Viennois. Rose, 18 Apr. 1360.

313 Will[215] of Matthew Redmane of Kendal (*Kendale*), kt. Commends soul to God, Blessed Mary and all saints. Burial in St. Peter's church, Heversham, with best animal for mortuary. All his goods, *viz.* horses, cattle, sheep, corn and household utensils, to his wife Margaret for her free disposal and to ordain for his soul. Executors: Christopher and Hugh de Moriceby.

Note of probate before M. Adam de Caldebek,[216] official of Carlisle, at Carlisle.[217]

[213] See *CFR*, VII.121. The previous sheriff had died (see **292, 313**)
[214] As in *CCR 1360–4*, 107.
[215] Printed in *Test. Karl.*, 27–8. He died in March 1360 (cf. **292, 309**).
[216] Cf. *Salkeld* in *Test. Karl.*, 28.
[217] With blanks left for date. There is no marginal note about the executors' account. As Heversham, Westm., was in York diocese, however, the will may also have been proved there.

314 [Fo.34; p.67] (i) Institution of John de Penreth, canon of Carlisle, to [Castle] Sowerby (*Sourby*) vicarage, vacant by the death of Bro. Patrick de Culwen;[218] presented by the prior and chapter of Carlisle. (ii) Archdeacon to induct. Rose, 27 Apr. 1360.

315 Note of letters dimissory to all orders to John de Alaynby, clerk with first tonsure. 3 May 1360.

316* Declaration by the bishop that the archdeacon of Carlisle may have a clerk attending chapters for the diocese to assist the bishop's official and ministers in making corrections and to make a copy of them. The archdeacon may call all subjects by letter to undergo visitation, and proceed by censures against absentees and non-payers of procurations due in his visitations. Whenever the bishop's deans account before the bishop's auditors, the archdeacon is to have a third of receipts for corrections, and also of *sinodalia* from the deans; he may proceed against them for non-payment.[219]

Memorandum that the bishop made this declaration in the principal chamber at Rose in the presence of M. William de Routhbury, archdeacon of Carlisle, and W[illiam] de Rag[enhill] clerk [with his signature]. 2 May 1360.

317 LICENCIA CONCESSA JOHANNI DE LYE INGREDIENDI RELIGIONEM. Letters patent. John de Lye, who had recently married Elizabeth daughter of Richard Bruyn, was ordered by the bishop to treat her with conjugal affection. Appearing before the bishop, with Elizabeth present, he said that he had avoided a sexual relationship because he wanted to be a monk.[220] After deliberation and investigation of the facts, and with Elizabeth's consent, the bishop licensed him to enter religion within a month, otherwise he would be excommunicated unless he returned to Elizabeth. Rose, 18 Apr. 1360.[221]

318 (i) Collation to M. John de Welton, clerk skilled in law, of Crosthwaite vicarage, now vacant.[222] (ii) Dean of Cumberland to induct. London inn, 19 May 1360.

319 (i) Commission to the prior of Carlisle, quoting a writ of Edward III (tested by Thomas, keeper of England, at Reading, 22 Apr. 1360), ordering the bishop to appoint a collector in Carlisle diocese of both halves of a tenth granted by the prelates and clergy of York province in their last convocation in St. Peter's, York, for the defence of the realm and the war in France; to be paid on 24 June and 2 Feb. [1361], under certain conditions, as was certified by John

---

[218] Instituted 1339 (*Reg. Kirkby*, I.94, nos.492–3).

[219] The (sole) archdeacon of Carlisle 'never had a court of his own' (*Reg. Halton*, II.xxix–xi, xxxiii); for his customary rights, see *Reg. Kirkby*, I.75, no.395. He apparently did not have an official (see **220, 255**).

[220] Printed to this point in Historical Manuscripts Commission, *Ninth Report*, I.191.

[221] See **376**.

[222] The vicarage was still being contested by a provisor (see **195**). On 14 July 1360, William de Essinden (of Lincoln dioc.) received papal confirmation as vicar. Like John Welton, he was unable to get possession because of a royal prohibition (i.e. **321**?; *Accounts*, ed. Lunt, 517).

[Thoresby], archbishop of York.[223] [Fo.34ᵛ; p.68] (ii) Certificate of the prior's appointment to the treasurer and barons of the Exchequer. Rose, 1 June 1360.

320* Letters patent. William de Stapilton and Alice daughter of Richard de Whytefeld were impeached before the bishop *ex officio* on the grounds that their marriage was unlawful and clandestine. This they admitted, as was confirmed by witnesses. The bishop therefore found that the marriage could not stand in law and declares it void.[224] Rose, 1 June 1360.

321 [Chancery] writ of prohibition ordering the bishop not to confer the vicarage of Crosthwaite, said to be vacant, until it is decided in the king's court whether the presentation belongs to the king or the bishop.[225] Westminster, 25 May 1360.
    Note that this writ was delivered to the bishop by a messenger, together with letters supplicatory from Queen Philippa. 4 June 1360.

322 Note of licence for one year to Adam Parvynk', kt., and Katherine his wife, for a chaplain to celebrate in an oratory in their manor of Blackhall (*Blakhale*); without prejudice etc. 30 June 1360.

323 Note of letters dimissory for all orders to John de Levenhowe, clerk with first tonsure. 6 July 1360.

324* Commission to M. William de Ragenhill, the bishop's familiar clerk, and the dean of Carlisle. The bishop has been told that some parishioners of Burgh by Sands, without his consent, dug round an arch attached to the new belltower,[226] removing stones and mortar, with the result that this arch and others adjacent collapsed. One or both [commissaries] are to go to the church and examine reliable parishioners under oath to find who had done this damage; whether parishioners had consented; whether the collapse of the arches had damaged the church and how much; whether those responsible had the means to recompense God, the church and parishioners. They are also to enquire into all other particulars and for the names of those responsible, certifying the bishop by letters patent under the dean's seal. Rose, 15 July 1360.

325* Sentence. While the bishop was visiting the diocese, William del Hall, claiming to be rector of Bowness, was called, with other rectors and vicars, to

---

[223] As in *CFR*, VII.123. Writs dated 28 May were sent to most collectors in both provinces asking for prompt payment of the half tenth due on 24 June, but seemingly not to the prior of Carlisle (*Foedera*, III(1).496–7; *CCR 1360–4*, 40–1). See also **296**.
[224] Cf. **328**.
[225] There was a royal presentation to the vicarage dated 15 Nov. 1359, of John Roberd of *Wylien*, chaplain, which was opposed by Thomas Inne, named as 'Juven' (*CPR 1358–61*, 307, 413); cf. **86, 195, 318** and note, **375, 382**).
[226] See J.F. Curwen, *The Castles and Fortified Towers of Cumberland, Westmorland and Lancashire North-of-the-Sands*, CWAAS extra ser.13 (1913), 323–5; D.R. Perriam & J. Robinson, *The Medieval Fortified Buildings of Cumbria*, CWAAS extra ser. 29 (1998), 62–3.

show his title to the church.[227] He made a statement (quoted) protesting his lawful occupation, as duly appointed and inducted, asking for its confirmation. He came on another day set to determine the matter [Fo.35; p.69] and showed many letters and instruments. On that day, for judgment, the bishop examined the documents with legal assistance, and pronounced that William had proved his case, confirmed his title and dismissed him from further impeachment. Rose, 20 May 1359.

326 Commission to M. William [de Salkeld], rector of a mediety of Aikton, and John Boon and John Maresshall, chaplains, to claim and receive clerks accused before the king's justices of gaol delivery in Carlisle [etc. as in **542**]. Rose, 4 Aug. 1360.

Note of similar commission to William Colyn and John Toke, vicars of St. Lawrence's and St. Michael's, Appleby, for gaol delivery at Appleby. [Same date?]

327 Note of a mandate to the dean of Allerdale to sequestrate all goods of Gilbert de Hothwayt', deceased, in the diocese, and publish the sequestration. 26 July 1360.

Note that custody of the sequestration was granted to Robert de Musgrave,[228] with a clause that he would account when required. 2 Aug. 1360.

328* Letters patent. William de Stapelton and Alice daughter of Richard de Whytefeld of Carlisle had contracted marriage by words of consent, and solemnised and consummated their marriage.[229] Although she had not been divorced, however, she had similarly contracted, solemnised and consummated marriage with John de Gaytescales of Carlisle. John and Alice were therefore cited before the bishop, who pronounced this marriage to be illegal, void and divorced. Rose, 8 July 1360.

329 Licence, during pleasure, to the prior and convent of Austin friars, Penrith, to provide one of themselves to celebrate in Newton Reigny chapel, which is vacant. Rose, 2 Aug. 1360.

330 Note of licence to William de Ebor', rector of Bolton, to be absent for two years while serving [Ralph] lord de Nevill (at his request); excused from synods. 26 June 1360.

331 Memorandum that, at his request, Richard de Segbroke, who was judicially condemned to pay the bishop £8, undertook in writing to pay the bishop or his attorney at Rose forty shillings annually for four years, in halves at Easter and Michaelmas from Easter next, under pain of excommunication. Richard swore to comply, and the bishop repeated the sentence. Present: Richard de Aslacby, vicar of Wigton, John de Dalston of Carlisle diocese,

---

[227] See **36** and note, also **42**, **604**.
[228] An executor of Gilbert's will (**371**).
[229] Cf. **320**.

John de Piperharowe of Winchester diocese, and William de Rag[enhill], clerk and notary, of York diocese [with his signature]. Rose (chapel), 11 Aug. 1360.

332 [Fo.35^v; p.70] Mandate to the dean of Westmorland, rector of Lowther (*Louthre*) and vicars of Morland, Shap and Crosby Ravensworth [with preamble as in **284**]. The bishop has been told that enemies of the Church have broken doors, windows and walls of a grange and buildings of Shap abbey called Sleddale and removed goods. Moreover many sons of iniquity, satellites of Satan, etc., attacked Abbot Lambert of Shap and his attendants while they were riding on the highway beside Lowther park, with swords, axes and bows and arrows, pursuing them with arrows and furious cries, intending to kill them. All involved are to be denounced, in English (*lingua materna vulgarique eloquio*), as excommunicate in the above churches and others in Westmorland, as required by the abbey, until they come to seek absolution from the bishop. Enquiries are to be made for their names and a report made. Rose, 12 Aug. 1360.

333 Note of letters dimissory to all orders to John de Soulby, rector of [Great] Musgrave. 16 Aug. 1360.

334 Note of signification to the king against Robert Beaucham of Sowerby Wood, excommunicate for 40 days. 12 Oct. 1360.

335 (i) Collation to Robert de Welton, clerk, of Ousby church, now vacant.[230] (ii) Archdeacon to induct. Rose, 15 Oct. 1360.

336 Will[231] of William de Appilby,[232] vicar of Doncaster, dated 24 Sept. 1360. Commends soul to God, Blessed Mary and all saints. Burial in St. George's [Doncaster], with his body as mortuary (*ut est juris*), with 20 pounds of wax for burning and £20 for a wake. Sir William de Hauley (*or* Hanley), 40s. and his best gown. Sir John de Barneley, 13s. 4d. and his second-best gown. Sir John de Mekesburgh, 13s. 4d. and his third-best gown. Sir William de Estthorp, 13s. 4d. and his fourth-best gown. Sir Thomas de Appilby, 13s. 4d. and his fifth-best gown. In dole for the poor, £10. Thomas Olifant, his wife and their children, £6 13s. 4d. Legitimate children of John son of Christine, 40s. [The testator's] sister Alice and her daughter living in Kirkby Stephen, 40s. Sir John del Okes, 3s. 4d. William Wrangwys, the 40s. he owes and 26s. 8d. Every chaplain celebrating in Doncaster church, save those named above, 40d. The church's two clerks, 3s. 4d. each. John Foxholes, 6s. 8d. M. John Burdon, 20s. Sir John de Marton, [the testator's] breviary, or the other which Sir William de Loundres has from him. Sir John, vicar of *Burgh*,[233] his little breviary. Godewill and his wife, 26s. 8d. they owe and 40s. Adam le Harpour, 13s. 4d. The Carmelite friars, Appleby, 8 marks at the disposal of Fr. William Garaun. A chaplain celebrating for the souls of his father, mother and friends in St. Michael's, Appleby, for three years, 18 marks.

---

[230] Presumably by resignation of John de Welton (see **255**, **318**).
[231] Printed in *Test. Karl.*, 28–31.
[232] Named 'William Nelson' in margin.
[233] Probably Brough under Stainmore, where the first known fully named vicar was John Rainold, 1369 (Nicolson & Burn, I.568).

St. Lawrence's, Appleby, a missal. St. George's, Doncaster, the breviary which belonged to John Gare, chaplain. William de Brampton, 20s. and a bed, *viz.* a canvas, two blankets, two sheets and a coverlet with a curtain. John del Hill and a bed [as above]. The high altar of Blessed Mary's, 6s. 8d. The altars of St Thomas the Martyr, St. Nicholas and St. Lawrence, 10s. in equal portions. Sir William de Hauley, a chest. Sir John de Lon[er]sale, 20s. The fabric of St. George's, 13s. 4d. His kinsmen William and John, £20 and two books, *viz.* a *Legenda Sanctorum* and a book of expositions of the Epistles; also a Flanders chest and everything belonging to his chamber not already bequeathed. His maid Agnes, 13s. 4d. William del Hill, 6s. 8d. Thomas le Carter, 6s. 8d. His page John, 6s. 8d. His page Thomas, 6s. 8d. Robert de Fulsham's children, 6s. 8d. Alice daughter of William Wodecok, [Fo.36; p.71] 6s. 8d. Thomas Cote's children, 6s. 8d. John de Stanford's children, 6s. 8d. William de Cauteley's children, 6s. 8d. The friars minor, Doncaster, 13s. 4d. The Carmelite friars, Doncaster, 13s. 4d. The anchorites of Doncaster, 6s. 8d. John Clerk, 40d. The residue to celebrate for his soul, as his executors dispose; they are empowered to increase or reduce in the foregoing as necessary. Executors: William de Hauley of Doncaster, chaplain, William Wodecok, Thomas Cote and William de Fisshelake. Under his seal and the seal of the deanery of Doncaster.

[Adding] bequest to Sir William de Hauley, chaplain, of 48 marks for celebrations for his soul and the souls of all the faithful departed for eight years, *viz.* 6 marks p.a., if his goods suffice.

Sentence of probate before the commissary-general of the official of the court of York, with grant of administration. Doncaster, 6 Oct. 1360.

APPROBACIO EJUSDEM TESTAMENTI. Sentence of approval by Bishop Gilbert, with grant of administration of the testator's goods in Carlisle diocese to William de Hauley and William de Fisshelak', reserving power to grant the same to the other executors. Rose, 16 Oct. 1360.[234]

337 Note that on 7 May 1360, at Penrith on the bishop's way to London,[235] he granted William de Pulhowe, rector of Melmerby, licence to be absent for two years in a suitable place. Letter sealed with the date 16 Oct. 1360.

338 Note of licence to William del Hall, rector of Bowness, to study in a *studium generale* for one year under the constitution *Cum ex eo*. 8 Oct. 1360.

339 Note of letters dimissory for all orders to Robert de Welton, rector of Ousby. 17 Oct. 1360.

340 Note of licence for one year to Nicholas Walays of Boroughbridge (*Burghbrig'*) and John de Lokton, proctors of the chapter of Ripon, for a collection for its fabric; as for the questors for Durham on the third folio above (**306**). 18 Oct. 1360.

341 Mandate to the dean of Cumberland. Adam Presteman of Blencarn (*Blencarne*) died intestate. His widow Alice is to be called and granted

---

[234] There is no marginal note about the executors' account.
[235] For parliament (**311**, **318**).

administration *in lieu* of executors, taking an oath to make an inventory, administer his goods and pay his debts, as means allow. A report is to be made. Rose, 24 Oct. 1360.

342 Letters patent. The bishop has appointed Emma, widow of Alan Williamson of Ireby (*Irby*) who died intestate, as administrator. She swore to make an inventory, administer his goods for the welfare of his soul and make an account when required. Rose, 24 Oct. 1360.

343 Letters patent.[236] Grant of indulgence of 40 days to all contributing to the repair of Salkeld bridge, which has been destroyed. Rose, 24 Oct. 1360.

344 Note of letters to deans and other clergy to order any persons who have taken goods bequeathed or given to the ruined bridge at Salkeld to deliver them to Roger de Salkeld or Richard Hunter, proctors for its fabric; under pain of excommunication. Same date.

345 [Fo.36ᵛ; p.72] Notice to the prior and chapter of Carlisle that the bishop intends to visit them in their chapter house on 4 November. They are to appear before the bishop or his commissaries [continuing as in **209**]. Rose, 24 Oct. 1360.

346 Mandate to the dean of Carlisle to prepare for visitation by the bishop or his commissaries of the city and deanery by citing all rectors, vicars [etc. as in **212**]. Rose, 24 Oct. 1360.
Note of similar mandate to the dean of Allerdale. Same date.

347 SUPERCESSIO HUJUSMODI VISITATIONIS. Undated memorandum that this visitation was suspended.

348 Note that the dean of Westmorland, rector of Lowther and vicars of Shap, Bampton and Crosby Ravensworth were told in writing to suspend execution of the bishop's mandate against delinquents who attacked the abbot of Shap and his entourage.[237] 5 Nov. 1360.

349 Mandate to the rector of Greystoke. Nicholas Swayn of his parish complained to the bishop that Emma, his lawful wife, has left him for trivial and fabricated reasons (*ex causis frivolis et confictis*). The rector is to order her to return within eight days and hold to Nicholas as her husband with marital affection in bed and board, obeying him in other conjugal duties, under pain of excommunication; reporting by 25 November. Rose, 12 Nov. 1360.

350* Mandate to the dean of Westmorland to receive the purgation of Robert Weror' and Isabel wife of William de Helton, each by the hands of eight good men and women likely to have knowledge of their alleged adultery. If they can be purged, their good name is to be restored. Otherwise, they are to be cited to

[236] Printed in Nicolson & Burn, II.415.
[237] See **332**, where the vicar of Morland, but not of Bampton, was addressed.

appear before the bishop in the chapel at Rose to receive a suitable penance. The dean is to report by 25 November. Rose, 13 Nov. 1360.

351 Licence to William de Loundres, rector of [Long] Marton, to be absent for one year while serving the noble lord, Thomas de Musgrave; excused from synods, etc., and required to have a proctor answerable to the bishop. Rose, 22 Nov. 1360.

352 INHIBICIO FACTA SINGULIS DECANIS. Note of letters to all deans ordering them not to make any payments of money from their perquisites of office before they have rendered accounts, unless they have other orders. Rose, 23 Nov. 1360.

353 [Fo.37; p.73] COMMISSIO ADMINISTRATIONIS BONORUM WALTERI MAUCHELL' AB INTESTATO DEFUNCTI THOME BEAUCHAM. Commission to Thomas Beaucham of administration of the goods of Walter Beaucham[238] who has died intestate; to make an inventory and account when required. Rose, 2 Dec. 1360.

354 Mandate to the dean of Carlisle. William Lenglys, kt., told the bishop that he released a falcon at Brunstock Beck (*Brunscaythbek'*) on Thursday after the feast of St. [omitted] the virgin;[239] it flew out of sight. An order is to be published in all churches as William requires for its return within eight days, or to tell him who has it, under pain of excommunication; saving lawful process. Rose, 2 Dec. 1360.

355 Commission to Martin de Brampton, canon of Lanercost. The bishop has learnt that Richard de Ridale, prior of Lanercost, has gone to distant places for his own reasons. To save the priory from loss in spirituals and temporalities, it is committed to Martin's custody in Richard's absence; he is to give an account to the bishop, or to the prior if he is present. Rose, 30 Nov. 1360.[240]

356 Mandate to the official of Carlisle quoting the king's writ of summons to a parliament at Westminster on 24 Jan. 1361, with *premunientes* clause (dated Westminster, 20 Nov. 1360),[241] for execution [as in **155**], reporting by 13 January. Rose, 22 Dec. 1360.

357* Letters patent. The Austin friars of Penrith have recently begun to kindle a light in honour of the Nativity of our Saviour and the Blessed Mary his mother in their conventual church on the feast of the Nativity at the mass when the office of *Lux fulgebit* is sung. They propose to do this annually, but lack the means without alms. Grant of 40 days indulgence to all going to that church at Christmas for the mass or making contributions for the light. Rose, 16 Dec. 1360.

---

[238] *Sic*, probably in error by repeating the administrator's surname,
[239] Possibly St. Katherine the virgin, the date set for reports in **349** and **350**, and thus 26 Nov. 1360.
[240] Also summarised in *VCH Cumberland*, II.161, note 9.
[241] As in *CCR 1360–4*, 147. The interval between the dates of **360** and **362** shows that the bishop could have attended.

358 [Fo.37ᵛ; p.74] Note of renewal, for one year, of the indulgence on behalf of the fabric of Carlisle cathedral, at the request of the prior and convent, who have appointed John Boon, chaplain, and Thomas Hogge of Carlisle their proctors in this matter. 2 Jan. 1361.

359 Note of letters dimissory for all orders to Robert de Louthre, clerk with first tonsure. Rose, 5 Jan. 1361.

360 Licence to Adam [de Wygton], vicar of Addingham. As his church is so far from his parishioners, they have services in the chapel at [Little] Salkeld, but this is now polluted by bloodshed. Until it is reconciled, he may celebrate in a decent place in his manse; without prejudice to the parish church. Rose, 7 Jan. 1361.

361* Sentence. M. William de Routhbury, archdeacon of Carlisle, has frequently complained that he has been impeded by the bishop and his ministers in the exercise of many parts of his office. In order to do him justice, the bishop made enquiries by sworn witnesses and other sources and found as follows. The archdeacon was entitled to have a clerk attending chapters held by the official and deans, ministers of the bishop, for the whole diocese, to make a counter-roll of all corrections made there. The archdeacon was also allowed to call subjects to his visitations by his letters, and to proceed by censures against absentees, and likewise against those not paying procurations then and their benefices. Having sufficient proof on these points, the bishop pronounces that the archdeacon should be allowed their exercise and not be impeded by him or his ministers.[242] Rose, 4 May 1360.

362 (i) Institution of John de Brounfeld, priest, to Bewcastle church, vacant by the death of Henry de Whytebergh; presented by the prior and chapter of Carlisle. (ii) Archdeacon to induct. Penrith, 4 Mar. 1361.

363 Mandate to the official to enquire by clerks and laymen about defects of the buildings, chancel, books and ornaments of Bewcastle church since Henry de Whytebergh was instituted as rector,[243] calling his executors and others interested; also what he received for defects then apparent from his predecessor's executors and what he spent on repairs, and what more will cost, sequestrating his goods to their estimated cost until ordered by the bishop; reporting when required by John de Brounfeld. Rose, 12 Mar. 1361.

364 Letters patent to make it known to everyone that William Parker attacked Thomas de Castello of East (*Este*) Drayton *alias* de Suthayk', chaplain, without provocation, striking his right hand with a sword and badly wounding him, as has been confirmed by an enquiry following Thomas's complaint. Rose, 12 Mar. 1361.

---

[242] Cf. **316*** of 2 May 1360.
[243] By exchange in 1356 (**133**).

365 Licence (for one year) to Adam Parvynk', kt., to choose a chaplain as his confessor to absolve him and order penance, even in cases reserved to the bishop. Rose, 15 Mar. 1361.

366 [Fo.38; p.75] Commission to Masters William de Routhbury, archdeacon, and John de Welton, clerk skilled in law, to proceed and pronounce in a divorce-cause pending or expected before the bishop, who is otherwise engaged, between William de Cowyk' [of Salkeld][244] and his wife Joan, reporting afterwards. Rose, 6 Apr. 1361.

367 (i) Institution of Thomas Roke, chaplain,[245] to Farlam (*Farlham*) vicarage, vacant by the death of Thomas de Derby;[246] presented by John, subprior, proctor of the prior *in remotis*, and convent of Lanercost. (ii) Archdeacon to induct. Rose, 5 Apr. 1361.

368 Letters patent. An enquiry has found that William de Stapelton is not married and is free to contract marriage.[247] Rose, 10 Apr. 1361.

369 (i) Institution of John de Bempton, priest, to Kirkandrews upon Eden (*Kirkandres*) church, vacant by the resignation of John Palmer;[248] presented by the prioress and convent of Marrick (*Marrig'*), in York diocese. (ii) Archdeacon to induct. Rose, 12 Apr. 1361.

370 Licence to Richard de Askeby, rector of Uldale, to be absent for two years in the service of the noble lord, Thomas de Lucy; excused from synods, etc., with a proctor answerable to the bishop, otherwise the licence will be void. Rose, 16 Apr. 1361.

371 Will[249] of Gilbert de Hothwayt, dated 13 July 1360. Commends soul to God, Blessed Mary and all saints. Burial in church of Blessed Mary the virgin, Cockermouth. Isabel his wife and children to have all goods, live and dead, after payment of debts. Executors: Alan, rector of Plumbland, and Robert de Musgrave.

Probate before the dean of Copeland, commissary of the archdeacon of Richmond, with grant of administration to executors named. Under his seal of office, Cockermouth church, 10 Aug. 1360.[250]

Sentence of approval by the bishop of Carlisle; administration for goods in the diocese granted to Robert, reserved for Alan. Rose, 17 Apr. 1361.[251]

---

[244] Supplied from margin.
[245] Ordained priest 1344 (*Reg. Kirkby*, I.161).
[246] *Alias* Rotheland (**174**)?
[247] See **320**, **328**.
[248] This is the only known institution to Kirkandrews before 1576 (Nicolson & Burn, II.226). One Thomas was rector in 1336. Palmer was ordained deacon on a title from John de Kyrkandres, 1344 (*Reg. Kirkby*, I.57, no.300, and p.160). See also **379**.
[249] Printed in *Test. Karl.*, 31–2.
[250] MS. *die lune in festo sancti Laurencii martiris* (misread in *Test. Karl.*).
[251] With marginal note, *reddider' compotum*, in same hand as main text. See also **327**.

372 Note of licence to M. Henry [de Sandford], rector of Crosby Garrett, to be absent for one year in a suitable place; excused from synods. 23 Apr. 1361.

373 Note of licence to M. Henry de Rosse,[252] rector of Cliburn, to be absent for two years. Same date.

374 Note of letters dimissory for all orders to Thomas de Hayton, clerk with first tonsure. 30 Apr. 1361.

375 COMMENDA VICARIE DE CROSTHWAYT. Commendation to Peter de Morland, vicar of Torpenhow, for six months, of Crosthwaite vicarage, so that it is properly served in its vacancy,[253] [Fo.38ᵛ; p.76] saving the rights etc. of the bishop and his church; provided that during this title the church and its parishioners are suitably served. Rose, 2 May 1361.

376 Commission to M. John de Welton, clerk skilled in law, to proceed and pronounce in the divorce-cause pending or expected before the bishop between Elizabeth, daughter of Richard Bruyn, plaintiff, and John de Lygh, son senior of William de Lygh, kt., deceased;[254] reporting his process. Rose, 4 May 1361.

377 Memorandum of dispensation of Thomas de Slegill, clerk (dioc. Carlisle), son of unmarried parents,[255] by authority of letters of Francis [de Aptis], cardinal-priest of St. Mark, penitentiary of Innocent VI; also requiring Thomas to do penance for being tonsured as a clerk without dispensation. An enquiry by the dean of Westmorland found that Thomas was continent, of good character and literate. He was dispensed to receive orders and a benefice with cure of souls, but the dispensation would be void if he did not reside and be ordained. He has letters sealed by the bishop. Rose (chapel), 5 May 1361.

378* Letters patent. William Whyteheved of Sowerby was sued before the bishop by Godiva, daughter of Nicholas de Motherby of Sowerby, in that he had contracted and consummated marriage with her and, although not divorced, contracted marriage with Alice, widow of John de Stokdale, as his *de facto* wife. William and Godiva appeared before the bishop. He denied her charge and swore to his truth. Godiva brought two witnesses, *viz.* Nicholas de Motherby and Alice, wife of John Yholehorne of Sowerby. They were sworn and examined, their testimony written and published with the parties' consent. Another day was set to challenge the witnesses and their words, when nothing new was said. On a further day for sentence, the bishop pronounced that, after full deliberation and consideration of the evidence, he found that Godiva had not proved her case; William was dismissed from further impeachment. Rose, 10 May 1361.

---

[252] *Alias* Heynes (**254**).
[253] See **318** and note, also **321**.
[254] John is not named in William's will (**91**). See also **317**.
[255] For a similar dispensation to John de Slegill, canon of Carlisle, by 1363, see *CPP*, I.438.

379   Letters patent. John Palmer, late rector of Kirkandrews, resigned the church to the bishop for lawful causes.[256] He has a good character and is not known to be defamed in the diocese. He has licence to depart in grace and return at will. Rose, 12 May 1361.

380   Memorandum that, in the principal chamber at Rose, Peter de Morland, vicar of Torpenhow, renounced the commendation of Crosthwaite vicarage [quoting his statement to this effect]. Present: M. John de Welton, John de Bylton *alias* Barker and Robert Trayll. Rose, 14 May 1361.

381   Note of licence to John de Bempton, rector of Kirkandrews, to be absent in a place of his choice for one year from Whitsun (16 May); excused from synods. 12 May 1361.

382   Note of grant to John Boon, priest, of commendation of Crosthwaite vicarage for six months; with a letter as in the last folio (i.e. **375**). Rose, 19 May 1361.

383   Note of licence to John de Brounfeld to be absent from Bewcastle church for one year from 20 May 1361; given the usual letter [date omitted].

384   Note of similar licence from 20 May to Robert de Bolton, rector of Stapleton.

385   [Fo.39; p.77] Note of renewal for one year of licence to Hugh de Jarum, nuncio of the hospital of Saint-Antoine-de-Viennois. Rose, 8 June 1361.

386   (i) Collation to Peter de Morland, chaplain, of [Great] Musgrave church, vacant by the death of John de Soulby. (ii) Archdeacon to induct. Rose, 18 July 1361.

387   (i) Institution of Robert de Wytton, chaplain, to a mediety of Kirkbampton church, vacant by the resignation of John de Thornton;[257] presented by Brian de Stapilton, kt. (ii) Archdeacon to induct. Rose, 8 Aug. 1361.

388   Will[258] (in French) of William, Lord Dacre. Memorandum of his debts when he went abroad on 29 Sept. 1359:[259] to Lord [Ralph] de Neville, 40 marks by a bond; to Hugh de Redehou, 80 marks by bond; to the king for a fine at the Exchequer (*Lescheqer*), £32 for himself and his mother; for queen's gold,

---

[256] Cf. **369**.

[257] *Alias* John atte Hurne of Thornton (**3**).

[258] According to the margin, where there is no note of executors accounting. Printed in *Test. Karl.*, 32–33. See also Introduction, xxi.

[259] He had letters of protection dated 1 Sept. 1359 and April 1360 while serving under the Black Prince in Edward III's last French campaign (*Foedera*, III(1).443, 482). Dacre died 18 July 1361, his wife Katherine (Neville) by 1 Sept. 1361, and his mother Margaret (Multon) 10 Dec. 1361 (*Complete Peerage*, IV.3–4).

10 marks; to the archdeacon of Durham,[260] £10 by a bond; to John de Hiltoft', £10 8s. by a sealed bond; to Sir Walter de Loughteburgh, £23 15s. 7d. by a bond;[261] to the bishop of Carlisle, 20 marks by a bond; to the abbot of Holm [Cultram], 20 marks by a bond; to Sir William de Salkeld, rector of Aikton, 20 marks by a bond; to the executors of John de Salkeld,[262]10 marks by a bond; to Roger de Mirescho, £10 by a bond; to William Suetmuth, £25 by a bond; to Adam de Blencou, 4 marks; to Thomas his son, 100s.; to Robert Haulay, 100s.; to Evirwyk'[263] in various amounts, £14 7s.; to Sir Henry de Craystok',[264] 10 marks; to Robert Bouchard of London, 47s. by a sealed bill; to John de Oxinford of London, 111s.; to the bakers of London, 11s.; to Simond de Worsted, mercer, 36s.; to Henry de Cove, 27s. 9d. Total: £289 16s. 8d. William has appointed his mother, Clement de Skelton, William de Salkeld, rector of Aikton, Robert de Kilhom and Sir Walter de Loughteburgh his executors, to dispose of his goods, pay his debts and keep the residue for his mother.

Sentence of probate, with grant of administration to Clement de Skelton and Walter de Loughtburgh, rector of Dacre; reserved for Margaret, Lady Dacre, M. William de Salkeld, rector of a mediety of Aikton, and Sir Robert de Kilhom. Rose (chapel), 16 Aug. 1361.

389 Probate of nuncupative will of John Pulter of Hawksdale,[265] commending soul to God, Blessed Mary and all saints; burial in the churchyard of St. Michael's, Dalston; his goods, after payment of debts, be given to his wife Agnes and children; appointing Richard de Botery as executor. Rose (chapel), 16 Aug. 1361.[266]

390 [Fo.39ᵛ; p.78] ORDINACIO CANTARIE IN ECCLESIA DE HOTON. Sentence.[267] Thomas de Hoton has told the bishop that a chantry was founded at Bramery (*Bramwra*) by episcopal authority to celebrate for the souls of Thomas de Capella and his parents and its chaplain endowed with the king's consent.[268] Because of the pestilence which lately afflicted all England, scarcity of tenants and other mischances and destruction, its lands became so sterile that they were unable to yield half a chaplain's needs and still do not suffice, so that no chaplain wishes to be instituted. The chantry has therefore been vacant for a long time, to the prejudice of the above souls. The right of founder of the chantry lately

[260] Thomas de Neville (*Fasti*, VI.112).

[261] Rector of Dacre, in his service (see **302**).

[262] See **231**.

[263] 'At York'(?), but preceded by *A*, as for all other creditors: possibly refers to William de Ebor', rector of Bolton, in Ralph Neville's service (see **330**).

[264] Master of hospital of St. Nicholas, Carlisle, 1349–68; baron of the Exchequer, 1356–62, after a career in the king's chamber (W.G. Wiseman, 'The hospital of St. Nicholas, Carlisle, and its masters; Part 2', *CWAAS*, 2nd ser. 96 (1996), 55–8).

[265] Printed in *Test. Karl.*, 33–4.

[266] The rest of this page (5 cm plus lower margin) was left blank blank and (later?) crossed with cancellations.

[267] Its initial *I* is decorated and 17 cm long, extending half-way down the margin to a second, large-written HOTON.

[268] For this chantry and the new one at Hutton in the Forest, see *VCH Cumberland*, II.35–6; Storey, 'Chantries' (as for **135**), 81–4.

descended to Thomas de Hoton. Some of these lands, rents and tenements in Hutton parish have been assigned as follows:

Charter of Thomas de Hoton in Foresta. With the king's consent, for the safety of the souls of himself, his wife Isabel, their parents and ancestors, and all the faithful departed, he has by this indented charter granted to Richard de Brampton, chaplain celebrating at the altar of the Blessed Mary in the church of St. James, Hutton in the Forest, 6 messuages and 44 acres of land and meadow in Hutton which Thomas acquired from John de Raghton, Hugh Page and Alan de Neuton, with their appurtenances and rights of common pasture; these are granted to Richard and succeeding chaplains celebrating for ever, by services to the chief lords of the fee, and which they are to preserve without waste. If any of the buildings are destroyed in war by enemies of the king and realm, Richard and his successors are to rebuild them as their means allow. In vacancies of the chantry, Thomas and his heirs will present chaplains to the diocesan. Thomas and his heirs will guarantee this grant. The tenements granted by his ancestor Thomas de Capella are no longer sufficient for the chantry in the chapel of the Blessed Mary, Bramery, of which he is now patron. He has therefore given them to Richard and his successors so they might be more fully supported in the chantry at Hutton where they will celebrate for the founders of both chantries according to an ordinance to be made by the bishop of Carlisle. Thomas has sealed the part of the indenture to be kept by Richard [etc.], and Richard the part for Thomas and his heirs. Witnesses: Christopher de Morysby, the present sheriff of Cumberland, Hugh de Louthre, kt., junior, William de Hoton Jon, Adam de Blencowe, John and William de Laton, William Vaux of Catterlen (*Caterlen*) Dated at Carlisle, Whitsun (16 May), 1361.

The bishop, being informed by Thomas, founder of both chantries, that neither can support a chaplain and that both are now vacant, has agreed to his request that they be united by his ordinance. After deliberation, he approves of this revival of services, making this decree for union with the consent of the chapter of Carlisle.[269] Hutton church will be a more honourable place for a chantry than the manifestly inadequate chapel at Bramery. There will now be a single chantry at the altar of Blessed Mary in Hutton church. Thomas is to present a chaplain now, and in future he and his heirs within a month of vacancies, to the bishop, his vicar-general or the keepers of the spiritualities, *sede vacante*, [Fo.40; p.79] to whom the presentation will otherwise devolve. Every chaplain is to say or sing canonical hours daily with the rector or parish chaplain and celebrate masses at the above altar (unless lawfully prevented), *viz.* of the day on Sundays, of the Blessed Virgin Mary with commemoration of the above named on Saturdays, and of the office of the dead and souls of founders, all the above and faithful departed on weekdays; except on double feasts, they shall also say the office of the dead, *Placebo* and *Dirige* with commendation for the above at suitable hours. The chaplain is to obey the rector of Hutton's lawful commands. He is also to keep the messuages, lands [etc.] of the chantry in good condition, and from time to time improve them as he is able, so that they remain after his death, resignation or removal. To ensure faithful compliance, every chaplain shall take an oath at his institution that he will leave the chantry in as good condition as he found it. Faculty to amend this ordinance is reserved to the

---

[269] Patrons of Hutton rectory.

bishop and his successors. Dated under the seals of the bishop and Thomas de Hoton, Rose, 10 July 1361.

391 (i) Institution of Richard de Brampton, chaplain, to the newly ordained chantry at the altar of the Blessed Mary in Hutton church, having taken the oath as required in its ordination; presented by Thomas de Hoton. (ii) Note of mandate for induction to the rector of Hutton. (iii) Note that the bishop released Richard from this oath until 11 November next, for reasons he alleged. Rose, 11 July 1361.

392 Note that Thomas [son] of John de Derwentwater, clerk, son of unmarried parents, was dispensed by authority of letters of Francis, cardinal-priest of St. Mark, penitentiary of the pope. Rose (chapel), 15 July 1361.

393 Commission to the official and M. John de Welton, clerk skilled in law, to be in Carlisle cathedral representing the bishop on 2 September and publish to abbots, priors, rectors, vicars and other ecclesiastics holding benefices in the diocese cited to appear there, letters of John [Thoresby], archbishop of York, containing papal mandates.[270] Both or either [commissary], acting as the bishop's deputy, is to bring their censures and orders to the notice of all present; certifying afterwards. Rose, 28 Aug. 1361.

394* Memorandum that the commissaries had the archbishop's letters read in the chapter house of Carlisle cathedral on 2 September before the prelates, rectors and vicars of Carlisle diocese cited there; the censures ordered in the papal letters were promulgated. They arranged that the expenses mentioned should be paid within 30 days at the rate of $\frac{3}{4}$d. in the mark from all benefices in the diocese, at the old rate of taxation, under the prescribed pains. The prior of Carlisle was appointed to collect, as follows:

395 Commission to the prior of Carlisle, referring to the archbishop's and papal letters, to collect the expenses [as above] of Androin [de la Roche], abbot of Cluny, and Hugh de Geneva (*Thebennis*), lord of Anton (*Anorn'*), papal envoys to the kings of England and France to treat between Charles [de Blois], duke of Brittany, and John, count of Montfort. [Fo.39ᵛ; p.80] Names of payers and non-payers are to be certified by 12 October. Rose, 3 Sept. 1361.

396 Certificate to the archbishop that his letters [said to be quoted] were received on 21 August. The bishop had accordingly called all the ecclesiastics of his diocese and had the letters read. Names of payers and non-payers are in an attached roN. Rose, [day omitted] Oct. 1361.

397 TRANSMISSIO VERE COPIE TAXE ANTIQUE BENEFICIORUM PRIORI KARL'. Letters patent. The bishop has inspected his and his predecessors' registers for the assessment of benefices, as are in the attached [list] which matches the assessment given to the bishop by the last cardinals in England, *viz.* [the cardinals] of Périgord and Urgel.[271] Rose, 3 Sept. 1361.

[270] For this papal mission, see Lunt, *Financial Relations*, 657–60, and see **412**.

Memorandum that this assessment, pensions and portions excepted, was sent to the prior of Carlisle under the bishop's seal, for collecting the expenses of the abbot of Cluny and Hugh de Geneva.

398 Signification to the king that John de Tuxford,[272] vicar of St. Michael's, Appleby, John Ricardson of Brougham, Thomas Cokeson of Aikton, Maud de Rokeby of Carlisle, Emma de Goldyngton, Agnes de Hothwayt' and Maud wife of Adam Taillour of Ivegill (*Yvegill*) have been excommunicate for 40 days at the instance of the bishop's office. Rose, 3 Oct. 1361.

399 Will[273] of William de Brigholm of Crosthwaite, dated 5 Aug. 1361. Commends soul to God, Blessed Mary and all saints. Burial where God shall provide, with his horse as mortuary to Crosthwaite church. John son of Geoffrey the cobbler, a bullock. Agnes de Lonnesdale, a heifer. His godson John, son of John de Derwentwater, kt., 6s. 8d., his sword, bow and arrow[s?]. The light of Blessed Mary, Crosthwaite, his best copper pot. Half the residue to his three children, the other half to John de Derwentwater and William Engayn of Clifton, who are appointed executors.
Memorandum of probate and grant of administration to William; reserved for Sir John. Rose (chapel), 20 Oct. 1361.

400 (i) Institution of John de Bouland, clerk, to Arthuret church, vacant by the resignation of Richard de Tissyngton;[274] presented by the king.[275] (ii) Archdeacon to induct. Rose, 29 Oct. 1361.

401 Probate[276] of nuncupative will of John de Hoghton, dated 8 Aug. 1361, commending soul to God, Blessed Mary and all saints; burial in the churchyard of St. Michael's, Arthuret, with best beast for mortuary and 16d. for lights and oblations; and residue to his wife and Robert de Riley, who were appointed executors. Rose (chapel), 5 Nov. 1361.

402 Note of licence for one year to Robert Jardyn, senior, and Robert Jardyn, junior, for the quest for the fabric of Durham cathedral. Rose, 8 Nov. 1361.

403 [Fo.41; p.81] Probate[277] of nuncupative will of John del Blamyre of Hawksdale,[278] as follows:
Dated 30 Oct. 1361. Commended soul to God, Blessed Mary and all saints.

[271] See **184–94**.
[272] *Alias* Toke (**268**). See *Reg. Kirkby*, I.131, no.645.
[273] Printed in *Test. Karl.*, 34.
[274] Presented by the king, 1351 (*CPR 1350–4*, 46). The previous known rector was Ralph de Lepyngton in 1348; he was instituted 1337 (*CPR 1348–50*, 176; *Reg. Kirkby*, I.69).
[275] By letters dated 22 Oct. 1361 (*CPR 1361–4*, 76).
[276] Printed (without the will's date) in *Test. Karl.*, 35.
[277] Printed *Test. Karl.*, 35–6.
[278] Possibly either the John son of Ralph del Blamire or the John son of Robert, tenants of Hawksdale in 1329: the oldest John then had sons Robert and Roger (*Reg. Kirkby*, II.10–11).

Burial in churchyard of St. Michael's, Dalston, with best beast for mortuary, 18d. for lights, an ox and a pig as a dole for the poor, and 24s. for a wake. The two children of his son William, two cows and a skep of oats each. The daughter of his son Thomas del Blamyre, a cow and a quarter of oats. John son of Thomas Hirde, a heifer. William son of John son of Simon de Gaytscales, a beast. The daughter of William son of Margaret, 18d. From the residue after payment of debts, enough should be paid to his sons Thomas and William for a pilgrim to St. James in the next seven years, or for one of them to go on his behalf, because he had vowed to visit that place or to pay another to go. Residue to Thomas son of Thomas Hirde,[279] Robert Stuble and his son William del Blamyre, appointed executors.

Administration to named executors. Rose (chapel), 7 Nov. 1361.

404 Note of licence with indulgence, for one year, for quest for the fabric of Calder (*Caldre*) [abbey] in York diocese. 15 Nov. 1361.

405 (i) Institution of John de Hayton, priest, to Brampton vicarage, vacant by the death of John Cugge;[280] presented by John de Nonyngton,[281] subprior of Lanercost, proctor of the prior *in remotis*, and its chapter. (ii) Archdeacon to induct. Rose, 18 Nov. 1361.

406 Probate[282] of nuncupative will of Isabel, wife of Richard de Thornethwayt' of Crosthwaite, as follows:

Dated 27 Oct. 1361. Commended soul to God and Blessed Mary. Burial in churchyard of St. Kentigern's, Crosthwaite, with best beast and cloth for mortuary, 2s. for oblations, a pound of wax and 4d. for lights, 6s. 8d., a cow and 2 sheep for a dole for the poor, and 15s. for a wake. Residue to her husband Richard de Thornethwayte and their children. Executors; her husband and John de Thornewayte

Administration to executors named. Rose (chapel), 22 Nov. 1361.

407* Letters patent licensing Robert de Burgham, chaplain, to keep schools in Penrith, teaching children and youngsters about the psalters, primer and song, during pleasure; forbidding anyone else from keeping schools in Penrith church or elsewhere in the parish without the bishop's licence. Rose, 29 Oct. 1361.

408 Memorandum that Robert de Welton, rector of Ousby, personally resigned the church to the bishop [quoting his statement]. Present: M. John de Welton, clerk, notary, Richard de Aslacby, rector of Levisham (*Levesham*),[283] and John de Grandon, vicar of Crosby on Eden, of the dioceses of Lincoln, York and Carlisle. Rose (chapel), 30 Nov. 1361.

---

[279] Thomas Hird and his sons John and Thomas appear in this rental (*ibid.*, 10, 12).
[280] Instituted as John Engge, 1346 (*Reg. Kirkby*, I.174, no.836).
[281] See **101**.
[282] Printed *Test. Karl.*, 36–7.
[283] He last occurs as vicar of Wigton (**331**); for his successor there, see **509**.

409 (i) Collation to Richard de Ulnesby, priest,[284] of Ousby church, vacant by the resignation of Robert de Welton. (ii) Archdeacon to induct. Rose, 2 Dec. 1361.

410 [Fo.41ᵛ; p.82] Probate[285] of nuncupative will of John de Lynton, vicar of Crosby Ravensworth,[286] as follows:
Dated 24 Nov. 1361. Commended soul to God, Blessed Mary and all saints. Burial in Crosby church, with 4 pounds of wax for lights. To the abbot and convent of Whitby, 3s. 4d. To repair the choir of Crosby church, 6s. 8d. For a dole to the poor, a skep of flour, 4 measures(?)[287]of salt and an ox. The children of his brother Thomas de Lynton, 11 sheep. His brother Thomas, all his household vessels save those he is bound to leave for his successor. Residue to Thomas de Lynton, son of William de Lynton. Executor: Adam Harpour of Crosby.
Administration granted to this executor. Rose (chapel), 9 Dec. 1361.

411 (i) Institution of Robert de Threlkeld, priest, to Crosby Ravensworth vicarage, vacant by the death of John de Lynton; presented by the abbot and convent of Whitby.[288] (ii) Archdeacon to induct. Rose, 15 Dec. 1361.

412* Letter missive to Archbishop [Thoresby]. Before Christmas, M. [Robert] de Hakthorpp[289] brought the bishop letters close and missive, and his credence, from the archbishop. The clergy of Carlisle diocese were unlikely to obey without seeing the archbishop's commission. They were called to a convocation in Carlisle on 20 December, trusting by then to have received it and news of the convocation at York.[290] None came, but the bishop overcame his clergy's reluctance and persuaded them to agree that they would pay [a papal subsidy[291]] at the same rates and terms as in the dioceses of York and Durham. Rose, 4 Jan. [1362].

413 Note of renewal for one year of letters to John Boon, chaplain, and Thomas Hogg', licensing the quest for the fabric of Carlisle cathedral, with indulgence. 5 Jan. 1362.

---

[284] He died soon after 25 Feb. 1362 (**434**). While rector, he witnessed the bishop's undated quitclaim to Lanercost priory of a pension from Carlatton church. The other named witnesses were M. William de Routhbery, the archdeacon, M. Nicholas de Qwitryg, rector of Caldbeck, and Adam de Byrkensyde (*Lanercost Cartulary* (cited in Introduction, xxii, *n*.71), 382–3).
[285] Printed (without the will's date) *Test. Karl.*, 37–8.
[286] Possibly the John de Lynton of Brampton, Westmorland, ordained subdeacon 1333 (*Reg. Kirkby*, I.17).
[287] MS. *ostr'*, perhaps for '[h]ostoria' (classical Latin), meaning 'strickle' – a stick for levelling corn etc. in measures.
[288] This and **499** are the only registered institutions to the vicarage before 1572 (Nicolson & Burn, I.496). Only John de Insula appears as an earlier vicar, 1300–4 (*Reg. Halton*, I.134, 190).
[289] Of Carlisle dioc., created notary 1344 (*CPL*, III.163).
[290] For an assembly at York on 15 Dec. 1361, see *HBC*, 596.
[291] See Lunt, *Financial Relations*, 95–103; also **461** below.

414 Will[292] of John de Soulby, clerk,[293] dated 5 June 1361. Commends soul to God, Blessed Mary and all saints. Burial in churchyard of St. Andrew's, Holborn. First, payment of debts which can be proved. Edmund de Sandford, his best green bed. William de Sandford, chaplain, a breviary. [John's] sister Joan, 10 marks towards her marriage. Residue for disposal by his executors, *viz.* Hugh Fissh and John Glasier of London, his father Robert and Thomas Dounay.

Note of probate by the archdeacon of London's official, with administration reserved for John's father; the other executors had refused to act. London, 26 Nov. 1361.

Sentence of approval by Bishop Gilbert in respect of goods in his jurisdiction, with administration granted to Robert Donkyn, John's father. Rose (chapel), 10 Jan. 1362.

415 Note of renewal for one year of letters to Thomas de Cokirton to make a quest for the fabric of the collegiate church of St. John, Beverley. 11 Jan. 1362.

416 [Fo.42; p.83][294] Letters patent of Edward III to Bishop Gilbert and Thomas de Luci.[295] As the king is about to go abroad to prosecute his war in France, he appoints them jointly and singly wardens of the west marches of England towards Scotland in the counties of Cumberland and Westmorland, both inside and outside liberties; and also conservators of truces made with Scottish enemies. They are to punish breaches of the truces by the king's subjects, arresting and imprisoning them until the king shall order. They are to seek reforms of the truces, and punish their breaches by Scots and their adherents. They are to enquire whether castles, fortalices and other places harbour breakers of truces and the law of the march, seizing castles etc. whose constables and keepers refuse to allow such scrutiny, arranging for their safe custody and arresting etc. opponents in them until the king and council order. When dangers threaten, [the wardens] are to choose and array all men-at-arms, hobelars, archers and other fencible men, knights, squires and others, in Cumberland and Westmorland, and the counties of Nottingham, Derby and Lancaster; organising them in companies and leading them against the Scots if truces are broken and England invaded. They are authorised to enforce military service by imprisonment, seizure of lands and goods, amercements and distraint; rebels are to be imprisoned until otherwise ordered. Sheriffs of the said counties, constables of castles etc., mayors of towns, bailiffs and other subjects in England and Scotland are commanded to obey and assist [the wardens], under pain of arrest for disobedience. Westminster, 8 July 1359.

---

[292] Printed *Test. Karl.*, 38–9; it omits *que rite probari poterunt* after *debita mea.*
[293] Described in margin as late rector of [Great] Musgrave; and see **290, 307–8, 386.** He was apparently employed, as a king's clerk, at Westminster.
[294] This folio, despite being out of date-sequence, is the second part of the first opening of the quire from Fo.31; p.61 (from **283**); and see second note under **422.**
[295] Printed in *Rot. Scot.*, I.841.

41   Commission (in French)[296] of Bishop Gilbert and Thomas de Lucy, lord of Cockermouth, wardens of the west march, to Roland de Vaux, senior, and Andrew de Laton to array fencible men of Gilsland to keep watch and arrest robbers entering England; under the pains ordered by common consent of all Cumberland.; during pleasure. Carlisle, 27 Oct. 1359.

Note of similar commissions to Robert Bruyn, Roland de Vaux, junior, Adam de Berwys, John de Dalston, John Grymbald, William de Arthureth, Roger Botycombe, John de Mulcastre, Walter de Ormesby, Thomas son of Stephen de Whelpdale and John Baron.

418   Letters patent (in French)[297] of Bishop Gilbert, warden of the march of Carlisle. Safe conduct until Easter for Stephen de Dounfrys and William Boyvill, two boys, their horses and harness, to pass through English marches into Scotland and return to wherever they wish with their merchandise without harm by the king's subjects, provided they do nothing against *la defense*. Rose, 29 Dec. 1359.

419   Note that this safe conduct for Stephen and William was renewed from 6 April 1360 until Christmas following. A letter was sent for them under the bishop's seal to Sir Thomas de Ros, keeper of Lochmaben, as follows:

Letter missive to *Treschier amy* [Thomas de Ros]. The bishop has appointed Stephen and William to purvey cattle, horses and other things, and asks that they be shown favour while passing through Annandale (*la vale Danand, in voz boundes*) and not molested when doing the bishop's business. Rose, 12 Apr. [1360].

420   [Fo.42ᵛ; p.84] Order[298] of Bishop Gilbert, as warden of the marches of Carlisle with Thomas de Lucy, to the sheriff of Cumberland. They have ordered a council (*colloquium*) about the state and defence of the marches at Carlisle on 4 Jan. 1361. The sheriff is to summon all knights and other trusty men of the county to make plans for the marches and consent to decisions. Rose, 11 Dec. 1360.

421   Commission[299] of Edward III to the bishop of Carlisle, Roger de Clifford and Thomas de Lucy, to survey all castles and fortalices in Cumberland and Westmorland, including liberties, to ensure that they are strongly manned and well victualled for the defence of the realm, as the king has ordered their lords by letters of privy seal; with authority to enforce their orders by forfeiture and imprisonment, and to command assistance from all prelates, lords, knights, other freemen and officials. Westminster, 5 May 1361.

422   Letters patent (in French)[300] of Bishop Gilbert, warden of the march of Carlisle. Safe conduct until 29 September to Gynot' de la Roche, canon of

---

[296] Printed in *Letters from Northern Registers*, ed. J. Raine, Rolls Series (1873), 406–7.
[297] Printed, with **419**, in *Letters . . .*, 407–8.
[298] Printed ibid., 408.
[299] Printed in *Rot. Scot.*, I.856.
[300] Printed in *Letters . . . .*, 409–10.

Glasgow, familiar of Cardinal Périgord, six men and their horses, to enter and pass the English marches and stay where they wish, without harm by the king's subjects, provided they do nothing against *la defense*. Rose, 16 July 1361.[301]

423 [Fo.43; p.85] Sentence. Some time before her death, Margaret, lady of Dacre and Gilsland, gave all her goods to M. William de Salkeld, Robert [de Kirkeby[302]], rector of a mediety of Aikton, and Andrew de Laton. They came to the bishop seeking to be exonerated from the administration of these goods: they had transferred their gift of them to Sir Ranulph de Dacre, son and heir of Lady Margaret.[303] The bishop confirmed this transfer and charged Ranulph, on peril of his soul, to dispose of the goods for Margaret's spiritual welfare. Rose, 11 Jan. 1362.

424 Note of signification to the king against John Armestrang', John Douson of Walton, William Champeney of Castle Carrock, Robert son of Alan de Bothecastre, Gilbert Gilyspynstepson of Lanercost and Christine Mauclerk' of Wetheral, excommunicates. 16 Jan. 1362.

425 Note of licence to Robert de Kirkeby, rector of a mediety of Aikton, to be absent for three years; excused from synods and chapters. 4 Feb. 1362.

426 (i) Institution of Adam Armestrang', priest, to Bewcastle church, vacant by the resignation of John de Brounfeld; presented by the prior and chapter of Carlisle. (ii) Archdeacon to induct. Rose, 16 Feb. 1362.

427 (i) Institution of William de Neuton, chaplain, to Barton vicarage, vacant by the resignation of John de Shirborne;[304] presented by the prior and convent of Warter. (ii) Archdeacon to induct. Rose, 18 Feb. 1362.

428 Mandate to [the dean of] Allerdale and vicar of Bridekirk to denounce as excommunicate, in all churches of the deanery, the unknown malefactors who polluted Bridekirk church and churchyard with bloodshed, enquiring for their names and reporting to the bishop by letters under the dean's seal by 6 March; their denunciations are to continue until further orders. Rose, 16 Feb. 1362.

429* Certificate to the official of the court of York. The bishop received his mandate on 10 February, as follows:
The official was told on behalf of Thomas Olifant of Hilton[305] and his wife Alice, John Olifant and his wife Emma, and William Olifant, that the bishop

---

[301] The remainder of the folio (nearly half) is blank, with crossings. The bishop was not reappointed warden in a new commission dated 21 Oct. 1361 (*Rot. Scot.*, I.857).
[302] See **425**. M. William was rector of the other mediety (**388**).
[303] He was rector of Prescot, Lancs., called to parliaments as Lord Dacre from 1362 (*Complete Peerage*, IV.4).
[304] Possibly in error for John de Wystowe (cf. **58**); but Sherborne could have been *alias* for Wystowe: Wistow, YNR, is 5 miles from Sherburn in Elmet.
[305] In the parish of Appleby St. Michael.

excommunicated them without legal process under the constitution *Siquis suadente diabolo* for violence to Robert de Appilby, brother of M. John de Appilby, doctor of laws; they were denounced in all churches of Westmorland deanery, by a pretended process before the bishop at M. John's instigation, without being lawfully cited and warned, in their absence and not for contumacy. They therefore appealed to the court of York. Order to the bishop to do nothing to their prejudice pending the appeal, and to cite M. John to appear before the official or his commissary in York minster on 26 February [Fo.43ᵛ; p.86] for proceeding in the appeal. The bishop may attend and should certify by that day. York, 5 Feb. 1362.

The bishop's enquiries have failed to find M. John so that he could not be cited;[306] he will otherwise obey the mandate. Rose, 19 Feb. 1362.

430 Mandate to the dean of Cumberland. Fr. James de Lancastre, monk of Dundrennan (*Dumdranyn*) in Whithorn (*Candida Casa*) diocese, has left his cloister and lives wantonly, wandering through Carlisle diocese, incurring excommunication and the penalties for apostasy yet still celebrating divine offices. He is to be ordered not to celebrate. This inhibition is to be published in the diocese, particularly in Renwick church, where he is said to stay; certifying by 12 March. Rose, 22 Feb. 1362.

431 Mandate to the dean of Cumberland. Richard [de Monte[307]], rector of Kirkoswald, is reported to be broken with age and infirmity, unable to attend to his cure or himself. He is to be cited before the bishop in Rose chapel on 3 March to show cause why the bishop should not appoint a coadjutor. Rose, 23 Feb. 1362.

432 Will[308] of William de Lancastre, dated Rydal, 10 Sept. 1361. Commends soul to God, Blessed Mary and all saints. Burial wherever God disposes. All the fittings of his chapel,[309] *viz.* books, vestments, chalices and other ornaments to his wife Alina, for her use and afterwards to his heirs. Residue of goods and household utensils, after payment of debts and funeral expenses, to Alina and his children. Executors, for the welfare of his soul: Alina, John Swaynson and Nicholas de Plesyngton.

Probate by the dean of Kendal and Lonsdale (*Kend' et Lon'*). As Nicholas had died and Alina refused to act, administration granted to John Swaynson. Under his seal of office, Kirkby Lonsdale (*Kirkeby in Lonesd'*) church, 8 Nov. 1361.

Approval by Bishop Gilbert, with administration in his jurisdiction granted to Alina and John Swaynson. Rose (chapel), 21 Feb. 1362.

433 Note of letters dimissory for all orders to John de Bouland, rector of Arthuret. Rose, 22 Feb. 1362.

---

[306] He was probably on his way to the Curia at Avignon (*BRUO*, I.40). See also **436**.
[307] Instituted 1323; certified an alien, from Normandy, 1346 (*Reg. Kirkby*, I.173, no.826). See also **441**.
[308] Printed *Test. Karl.*, 39. William died 7 Oct. 1361 (*CIPM*, XI.87–8).
[309] See **293**.

434 Will[310] of Richard de Ulnesby, rector of Ousby, dated 25 Feb. 1362. Commends soul to God, Blessed Mary and all saints. Burial in churchyard of friars preachers, Carlisle, with 5 pounds of wax for lights and 20s. for the poor. Bishop Gilbert, if he pleases, 2 oxen. His sister Cecily, 13s. 4d. Her daughter Margaret, 20s. Her daughter Joan, 20s. Her daughter Mariota, 20s. His sister Enota, 13s. 4d. Her son John, 20s. Her younger son John, 20s. Her son William, 20s. Richard son of Enota, 20s. Clement de Crofton, a cow and 40s. from his debt. John de Mydelton, chaplain, his murrey robe with his purse and little psalter. Sir Richard de Aslacby, his robe of the livery of his lord the bishop. Sir John de Crosseby, his cloak. Sir Robert de Bolton, his saddle with bridle. Sir Richard de Denton, [Fo.44; p.87] a small silver cross. Joan de Layborne, a gold ring with 40s. from his debt. John Vaux, a gold ring with a red stone. A chaplain celebrating for one year, £4 in silver. The friars preachers, Carlisle, 13s. 4d. Fr. John de Ermithwayt, OP, 4s.[311] Fr. Richard de Barton, 40d. The friars minor, Carlisle, 6s. 8d. His servant Robert, 2 heifers at *Les Lathes*. Adam Hunter, a cow there. To repair buildings of Ousby rectory, 18 oaks. The nuns of Armathwaite, a cow at Ousby. The nuns of Lambley, a heifer at Denton. The prioress of Lambley, 6s. 8d. Robert Dyvok', all the wood for a wagon which he has in hand. The friars of Appleby and Penrith, 6s. 8d. equally divided. Ousby church, a new chalice in place of a fourth portion claimed by the friars among whom he is to be buried. Farlam church, his new vestment. John son of Reginald Meke, his breviary and other books. Every priest at his exequies, 6d. John de Dolfanby, 40d. of 6s. 8d. which he owes. John de Alaynby, chaplain, a furred tunic of blue cloth with a hood. The above Fr. John de Ermythwayt, a ram at *Les Lathes* The children of his sister Cecily, 4 marks owed by John del Mosse. Legitimate children of his sister Enota, 2 marks owed by Reginald Meke. His sister Cecily, a new hood in John de Dolfanby's custody. Enota, another cow in Clement de Crofton's custody. Money remaining with the executors is to be given to a priest to celebrate for his soul for as long as it lasts. For a wake, 10s. Residue to his sisters Cecily and Enota and their children; if any of the children should die, his portion is to be divided among all the children of both sisters. Executors: John de Midelton, chaplain, Reginald Meke and John del Mosse. Witnesses: Thomas del Bek', Robert Wakeman and many others.

Probate, with administration to the named executors. Rose (chapel), 3 Mar. 1362.

435 Note of letters dimissory for sacred orders to John de Arthureth, acolyte. 8 Mar. 1362.

436 Certificate to the official of the court of York. The bishop received his mandate (dated York, 26 Feb. 1362) on 5 March, quoting it [a repetition of **429** until:] Order to cite M. John de Appilby if he is found in the diocese, his proctor if he left one, or by public edict in Carlisle cathedral, Appleby parish church and other public places, so that it reaches the notice of his friends and acquaintance, for him to appear in York minster on 19 March. The bishop has not found M.

---

[310] Printed *Test. Karl.*, 40–2.
[311] Ordained subdeacon and deacon in Carlisle, 1345 (*Reg. Kirkby*, I.163–4).

John or a proctor, but he had the citation made so that his friends could learn. Rose, 12 Mar. 1362.

437 Note of letters dimissory for all orders to John de Cokden of Carlisle, clerk with first tonsure. 18 Mar. 1362.

438 [Fo.44ᵛ; p.88] (i) Institution of Adam de Crosseby, priest, to Bolton church, vacant by the resignation of William de Ebor'; presented by Alexander de Moubray, kt., lord of Bolton in Allerdale. (ii) Archdeacon to induct. Rose, 17 Mar. 1362.

439* Mandate to the dean of Westmorland. Ellen daughter of Richard, son of Robert del Hall of Maulds Meaburn, has petitioned the bishop. She claims to be the legitimate daughter and heir of Richard, who was brother and heir of Stephen de Meborne, a former clerk of King's Bench, and she should therefore inherit the lands and tenements of which Stephen died seised. Some envious people, however, have alleged publicly that she was not Richard's legitimate daughter and heir, and thus not Stephen's heir. She has therefore asked the bishop to enquire into the truth of these allegations and he favours her request. Six or four trustworthey men of the deanery, not related to Ellen, are to be cited before the bishop in Rose chapel on 4 April to give evidence; their names and surnames are to be certified.[312] Rose, 18 Mar. 1362.

440 Note of letters dimissory for all orders to Thomas Stedeman of Colby, clerk with first tonsure. 21 Mar. 1362.

441 Probate[313] of nuncupative will of Richard de Monte, rector of Kirkoswald,[314] commending soul to God, Blessed Mary and all saints; burial in Kirkoswald church, with residue (after paying funeral expenses and debts) to John de Laysyngby; appointing Adam de Alaynby executor. Administration granted to Adam. Rose (chapel), 24 Mar. 1362.

442 Note of licence to Robert Boyvill, rector of Thursby, to farm the revenues of the church for two years. 8 Mar. 1362.

443 (i) Institution of M. John de Appilby, rector of Ormside (*Ormesheved*),[315] to Kirkoswald church, vacant by the death of Richard de Monte; presented by Ranulph de Dacre, lord of Gilsland. (ii) Archdeacon to induct. Rose, 7 Apr. 1362.

---

[312] See **444**. It was usual for parties in common law courts alleged to be illegitimate to obtain writs *de bastardia* ordering bishops to enquire into the question (e.g. *Reg. Kirkby*, II.134, index *s.n.* Bastardy).

[313] Printed *Test. Karl.*, 42.

[314] See **431**.

[315] Another John de Appilby (cf. **429**), rector of Ormside in 1352 (*BRUO*, I.41); the previous known rector was Robert de Risindon, ordained subdeacon, 1340, and licensed to study, 1343 (*Reg. Kirkby*, I.108, 154 no.735).

444 Letters patent to bring knowledge of truth to the ignorant, certifying that Ellen, daughter of Richard, son of Robert del Hall of [Maulds] Meaburn, is the legitimate daughter and heir of Richard, born of the marriage of Richard and Mariota daughter of William Smyth, now deceased. Stephen de Meborne, a clerk of King's Bench, now deceased, was Richard's brother; they were sons of the marriage of the said Robert del Hall and Sillota daughter of Adam Grayne, and publicly reputed their legitimate children. The truth was learnt from trustworthy men examined under oath. Rose, 6 Apr. 1362.

445 Probate[316] of nuncupative will of Thomas, rector of Croglin,[317] commending his soul to God, Blessed Mary and all saints; burial in Croglin church; his best beast, an ox, if it were owed to the bishop for mortuary; and residue, after payment of his debts of 40s., for disposal by his executors, John called 'Littel Jon' de Knaresdale and John de Croglin. [Fo.45; p.89] Administration granted to executors named. Rose (chapel), 8 Apr. 1362.

446 Probate[318] of nuncupative will of William called the hermit of St. Peter's chapel by Linstock, as follows:
Commended soul to God and Blessed Mary. Burial in churchyard of Carlisle cathedral, with a cow for mortuary. One cow each to the cathedral fabric, Stanwix church for mortuary, the vicar of Irthington, Sir John Boon, and for his executors to divide among priests and clerks at his exequies. Eden bridge, 20s. William de Stirkland, clerk, 12d. Sir Robert de Louthre, priest, 12d. Residue for disposal by his executors, John Nicolson and Patrick Bakester (both) of Carlisle.
Administration granted to John; reserved for Patrick. Rose (chapel), 17 Apr. 1362.

447 (i) Letters of Richard de Aslacby, rector of Levisham, as the bishop's commissary, to Patrick de Edenham, clerk, instituting him to Croglin church, vacant by the death of Thomas; presented by Hugh de Querton. Under the bishop's seal, his own being little known; confirmed by the bishop. (ii) Note that the commissary wrote to the archdeacon to induct Patrick. Rose, 25 Apr. 1362.

448 Probate[319] of nuncupative will of Adam Louson of Brisco, *viz.*: ecclesiastical burial; residue, after payment of debts, to his wife Maud and their children. Administration granted to Maud, as no executors were appointed. Rose (chapel), 29 Apr. 1362.

449 (i) Collation to John de Grete, chaplain, of Ormside church, vacant by the resignation of M. John de Appilby. (ii) Archdeacon to induct. Rose, 29 Apr. 1362.

---

[316] Printed *Test. Karl.*, 43.
[317] The previous known rector was John de Wetewang, instituted 1335 (*Reg. Kirkby*, I.46, no.275).
[318] Printed *Test. Karl.*, 43–4.
[319] Printed *Test. Karl.*, 44.

450 (i) Commission of John [Thoresby], archbishop of York, for an exchange of benefices between William de Loundres, rector of [Long] Marton, and Robert de Wolselay, rector of Addingham (*Adyngham*; York dioc.), sending the report of an enquiry by the archdeacon of York's official. Cawood, 6 May 1362. [Fo.45ᵛ; p.90] (ii) Institution of Robert, priest, to Marton, vacant by the resignation to Bishop Gilbert of John Lytster, priest, as William's proctor; presented by Thomas de Musgrave, kt., in right of his wife Isabel's dower. (iii) Archdeacon to induct. (iv) Institution of William, priest, to Addingham, vacant by the resignation of Henry de Mallerstang', clerk, as Robert's proctor;[320] presented to the archbishop by William Vavasor. (v) Certificate to the archbishop. Rose, 19 May 1362.

451 Probate[321] of nuncupative will of Gilbert Smyth of Eamont Bridge, *viz.*: ecclesiastical burial; residue to his wife Agnes and their children, appointing her executrix. Grant of administration. Rose (chapel), 13 May 1362.

452 Probate[322] of nuncupative will of William de Stapelton, senior, as follows: Commended soul to God and Blessed Mary. Burial in Edenhall churchyard, with best beast for mortuary. His son William to take what he pleases from his armoury (*armatura*), and the remainder to the vicar of Edenhall to repair the church's vestments. His daughter Emma, 10s. and 4 stones of wool, for her portion. From the residue, after payment of debts[323] and funeral expenses, chaplains are to be employed to celebrate for his soul. Executors: his sons William and John, and William de Whytelawe.
      Administration granted to John and William de Whytelawe; reserved for William the son. Rose (chapel), 20 May 1362.

453 Probate[324] of nuncupative will of Hugh de Cressopp', as follows:
[Fo.46; p.91] Commended soul to God. Burial in Edenhall churchyard, with saddle and sword for mortuary, and 3s. for lights and vigils at night. The vicar of Edenhall, 6s. 8d. Residue to the friars minor, Carlisle, to celebrate for his soul if they are willing to accept the responsibility, otherwise to employ a chaplain for this purpose. Executors: Henry Shepehird and Simon de Kendale.
      Administration granted to them. Rose (chapel), 20 May 1362.

454 Memorandum of probate of nuncupative will [not quoted] of Isolda, wife of John Scot' of Edenhall. Administration granted to John Scot', named as executor. Rose (chapel), 20 May 1362.

455 Probate[325] of nuncupative will of Isabel, widow of William de Stapilton, senior:

---

[320] Both rectors were also instituted by proxy.
[321] Printed *Test. Karl.*, 45.
[322] Printed ibid., 45–6. William died 6 May 1362 (*CIPM*, XI.333).
[323] MS. .. *de residuo bonorum porcionem suam concernent' debitis suis* .. (amending the text in *Test. Karl.* but still unsatisfactory).
[324] Printed *Test. Karl.*, 46.
[325] Printed *Test. Karl.*, 47.

Commended soul to God. Burial in Edenhall churchyard, with best beast for mortuary. Ten marks left with her by Gilbert Palfrayman, once servant of Sir John de Lancastre, lord of Stansted, kt., to be spent for his soul. Euphemia del Castell, her former maid, 20s. which she owes. Sir Richard de Langwathby, a psalter. Isabel wife of William de Stapilton, junior, her best saddle. Emma daughter of William de Stapilton, senior, her best robe, coffer with coverings and a saddle. Residue to be spent for her soul by Thomas de Sandford and William de Whytelawe, executors.

Administration granted to them. Rose (chapel), 23 May 1362.

456 (i) Institution of John Maresshall, priest,[326] to Edenhall (*Edenhale*) vicarage, vacant by the death of John de Loudham;[327] presented by the prior and chapter of Carlisle. (ii) Archdeacon to induct. Rose, 4 June 1362.

457 Probate[328] of nuncupative will of Henry Martyn, rector of Scaleby:

Commended soul to God, Blessed Mary and all saints. Burial in choir of All Saints', Scaleby, with 3 pounds of wax for lights. His servant Agnes, 2s. Sir John del Denes, chaplain, 3s. 4d. Residue to William Martyn and John del Hall. Executors: Sir John and William.

Adminstration granted to them. Rose (chapel), 23 June 1362.

458 Note of licence to M. Henry de Sandford, rector of Crosby Garrett, to be absent for one year; excused from synods and chapters. Rose, 26 June 1362.

459 [Fo.46ᵛ; p.92] Licence for one year to William Whyte of Crosthwaite parish for a chaplain to celebrate in an oratory in his house at Naddle (*Naddale*) which is far from the parish church; without prejudice etc. Rose, 26 June 1362.

460 (i) Collation to John de Grandon, priest, of Scaleby church, vacant by the death of Henry Martyn. (ii) Archdeacon to induct. Carlisle, 28 June 1362.

461 Commission to the prior of Carlisle. The bishop has received letters from Archbishop [Thoresby] of York containing a papal mandate ordering all parsons with goods and benefices in the diocese to pay a tenth, half by 8 August and half by 25 Jan. [1363], to be paid to the archbishop as the receiver in his province appointed by these papal letters; this arises from a subsidy of 100,000 florins granted to the Roman church by the archbishops of Canterbury and York.[329] As the bishop is too busy, the prior is appointed collector in the diocese; he is to report the names of payers and non-payers by 10 August and send his receipts to the bishop. Rose, 30 June 1362.

---

[326] Possibly parish chaplain of St. Cuthbert's, Carlisle (**267**, note).
[327] The previous known vicar was Adam de Warthecop, said to be incurably ill in 1341 (*Reg. Kirkby*, I.122, no.603).
[328] Printed *Test. Karl.*, 47–8.
[329] See Lunt, *Financial Relations*, 98–103; also **412**.

462 (i) Collation to Thomas de Kirkland, priest,[330] of Crosby on Eden vicarage, now vacant.[331] (ii) Archdeacon to induct. Rose, 3 July 1362.

463 Licence for one year to Thomas de Helton for a chaplain to celebrate in his chapel at Burton, because of his home's distance from his parish church [at Warcop], provided he and his household attends it on Sundays and feast days. Brough (*Burgus subtus Staynesmore*), 18 July 1362.

464 (i) Institution of John Bone, priest,[332] to Kirklinton (*Levyngton*) church, vacant by the death of Thomas de Barton;[333] presented by Robert Tilliol, kt. [Fo.47; p.93] (ii) Archdeacon to induct. Carlisle, 5 July 1362.

465 Will[334] of Adam de Wygeton, vicar of Addingham, dated 18 July 1362. Commends soul to God, Blessed Mary and all saints. Burial in choir of St. Michael's, Addingham, with 5 candles for lights and 40d. for oblations. A silver-gilt chalice to the altar of St. Mary's, Carlisle, where the mass of Our Lady is sung daily. Forty marks for the celebration of divine services or in other alms, at his executors' discretion. Residue to Richard Vaux and Alan de Blenerhasset, appointed executors.

Grant of probate and administration to these executors. Rose (chapel), 22 July 1362.

466 Probate[335] of nuncupative will of Nicholas del Hall of Crosby [on Eden]: Commended soul to God, Blessed Mary and all saints. Burial in churchyard of St. John's, Crosby, with best beast for mortuary and 2s. for oblations and vigils at night. The fabric of Carlisle cathedral, 3s. 4d. The lights of Crosby church, 3s. 4d. Each order of mendicant friars, Carlisle, 3s. 4d. Residue to his wife Godiva and their children. Executor: William Robynson of Linstock.

Administration granted to William before the bishop in the chapter house, Carlisle cathedral, 25 July 1362.

467 Will[336] of M. William de Fenton, clerk,[337] dated 22 July 1362. Commends soul to God, Blessed Mary and all saints. Burial in St. Mary's churchyard, Carlisle, with best beast for mortuary and 5s. for light. The cathedral fabric, 6s. 8d. St. Mary's, 20s. for forgotten tithes and other [dues?]. The fabric of St. Mary's, Holm Cultram, 40s. Lanercost church, 5s. The friars preachers and minor, Carlisle, to celebrate for his soul and the souls of those whom he

---

[330] Parish chaplain, Torpenhow, 1357 (**169**); and see **495**.
[331] Probably by resignation of John de Grandon (see **180, 308, 460**).
[332] Parish chaplain of St. Mary's, Carlisle, by 1354 (**17**).
[333] Instituted 1333 (*Reg. Kirkby*, I.25–6).
[334] Printed *Test. Karl.*, 48–9.
[335] Printed *Test. Karl.*, 49.
[336] Printed ibid., 49–51.
[337] His title is supplied from the margin. He was a notary, possibly the registrar of the consistory court (see **79**), as the sealing clause here also suggests. For married notaries in this period, see C.R. Cheney, *Notaries Public in England in the Thirteenth and Fourteenth Centuries*, Oxford (1972), 79–81. This explains why Fenton was unbeneficed (cf. Summerson, I.306).

wronged, 13s. 4d.; likewise as much to the friars of Penrith and Appleby. Robert Ussher, 6s. 8d. His wife Margaret, 6s. 8d. Eden bridge by Carlisle, 3s. 4d. Petteril bridge between Carlisle and Harraby, 6s. 8d. Kirkoswald, Salkeld and Temple Sowerby bridges, 10s. equally divided. The schoolmaster and 11 other priests in Carlisle city, 24s. equally divided, to celebrate as above. Elias Martyn of Crosthwaite, 12d. Henry son of Adam Wyllyknaf of Crosscanonby, 12d. William Whytheved, 6s. 8d. and the six lambs the vicar of Addingham gave [the testator]. John son of Ada, daughter of Roger Skinner, his lawful son by their [marriage], is recognised as heir to his tenements in Fenton and Carleton. To celebrate for his and Ada's souls, his tenement or burgage in Castle Street, Carlisle. His household utensils and vestments to the said Ada daughter of Roger, her son John and daughter Mariota, if they live; if any of them dies from the present mortality, the survivor or survivors are to have them. William son of Thomas, 2s. and his tunic, hood and tabard of blue cloth. John and Isabel, children of Robert Usshar, 6s. 8d. equally divided. All his books are to be sold and their price, with the residue, to be used to celebrate for his soul and the souls above and of all faithful departed, in the form as above. Executors, together and singly: M. Adam de Caldbeck,[338] John Bovell, John de Mydelton, priests, and Robert Goldsmyth. Under his seal and the seal of the official of Carlisle, at present in his hands.

Probate, with grant of administration to M. Adam and Robert Goldsmyth; reserved for the other executors. Rose (chapel), 26 July 1362.

468 [Fo.47ᵛ; p.94] Will[339] of Henry de Asbrigg' (sane of mind and memory) dated 29 April 1362. Commends soul to God, Blessed [Mary] and all saints. Burial in churchyard of Sebergham chapel, with best beast for mortuary, 2s. for oblations, 6d. for wax, and an animal and skep of flour for the poor. The prior and convent of Carlisle, 13s. 4d. The friars preachers there, 6s. 8d. The friars minor there, 40d. Sebergham bridge, 6s. 8d. Robert son of Adam de Berwyse, 13s. 4d. Margaret daughter of Adam de Berwyse, a cow with calf. Henry son of John de Monkhowys, an animal 3 years old. William his groom, a heifer of 3 years or more. Thomas his groom, a bullock of 3 years. Henry son of Thomas Milner, a sheep with lamb. The wife and daughters of William Colthird, a heifer of 2 years. William de Langrygg, a coat. The children of John Redheved, 2 marks. John de Gil[sl]land, priest, 40d. A priest celebrating for his soul for a year, 7 marks. Six pairs of shoes to the poor, for his soul. Residue to his wife and daughter Agnes; if she should die, her share to revert to his wife, to dispose for his soul. Executors: Adam de Berwyse and (Henry's) wife Annabelle. Witnesses: John de Tympron and John Stalker.

Probate; administration granted to both executors. Rose (chapel), 7 July 1362.

469 Probate[340] of nuncupative will of Ellen wife of John del Monkhous of Sebergham:

Commended soul to God and Blessed Mary. Burial in churchyard of Sebergham chapel, with best beast for mortuary in respect of her portion

---

[338] Official of Carlisle from 1355 (**89**).
[339] Printed *Test. Karl.*, 51.
[340] Printed ibid., 52–3.

(*porcionem suam concernens*), 6d. for lights and 6d. for oblations. Sir Nicholas, parish chaplain of the said church [*sic*] of Sebergham, to pray for her soul, 12d. Each order of mendicant friars, Carlisle, 3s. 4d. Residue, after burial fitting her estate, to John del Monkhous and their children, appointing him executor.

Administration granted. Rose (chapel), 27 July 1362.

470 (i) Institution of Walter de Helton, priest, to Addingham vicarage, vacant by the death of Adam de Wygton; presented by the prior and chapter of Carlisle. (ii) Archdeacon to induct. Rose, 27 July 1362.

471 Note of licence to John Bone, rector of Kirklinton, to be absent for a year in a suitable place in England; excused synods, etc. Same date.

472 Probate[341] of nuncupative will of Thomas Barton, rector of Kirklinton:

Commended soul to God, Blessed Mary and all saints. Burial in Kirklinton choir, with 6s. 8d. for light, 6s. 8d. for bread and the carcasse of an ox for the poor, and 2 cows, 6 sheep, a skep of malt and 10s. to buy bread for funeral expenses. The friars minor and preachers, Carlisle, 6s. 8d. equally divided. A chaplain to celebrate for his soul and all faithful departed, 6s. 8d. Carlisle cathedral fabric, 3s. 4d. [Fo.48; p.95] To repair the choir of Kirklinton church, 40s. His servant Cecily, 2 cows and 2 calves. His servant Agnes, 8 sheep. Mariota daughter of John son of William de Patrikdale, 6 sheep. His son Thomas,[342] 3 oxen, 3 cows, a bullock and 40 sheep. Each of his servants, a cow. Juliana wife of Adam de Agillonby, 2 stones of wool. Hugh de Levyngton, a 'Hakyney Dun'. Sir Adam Wyse, chaplain,[343] a chest which is in the house of Sir John de Wylton. Sir John de Wylton, two mazers. Thomas and Agnes, children of William Biset', 12 sheep. Half the residue to the said Thomas his son; the other half to hire a chaplain to celebrate for his soul and all faithful departed. Executors: Sir Henry de Craystok',[344] Adam de Agelonby and Thomas his son.

Administration granted to the last two; reserved for Sir Henry. Rose (chapel), 27 July 1362.

473 Note of letters dimissory for all orders to Thomas son of Hugh de Helton, clerk with first tonsure. Penrith, 19 July 1362.

474 Probate[345] of nuncupative will of Matthew Taillour of Wigton:

Commended soul to God, Blessed Mary and all saints. Burial in Wigton churchyard, with best beast for mortuary, 8d. for vigils at night, 18d. for oblations, 16d. for light, and 2s. and a cow for the poor. Twelve masses to be celebrated for his soul in the fortnight after his death. His servant Nicholas, 8s.

---

[341] Printed *Test. Karl.*, 53–4.
[342] Presumably the testator's son in view of the other large bequest, and his appointment as executor.
[343] Ordained priest 1344 (*Reg. Kirkby*, I.160).
[344] Baron of the Exchequer (see last note to **388**). For Barton's connection with the Exchequer, see *Reg. Kirkby*, I.111, no.549, 154, no.736.
[345] Printed *Test. Karl.*, 54–5.

Matthew son of Patrick Lytster, 12d. Robert son of Godiva, 12d. Residue to Robert de Wampole and his wife Alice, appointed executors.

Administration to them. Rose (chapel), 29 July 1362.

475 Probate[346] of nuncupative will of Thomas Bredeman of Wigton:

Commended soul to God, Blessed Mary and all saints. Burial in Wigton churchyard if he should die there, with best beast for mortuary, 8d. for vigils at night, and 10s. in silver and a cow for the poor and a wake for neighbours. Thirty masses for his soul. Residue to Alice wife of Henry Walker of Wigton, appointed executrix, to dispose of for his soul, and for herself if she has a similar fate.

Administration granted to her. Rose (chapel), 29 July 1362.

476 Probate[347] of nuncupative will of Gilbert Anotson of Dalston:

Commended soul to God, Blessed Mary and all saints. Burial in Dalston churchyard, with best beast for mortuary, 12d. for oblations and 2s. for lights. The vicar of Dalston, 12d. The parish chaplain, 12d. The parish church, 6d. Residue, after ecclesiastical burial and payment of debts, to his wife and children. A quarter of barley to St. Mary's lights in [Dalston] church. Executors: Robert Anotson and John del Grene.

[Fo.48ᵛ; p.96] Administration granted to John; Robert had died. Rose (chapel), 29 July 1362.

477 Probate[348] of nuncupative will of Robert Anotson of Dalston: commended soul to God; burial in Dalston churchyard, with best beast for mortuary; residue, after ecclesiastical burial and payment of debts, to his wife and children; executor: John del Grene of Dalston. Administration to him. Rose (chapel), 29 July 1362.

478* Commission to Thomas [de Sourby[349]], rector of Beaumont, to prove wills of subjects in the deanery of Carlisle and grant administration to their executors. Rose, 29 July 1362.

479 (i) Institution of William de Corbrig', clerk, to Kirkby Thore church, vacant by the death of Adam de Hoton; presented by Roger de Clifford, lord of Westmorland. (ii) Archdeacon to induct. Rose, 3 Aug. 1362.

480 Will[350] of Adam de Hoton, rector of Kirkby Thore, dated at Kirkby Thore, 7 Oct. 1361. Commends soul to God, Blessed Mary and all saints. Burial where God disposes, with £6 13s. 4d. for oblations, wax and other funeral expenses, and 40s. for the poor. Chaplains celebrating for his soul, £20. The four orders of friars, at Carlisle, Appleby and Penrith, 5s. each. His mother Christine, his

---

[346] Printed ibid., 55.
[347] Printed ibid., 56.
[348] Omitted from *Test. Karl.*
[349] Died 1365 (*Test. Karl.*, 76). The previous known rector was Richard Broun, instituted 1339 (*Reg. Kirkby*, I.98, no.513).
[350] Printed *Test. Karl.*, 56–7.

brother John and John's children, £6 13s. 4d. His lord, Sir Roger de Clifford, 40s. Sir Henry de Craystok', his master,[351] 40s. Nicholas de Whyterigg, lately his clerk, 20s. William de Hoton, his proctor, 40s. John de Sourby and John Donkyn, his chaplains, 13s. 4d. each. His other servants to be reasonably rewarded at his executors' discretion, according to their status and time in his service. Residue to be distributed by his executors for his soul, as they will answer before God; appointing Henry de Craystok, rector of Rowley, John Parvyng', rector of Skelton, Henry de Mallerstang, John Donkyn, chaplain, John Barker of Wigton and William de Hoton, his proctor. Under his seal.

Sentence of probate, with grant of administration to Craystok, Parvyng, Donkyn and Hoton; reserved for Mallerstang and Barker. Rose (chapel), 4 Aug. 1362.

481 Will[352] of Thomas de Alaynby, [citizen and mayor[353]] of Carlisle, dated Carlisle, 30 July 1362. Commends soul to God, Blessed Mary and all saints. Burial in St. Cuthbert's churchyard, Carlisle, with best beast and cloth for mortuary, and 5s. for wax. The friars preachers and minor, Carlisle, 26s. 8d. equally divided. The parish priest of St. Cuthbert's, 2s. Holm Cultram convent, 20s. Every secular priest celebrating in Carlisle, 12d. in equal portions. The tenement where he lives to his wife Mary, for her life, and afterwards to his heirs. St. Mary's convent, Carlisle, a pittance of 13s. 4d. St. Mary's light in St. Cuthbert's, 4 skeps of barley, one of corn and an ox. His wife Mary and her heirs, the rent from shops and upper rooms which he had by grant [Fo.49; p.97] of Henry de Staunton; also all the tenement in Rickergate once William de Logthmabane's. His daughter Christine and the heirs of her body, all tenements and lands once belonging to her mother Margaret; with successive remainders, should they die without issue, to his sons Adam, then Thomas, and [the testator's] rightful heirs in perpetuity. Also to Christine, all his share of household utensils, 20 skeps of corn, 4 of oats, 2 of rye, 4 oxen, half a sack of wool, a basin, jug, mazer cup and covered silver cup, with £6; should she die before next Whitsun, all these utensils are to remain with his other children still living. His brother Richard, 33s. 4d. His mother, 13s. 4d. Stephen de Karl', 6s. 8d. Residue to Sir Peter de Morland, Adam de Alaynby, his wife Mary and Stephen de Karleolo, appointing them executors. Under his seal.

Probate, with administration to the named executors. Rose (chapel), 4 Aug. 1362.

482 Will[354] of John de Seburgham, [vicar of Walton,[355]] dated 28 July 1362. Commends soul to God, Blessed Mary and all saints. Burial in church of friars minor, Carlisle, with 3s. 4d. for light, 60s. for the poor, 20s. for a wake, and 6s.

---

[351] Baron of the Exchequer (see last note to **388**). For his patronage of Adam, in 1354, see note to **49**. Like Thomas Barton (**472**), Adam had been a victualler for the king in the west march (*Reg. Kirkby*, I.111, no.549).

[352] Printed *Test. Karl.*, 58–9.

[353] Supplied from margin. Writ for inquest, 23 Aug. 1362; date of death not given (*CIPM*, XI.218–19).

[354] Printed *Test. Karl.*, 60–1.

[355] Supplied from margin.

8d. for a vestment to be buried in. Elmota daughter of Alice, 5 marks. John son of Margaret de Hubrigthby, 40s. to be entrusted to John Marchale. The friars preachers, 6s. 8d. The minorites, 20s. John son of Thomas de Alaynby, 13s. 4d. Christine daughter of the same Thomas, 13s. 4d. Thomas de Alaynby, his breviary. Stephen de Karl', 6s. 8d. John Marschale's wife, 13s. 4d. Alice de Ullaik', 13s. 4d. Margaret de Hubrightby, 6s. 8d. Alice Barker, 6s. 8d. A priest celebrating for his soul for one year, 100s. Each priest, religious and secular, coming to his exequies, 6d. Nally servant of Sir Thomas de Lucy, 3s. 4d. John Marschale, 20s. Thomas Hog', 6s. 8d. Residue to Thomas de Alaynby, John Marschale, Stephen de Karlo', and Thomas Hog'; appointing them executors. Under his seal.

Probate, with administration to John Maresshall and Thomas Hog' of Carlisle; Thomas de Alaynby has died; reserved for Stephen. Rose (chapel), 5 Aug. 1362.

483 Memoranda of probate etc. of eleven nuncupative wills [not quoted]:[356]
(i) William Lademan of Kirkby Thore; executor, Thomas Johnson [of the same].
(ii) Joan wife of William Lademan; executor, Thomas de Yhanewyth.
Rose (chapel), 4 Aug. 1362
(iii) John de Culgayth of Thursby; executor, Adam Page, his co-executor John All' Ale being dead.
(iv) Ada wife of John de Culgayth; executor as the last.
(v) [Fo.49ᵛ; p.98] Adam Emmotson of Thursby; executrix, his mother Juliana.
(vi) Joan his wife; executor, John Smyth of Thursby.
(vii) Richard de Shortrigges of Thursby; executor, Robert de Crofton, junior, his co-executor John de Shortrigges being dead.
(viii) Agnes his wife [executors as for last].
(ix) Joan widow of Adam Wilkynson of Thursby; executor, John Smyth.
(x) John All' Ale of Thursby; executor, Robert de Crofton, junior.
(xi) William Wilkynson of Thursby; executor, William Jonson of Cardew.
Rose (chapel), 5 Aug. 1362.

484 (i) Institution of William Beauchamp, clerk, to a mediety of Aikton church, vacant;[357] presented by Ranulph de Dacre, lord of Gilsland. (ii) Archdeacon to induct. Rose, 7 Aug. 1362.

485 Memoranda of probate etc. of nuncupative wills [not quoted] of (i) William Bowman of Addingham; executors, William de Farnham and John Bowman; and (ii) John son of Thomas Dobynson of Wigton; executor, Thomas Whyteheved of Wigton, his co-executor Henry de Assebrig' being dead. Rose (chapel), 8 Aug. 1362.

---

[356] See *Test. Karl.*, 61–3.
[357] The remainder of the line, 7.5 cm, erased; the next starts [ult]*imi rectoris*. The Dacres were patrons of both moieties. Both rectors occur in **423**. As Robert de Kirkeby continued to 1372 (*Test. Karl.*, 101–3), the vacancy was left by M. William de Salkeld; see also **513**, note.

486 Will[358] of John Maresshall, vicar of Edenhall,[359] dated 29 July 1362. Commends soul to God, Blessed Mary and all saints. Burial in churchyard of St. Andrew's, Penrith, with 4 pounds of wax for lights, 2s. for oblations, 13s. 4d. for the poor, and 10s. for a wake for chaplains and friends. The bridges of Eamont, Lowther, Salkeld, Kirkoswald, [Temple] Sowerby and Wragmire,[360] 6s. in equal portions. The four orders of friars, 4s. The convent of Carlisle, an ox for a pittance. For work at the cathedral, an ox. For the roof of Edenhall church, 40d. For the roof of Penrith church, 2s. His executors, 10s. For a linen cloth for his burial, 2s. 6d. For the roof of Langwathby chapel and a chalice there, 2s. The light of Blessed Mary, Penrith, 2s. His servant Beatrice, 40s. and a heifer. William Wryngster, 2s. Adam Malson', a cow and 10s. Idonea daughter of Adam, a cow and 10s. John son of Adam, a cow. The wife of William dell Vycares and her children, a cow. Residue to Adam Malson' and Idonea. Executors: John son of Adam and William Dautry.

Probate, with administration to John son of Adam; reserved for William Dautri. Rose (chapel), 24 Aug. 1362.

487* Sentence. After the death of Isabel, prioress of Armathwaite (*Ermythwayt'*), Cecily Dryng', subprioress, and the other nuns met in the chapter house on 25 Aug. 1362. With the exception of Katherine de Lancastre, they unanimously agreed to her [Fo.50; p.99] election as prioress, as they signify under their common seal to Bishop Gilbert and others interested, on the same date.

Memorandum that this election was delivered to the bishop, examined, and its defects graciously made good. He conferred the cure and administration on her, and she swore obedience to him.

Note of mandate to the archdeacon to assign her stall in choir and place in chapter. Rose (chapel), 2 Sept. 1362.

488 Will[361] of Thomas [del Close], rector of Brougham, dated 14 Aug. 1362. Commends soul to God. Ecclesiastical burial, with 6s. 8d. for light and 3s. 4d. for oblations. Thomas de Gryndoun, a bullock and an ox. John de Gryndon, son of Thomas de Gryndon, 2 cows. Residue to his father and John de Redyng', his servant. Executors: John de Bowes, vicar of Kirkby Stephen, William de Carleton, chaplain, his father and John Redyng'.

Probate, with administration to the two last; reserved for the others. Rose (chapel), 30 Aug. 1362.

489 Will[362] of Richard de Hanyngton, vicar of Morland,[363] dated 23 Aug. 1362. Commends soul to God, Blessed Mary and all saints. Ecclesiastical burial, with 3s. 4d. for oblations, 4 pounds of wax, 40s. for the poor and 40s. for a wake for

[358] Printed *Test. Karl.*, 64–5.
[359] See **456** for his institution.
[360] See **546**.
[361] Printed *Test. Karl.*, 65–6.
[362] Printed *Test. Karl.*, 66.
[363] Instituted 1335 (*Reg. Kirkby*, I.42, no.253, where his name is shown as Havingdon).

neighbours. £40 for the celebration of services. Residue to executors: John de Bowes, junior, vicar of Kirkby Stephen, and Roger his domestic servant.

Probate, with administration to Roger; reserved for John. Rose (chapel), 30 Aug. 1362.

490 Presentation by the bishop to Thomas [Hatfield], bishop of Durham, of Peter de Morland, priest,[364] to Warkworth (*Werkworth*) vicarage (dioc. Durham), now vacant. Rose, 9 Aug. 1362.

491 [Fo.50ᵛ; p.100] (i) Institution of John Marrays, priest, to Morland vicarage, vacant by the death of Richard de Haynyngton; presented by the abbot and convent of St. Mary's, York. (ii) Archdeacon to induct. Rose, 14 Sept. 1362.

492 (i) Institution of John de Danby, priest, to Kirkby Stephen vicarage, vacant by the death of John del Bowes; presented by the abbot and convent of St. Mary's, York. (ii) Archdeacon to induct. Rose, 14 Sept. 1362

493 (i) Collation to Richard de Aslacby, priest,[365] of the vicarage of St. Michael's, Appleby, now vacant.[366] (ii) Archdeacon to induct. Rose, 14 Sept. 1362.

494 Mandate to the official of Carlisle quoting the king's writ of summons to a parliament at Westminster on 13 October, with *premunientes* clause (dated Windsor, 14 Aug. 1362),[367] for execution [as in **155**], reporting by 29 September.[368] Rose, [. . .] Sept. 1362.

495 (i) Collation to Thomas de Kirkland, priest,[369] of Ousby church, vacant by the death of Richard de Ulnesby. (ii) Archdeacon to induct. Rose, 18 Sept. 1362.

496 (i) Institution of Thomas de Derby, clerk, to Brougham church, vacant by the death of Thomas del Close; presented by Roger de Clifford, lord of Westmorland. (ii) Archdeacon to induct. Rose, 18 Sept. 1362.

497 [Fo.51; p.101] (i) Collation to John called Fitz Rogier, priest, of Crosby on Eden vicarage, now vacant.[370] (ii) Archdeacon to induct. Rose, 23 Sept. 1362.

---

[364] Rector of Great Musgrave (**386**).
[365] Rector of Levisham (**408**, **447**). The king presented Richard de Upton to this church, 10 Jan. 1363 (*CPR 1361–4*, 278; and see Nicolson & Burn, I.589).
[366] Possibly by deprivation of John de Tuxford (see **398**).
[367] As in *CCR 1360–4*, 421.
[368] The clergy's proctors were Richard de Tissyngton and John de Bowland, both royal clerks (PRO, S.C.10, file 28, no.1390; and see **400** and note).
[369] Vicar of Crosby on Eden (**462**).
[370] See **495** and note.

498   (i) Institution of John de Regill, priest, to Crosby Ravensworth vicarage, vacant by the death of Robert de Threlkeld; presented by the abbot and convent of Whitby. (ii) Archdeacon to induct. Rose, 25 Sept. 1362.

499   Sentence[371] of probate of the will [not quoted] of Katherine wife of William de Brounfeld, with grant of administration to William de Brounfeld, chaplain; his co-executors, John de Ireby and John called the forester's clerk (*Clerk' Forestar*'), had refused to act. Rose (chapel), 26 Sept. 1362.

500   Note of probate of the nuncupative will of Thomas Blome of Gatesgill (*Gaytscales*); administration granted to his son Thomas and Simon Taillour. Rose (chapel), 29 Sept. 1362.

501   Will[372] of John del Bowes, vicar of Kirkby Stephen, dated 30 Aug. 1362. Commends soul to God, Blessed Mary and all saints. Ecclesiastical burial, with 4s. for oblations and 6 pounds of wax. The four orders of friars, 20s. equally divided. A dole for the poor on his burial day, 40s. Each priest celebrating in the deanery of Westmorland, 12d., if his goods suffice. The abbot of Shap, 30s. John, vicar of Brough under Stainmore, 2 good young horses. Sir John de Merton, an ox, a cow and a young horse. John de Fisshwyk, rector of Barningham, a bed and fur-edged tabard. John de Fisshwyk the tailor, 2 cows and a beast of burden. John de Warthecopp, 3 oxen and 3 cows. Adam Bradebell, a cow. John de Bowes his brother, a sack of wool with a bed. Roger de Morland his household servant and John his brother, 200[373] sheep. William de Kirkbride, a cow. Sir William Colyn, a robe and an ox. Sir John Yve, a beast of burden and a robe. Thomas son of John Coke, a cow. Crane, a cow. Sir John de Shirborne, 4 oxen and 2 bullocks. Christine de Warthecopp, a cow and a bullock. His household servants, 2 skeps of malt. Robert his household servant, a cow and a beast of burden. Thomas Bateson, 40d. John the clerk his foster-son, the residue except for 100s. towards the roofing of Kirkby Stephen church by his parishioners. Executors: John de Fisshewyk, rector of Barningham, John de Warthecopp, Roger de Morland his servant and John his brother; they are also appointed to collect tithes due to him and pay his debts from his goods and those which the vicar of Morland bequeathed to him.[374] Item, to Adam Grayne, a cow.
   Note of probate and grant of administration to the executors named. Rose (chapel), 10 Sept. 1362.

502   Will[375] of John de Askeby, vicar of Bampton,[376] dated 8 Sept. 1362. Commends soul to God. Burial in the choir of St. Patrick's, Bampton, with what is owing to God and the church, with 3 pounds of wax for light and 40d. for oblations. The light of the Blessed Mary of Carlisle, 2s. The chapel of St.

---

[371] Omitted from *Test. Karl.*, as is **500**.
[372] Printed *Test. Karl.*, 67–8.
[373] MS. *xx* over *X*
[374] See **489**.
[375] Printed *Test. Karl.*, 68–9.
[376] Cf. **225–6** for the last institution to Bampton, of John de Morland.

Thomas in Bampton church, 2s. Bampton bridge[s?], 3s. in equal portions. Eve his sister, 2 cows, a mare, his big cauldron, his smaller pot, all his bedclothes, a tripod with a griddle. Beatrice Bradebelt', 2 cows, and her children, 2 cows, an *otterbe*, his larger pot, smaller cauldron and all his personal clothing. Margaret her daughter, a little pan. Thomas de Karlo', a cow. John the clerk of Bampton, 2s. For a wake for those who were busy at his funeral, [Fo.51ᵛ; p.102] 20s. and an animal. Eve his sister, Beatrice Bradebelt' and her children, all his crops and meadows. Eve, his basin and jug. Eve and Beatrice, all grain and flour, in equal portions. Residue to Gilbert Dedyng' and Roger de Borghdale, to spend for his soul, appointing them executors. Under his seal. Witnesses: Thomas de Carlill, Roger de Cundale, Henry Watson, and others.

Note of probate, with administration granted to Gilbert, Roger having died. Rose (chapel), 10 Sept. 1362.

503 Will[377] of Walter Maresshall of Carlisle, dated 16 Aug. 1362. Commends soul to God, Blessed Mary and all saints. Burial in churchyard of St. Cuthbert's, Carlisle, with best beast for mortuary, and 6s. for wax. Marjory his wife, his tenement between those of Adam de Blencowe and Thomas Malmayns, and the residue of his goods, appointing her executrix. Witnesses: William son of Richard Bresewode, John de Dundragh and Gilbert Taynturell.

Note of probate, with administration to executrix. Rose (chapel), 30 Aug. 1362.

504 Will[378] of Nicholas de Motherby of [Castle] Sowerby, dated 23 Sept. 1362. Commends soul to God and Blessed Mary. Burial in churchyard of St. Kentigern's, Sowerby, with best beast for mortuary, a stott to its high altar for forgotten tithes, 2s. for wax, 16d. for oblations, an ox and skep of oatmeal to the poor, and 20s. for a wake. Chaplains celebrating for his soul, £8. The four orders of friars, 20s. Bridges over the Eden by Carlisle and Warwick, 20s. The light of Blessed Mary in Sowerby church. Its roof, 2s. William Tomlynson, an ox. Sir Hugh de Jar', an ox. Thomas de Richardby, a stott. Two of his oxen are to be hired from year to year, the receipts spent for his soul. John son of Alexander de Motherby and his sister, 6s. 8d. Adam son of John Dyxson, 5s. Alexander son of Peter le Wryght of Penrith, an ox. William de Stokdale, 3s. Alice daughter of Isabel de Raubankes, a heifer. Nicholas de Bresceby, 12d. *Le vaute* of Blessed Mary in Sowerby church, 12d. Upkeep of the Holy Cross there, 12d. Emma his wife, all his portion of household utensils, wagons and ploughs with gear. Alexander son of Peter le Wright of Penrith, the lands called 'Michelfeld' and 'Dokfeld'. John de Aldeby, the meadow once belonging to William de Aldeby his father. Alexander de Ricardby, 20s. Executors: Hugh de Jar', priest, William Michelson and Emma his wife; they are to have the residue and dispose of it for his soul, as they would answer to God.

Note of probate; administration to the executors named. Rose (chapel), 4 Oct. 1362.

---

[377] Printed *Test. Karl.*, 69–70.
[378] Printed ibid., 70–1.

505 Memoranda of probate etc. of the wills [not quoted] of (i) the wife of Hugh Mareshall; executor, her husband; and (ii) the widow of Robert Anotson of Dalston;[379] executor, John del Grene of Dalston. Rose (chapel), 11 Sept. 1362.

506 The like of (i) Ellen daughter of William Huetson of Blennerhasset; executor, Thomas del Gill; and (ii) John de Seburgham; executors, John de Tymparon and John's widow. 12 Sept. 1362.

507 (i) Institution of Walter de Well, priest, to Lowther church, vacant by the death of Thomas de Hurworth;[380] presented by Thomas de Stirkland, kt. (ii) Archdeacon to induct. Rose, 14 Oct. 1362.

508 Note that William de Corbrigg', rector of Kirkby Thore, was licensed to attend a *studium generale* in England for one year, be ordained subdeacon only, and excused from synods, etc.[381] 14 Oct. 1362.

509 [Fo.52; p.103] Commission to John [de Horncastre], prior of Carlisle, and M. Adam de Caldebek', skilled in law, to proceed singly or together and decree in the cause or causes coming before the bishop or his commissaries, by his citation, on the Friday after the synod at Carlisle, between Robert, abbot, and the convent of Holm Cultram, and William [de Cressop], vicar of Wigton;[382] and also against John de Irby, William called Proktor, priest, and William Somer, executors of William de Brounfeld, late parishioner of Wigton,[383] and with other citations arising in this matter, certifying the bishop about their decisions. Rose, 17 Oct. 1362.

510 Commission to the prior of Carlisle and M. John de Welton, clerk skilled in law, official of Carlisle, to preside singly or together at the synod due to be held in the cathedral after St. Luke's [18 Oct.], and attend and act in the name of the bishop, who is detained by other matters. Rose, 17 Oct. 1362.

511 Letters granting an indulgence of 30 days remission for supporting Richard Coupar of Carlisle, a pauper, so that he may visit the Holy Land and other places to fulfil his vows. Rose, 18 Oct. 1362.

512 (i) Collation to M. William de Ragenhill, clerk, of Caldbeck (*Caldebek'*) church,[384] vacant by the death of Nicholas de Whyterig'. (ii) [Blank] to induct. Rose, 22 Oct. 1362.

---

[379] See **477**.

[380] The first recorded institution to Lowther, which had alternating patronage (Nicolson & Burn, I.438). A Thomas de Hurworth was ordained acolyte, 1307 (*Reg. Halton*, I.275), and Walter de Welle priest, 1344, with a title from one of the patrons (*Reg. Kirkby*, I.166).

[381] See *BRUO*, I.486.

[382] Probably since 1361, in succession to Richard de Aslacby (**408** and note); until 1367 (Reg. Appleby, fo.9; p.157).

[383] His will is not in this register, but see **499**. He died 8 Sept. 1362 (*CIPM*, XI.439).

[384] Confirmed by the pope, 26 Jan. 1363 (*CPL*, IV.29; *CPP*, I.399).

513 Licence to M. John Burdon, clerk, to keep grammar schools in Carlisle city, teaching children, adults and others in grammatical science and other subjects within his knowledge; during pleasure.[385] Rose, 23 Oct. 1362.

514 Will[386] of Robert de Whyterig', senior, dated Caldbeck, 21 Oct. 1362 (being well in mind and memory). Commends soul to God and Blessed Mary. Burial in the choir of Caldbeck church before the statue of the Blessed Mary Magdalene, with mortuary due by law and custom, 6s. 8d. for oblations, 6 pounds of wax for lights, 40s. for a wake for neighbours and 40s. for the poor. Priests celebrating for his soul, £20. The four orders of friars in Carlisle diocese, 26s. 8d. equally divided. Lights of the Blessed Mary in Caldbeck church, a mark. John his brother, 100 marks. His mother, 20 marks. His son Nicholas, 10 marks. Lady Margaret de Malton, a mazer cup. Alice wife of John de Bampton, a cup. Both ladies, all his furs. Lady Ellen de Whiterig', a furred cloak. His 60 best oxen are to be selected, and from them 40 are to be divided equally between Henry de Malton and Thomas de Whiterig', knights. His executors are to be allowed reasonable expenses. Residue to the said Henry and Thomas. Executors: Robert de Bampton, Nicholas Saunderson and John [Fo.52ᵛ; p.104] de Whyterig', who are to act with the counsel of the said Henry and Thomas. Under his seal.

Note of probate, with administration to the executors named. Rose (chapel), 26 Oct. 1362.

515 (i) Institution of John Baynard, priest, to Isel vicarage, vacant by the death of John Wauton;[387] presented by the prior and convent of Hexham. (ii) Archdeacon to induct. Rose, 28 Oct. 1362.

516 Note of licence to William de Ragenhill, rector of Caldbeck, to study for 3 years in a *studium generale*, according to the constitution [*Cum ex eo*]; also granted letters dimissory to all orders. 6 Nov. 1362.

517 NOVA TAXACIO ECCLESIE DE HORNCASTRE UT PATET. Letters patent [of Edward III] confirming, at the request of his dear clerk, M. Simon de Islip, its rector, a reduced assessment of the rectory of Horncastle church (dioc. Lincoln). Westminster, 14 June 1344.

[This is a later insertion occupying most of the space (20 cm deep) following **516**, Welton's last recorded episcopal act. It was written earlier than the table of contents for Welton's register, which includes its above marginal description (Fo. vii). On Fo.52ᵛ this is followed by a drawing of a pointing hand, next by STIRKELAND in the same script as the description, and finally in the margin by a jejune drawing of a keep (2.5 cm square) with a horn on its centre, i.e. a rebus for

---

[385] He was still schoolmaster at his death, 1371 (*Test. Karl.*, 101). The previous known reference to a schoolmaster was the appointment of M. William de Salkeld, 1333 (*Reg. Kirkby*, I.33, no.193). For his probable death earlier in 1362, see **484**. He had been available for services in Carlisle, 1354–60 (**220, 267, 326, 542, 579**).

[386] Printed *Test. Karl.*, 72–3.

[387] The previous known institution was of William de Burton, 1341 (*Reg. Kirkby*, I.124, no.616).

Horncastle. All the writing and drawings appear to have been made with the same pen and ink.

The text was probably taken from a transcript of the Chancery roll (see *CPR 1343–5*, 267–8). The address clause here is *Rex omnibus ad quos etc. salutem*, and at the end the year of the date (*anno xviii E. tercii*) appears to be an editorial addition, after the warranty clause *Per ipsum regem*.

Bishops of Carlisle had aspired to appropriate their rectory of Horncastle since 1313, but were frustrated by a succession of rectors favoured by kings, popes and episcopal nepotism (*Reg. Halton*, I.240–1; *Reg. Kirkby*, I.40–1, 85 no.450, 155 no.746*n*.). William Strickland was rector from 1388 until he became bishop of Carlisle in 1400, with papal licence to retain the church for two years (*BRUO*, III.1806; *CPL*, V.317). In 1402 he received the king's licence to appropriate it to the bishopric (*CPR 1401–5*, 185). It is likely that this transcript was put in the register between 1388 and 1400, as the marginal note of Strickland's surname, if made later, might be expected to refer to him as bishop. He was vicar-general of Bishop Reade in 1396 (PRO, Gaol Delivery Rolls (J.I.3), 70/2, m.3)]

518* Notarial instrument dated 18 July 1353.[389] Bishop Gilbert asserted that at the time of his promotion, he was a canon of York and prebendary of Osbaldwick (*Osbaldewyk'*), which Pope Innocent VI licensed him to retain for a certain time after his consecration.[390] Appointment of M. Simon de Bekyngham, chancellor of York, Ralph de Drayton, Robert Swetemouth, Richard de Aslacby and Nicholas de Bautre, priests; Richard de Meaux, John de Midelton, John de Wyrkesope, Gerlac called de Clave and John de Piperharowe, clerks, to publish his letters of provision to Carlisle and others conferring graces, to prelates, chapters and their members with an interest, and having them effected and defended by judicial process if necessary; producing witnesses etc., seeking the relaxation of sentences, absolution and damages, and making appeals. Dated as above, in the bishop's house in the close at York. Witnesses: John de Coke, Richard de Babelak' and others.

Subscription by Richard de Wysebech, clerk (dioc. Ely), notary by papal and imperial authority.

519* Letters patent appointing M. John de Welton, clerk, to seek and receive from the prior and convent of Carlisle cathedral the episcopal chapel and all its ornaments, books and vessels, etc., necessary for the performance of the episcopal office; also all registers of his predecessors and pertinent *acta*, rolls and other memoranda. York, 12 July 1353.

520* The like appointing M. John to seek and receive the temporalities of the bishopric from escheators in Cumberland, Westmorland and Northumberland;[391] also to convoke tenants and subjects and hold courts and sessions; receive fealties, rents, farms and other services from tenants, and tithes of churches in and outside the diocese from appropriated churches; and to grant farms for the bishop's profit. Same date.

---

[388] This is the first folio of a new quire (ending with Fo.62; no.604). Its title is given in **27**, which refers to **530**. A note in a sixteenth-century hand on the facing folio (52ᵛ) suggests that the quire is out of place: *Nota. Hee xii paginae seqq. inserendae sunt ad hujus Registri initium; continent enim ea quae gesta sunt primo, 2, 3, 4 Gilberti Episcopi anno.* The total *xii* must include the 2 folios of ordinations (**605–22**). See also Introduction, xv.

[389] The initial *I* is decorated with a tail 10 cm long.

[390] Until 1 Nov. 1353; also Eaton prebend in Southwell (*CPL*, III.513; *CPP*, I.241).

[391] Their orders to give livery were dated 26 June, as were others for temporalities in Middlesex, Derbyshire and Lincolnshire (*CPR 1350–4*, 470). The bishop is not known ever to have visited his manors at Melbourne (Derbs.) and Horncastle (Lincs.).

521* The like appointing M. John to seek and receive from all tenants and subjects the services, fruits and rents due to the bishop and bishopric, by distraint if necessary. Same date.

522 Writ of Edward III requiring the bishop to grant the pension due to a royal clerk, because of his recent creation, [Fo.53ᵛ; p.106] to M. Michael de Northburgh. Westminster, 30 June 1353.

523 Letters patent of the bishop granting M. Michael de Northburgh, clerk, doctor of laws, secretary of King Edward III,[392] an annual pension of 5 marks at Carlisle at Christmas, until the bishop has provided him with a competent benefice. The bishop's manor by Westminster, 6 Oct. 1353.[393]

524 Letters patent of Michael de Northburgh, doctor of laws, the king's secretary, acknowledging that on this day he received 5 marks from Bishop Gilbert for the Christmas term. London, 26 Dec. 1353.

525* Letter missive to the prior and chapter of Carlisle. On the previous day, the bishop received their fellow-canon and envoy Thomas de Appelby,[394] to whom he replied more kindly than reasonably. Thomas next went stealthily to the auditor of the court of York, raising the case of a mortuary he claimed to be due to [the prior and chapter] from the previous bishop [John Kirkby]. He obtained letters of monition and citation in their name sent to the vicar of Masham, which is in the immediate jurisdiction of the chapter [of York], under that chapter's seal. These letters are injurious to the bishop and church of Carlisle, which they should defend, and also prejudicial to the archbishop, for the chapter [of York] should not meddle in such causes while the sees of York and Carlisle are occupied. It is also a great injury to their late bishop and his successor to intervene while there is no protector of the defunct's goods; it is well known that he died intestate. If they have decided to grieve him, the bishop will consider counter-measures. He is certain that their envoy had spoken to him with peaceful words, deceitfully, in their name. He doubted, however, whether they had intended and agreed to what was done, and asks to be made sure. York, 26 Aug. [1353].

526* To the same. The bishop has received their letter, with an explanation for Thomas de Appelby's singular excess in their conversation; they are excused on the matters in his last letter. While such conduct, particularly against his own church and pastor, demands apppropriate and swift punishment, the bishop does not wish to be too hasty; it should be deferred until Thomas is with them. The bishop is sending him back, contrite and humbled, in expectation of his reform. York, 4 Sept. [1353].

---

[392] Actually DCL and keeper of the privy seal; bishop of London, 1354 (*HBC*, 94; *BRUO*, II.1368–70).
[393] Welton was presumably attending the parliament of 23 Sept.–12 Oct. The writ of summons (dated 15 July) is not recorded in the register (*HBC*, 562; *CCR 1354–60*, 610).
[394] Bishop of Carlisle, 1363–95; see *BRUO*, III.2144.

527 Licence for one year for questors for the hospital of St. Lazarus, Jerusalem. York, 7 Sept. 1353.

528 Letters patent appointing M. Hugh de Fletham, clerk, as the bishop's attorney in all causes concerning him and his church before judges ordinary or delegate. [Fo.54; p.107]. York, 14 Nov. 1353.

529 Letters patent appointing M. John de Welton as the bishop's attorney to lease and farm all his lands and tenements in Eaton (*Eton*) by Retford, Sturton le Steeple (*Stretton*) and Littleborough (*Littelburgh*).[395] Rose, 23 Mar. 1354.

HIC INCIPIT ANNUS DOMINI MILLESIMUS CCC^{mus} QUINQUAGESIMUS QUARTUS.

530 Writ *dedimus potestatem* of Edward III for the bishop to receive the oaths of William de Lye as sheriff of Cumberland and escheator of Cumberland and Westmorland, to which and the custody of Carlisle castle he has been appointed (during pleasure) by letters patent.[396] Westminster, 4 Mar. 1354.
  Memorandum that William appeared before the bishop in the chapter house of Carlisle cathedral and took the oaths (*humiliter et devote*) on the Gospels, as follow: oath as sheriff [as in **292**]; oath as escheator:
  He will serve faithfully as escheator of Cumberland, saving the king's rights and preventing concealments, informing the king or his council if he cannot; he will treat all people of his bailiwick lawfully, nor harm any for gift, promise or hatred; return and serve writs; personally make and report extents of lands (in their true value) and inquests; appoint only lawful bailiffs under oath; and account to the Exchequer for issues.[397]
  The letters patent were then delivered to him. Carlisle, 3 Apr. 1354.

531 [Fo.54^v; p.108] (i) Mandate to the prior and chapter of Carlisle quoting the king's writ of summons to a parliament at Westminster on 28 April (dated Westminster, 15 Mar. 1354).[398] The prior is to attend in person and the chapter by a proctor; certifying the bishop by 29 March. (ii) The like to the official of Carlisle, to summon the archdeacon in person and the clergy by two proctors. Rose, 4 Apr. 1354.

532 Licence for one year to John de Botehill, proctor of the chapter of St. John's, Beverley, to seek alms for the sumptuous work of building and repair of their church, already begun, at a cost beyond their means. Rose, 7 Apr. 1354.

---

[395] All in east Nottinghamshire; and see second note under **518**.
[396] These appointments were revoked and Hugh de Louthre (re)appointed, 15 Mar. 1354 (*CFR*, VI.408, 410; *VCH Cumberland*, II.315). Cf. **27**, **551**.
[397] In same form as for escheator of Lincolnshire, 1391, which has two additional clauses (*Royal Writs*, as cited under **292**, 125–6).
[398] As in *CCR 1354–60*, 64. For the bishop's possible attendance see Introduction, xv.

533   Commission to the prior of Carlisle to deputise for the bishop (who is detained by business) on Maundy Thursday [10 April], when it is customary for penitents to come to the cathedral and be reconciled to God. Rose, 8 Apr. 1354.

534*   Licence addressed to abbots, priors and clergy of the diocese. The prior and chapter of Carlisle have begun to build the choir of the cathedral. All are urged to contribute, for the remission of their sins. William Bell, the chapter's proctor, will carry these letters when he comes seeking alms. He should be preferred to all other [questors] until this work has been completed, and allowed to collect from parishioners and retain all receipts, under pain of excommunication. [Fo.55; p.109] An indulgence of 40 days is granted to all donors and assistants. This licence is valid for one year. Rose, 21 Apr. 1354.

535   Licence for one year to Hugh de Jarum, questor for the hospital of Saint-Antoine-de-Viennois. Rose, 19 Apr. 1354.

536   Note that the same Hugh was granted similar letters for a quest for the hospital of St. Thomas the martyr of Canterbury of Acon (*sic*), London. Same date.

537   Commission to the prior of Carlisle to collect a tenth, quoting a writ of Edward III (dated Wilford by Westminster, 6 May 1354) ordering the bishop to appoint a collector in the diocese of the second tenth granted to the king for the defence of the English church and realm, by John [Kirkby], late bishop of Carlisle, and other bishops and clergy of York province in their last convocation in York minster;[399] the first tenth was to be paid in halves on 30 November following and 24 June [1352], the second on 2 February and 24 June [1353], as was certified by William [Zouche], late archbishop of York.[400] Rose, 20 July 1354.

538   Commission of John [Thoresby], archbishop of York, for the bishop to consecrate oil and chrisms in the fifth week before Easter in York cathedral or another church in the city or diocese of York. His house at Westminster, 28 Feb. 1354.

539   Commission of the archbishop [Fo.55ᵛ; p.110] for the bishop to ordain beneficed clergy, religious and others, of York diocese or having letters dimissory of their diocesans, in York cathedral or any other church of his choice wherever he happens to travel, at suitable times, until 29 September. Westminster, 11 Feb. 1354.

---

[399] In May 1351, when Kirkby and Welton (then official of York) presided as the archbishop's commissaries (*Records of Northern Convocation* (cited under **296**), 84–9).

[400] Died July 1352. An earlier writ ordering collection of this second tenth issued 20 Oct. 1352; it stated that convocation's conditions for its payment had been met in the last parliament (*CCR 1349–42*, 449; see also Storey, 'Simon Islip' (cited under **125**), I.142–5. The Chancery enrolment of the writ in **537** has not been traced.

540 Letters patent. Bro. Jordan de Bosdon', abbot-elect and confirmed of Cockersand (*Cokersand*), of the Premonstratensian order, came to the bishop with letters of M. Robert de Beverl', vicar-general of the archbishop of York (quoted; dated York, 28 July 1354), licensing him to receive blessing from any suffragan of York; provided that within a month of the archbishop coming into the province, Jordan in person visits him to do what is lawful and customary. He was blessed, as the bishop certifies, in the chapel of Rose, 3 Aug. 1354.

Memorandum that the abbot took an oath of reverence and obedience, as laid down in the rule of St. Augustine, to the bishop as the archbishop's deputy. [Same day.]

541 Commission of the archbishop for the bishop to consecrate chalices, patens, corporals, portable altars and other ornaments and dishes serving altars and churches in the diocese [of York]; also to confer first clerical tonsures and confirm children and adults. Bishopthorpe (*Thorp juxta Ebor'*), 12 Sept. 1354.

542 Commission to M. William [de Salkeld], rector of a mediety of Aikton, Richard [de Aslacby], vicar of Stanwix, John Boon and John Mareshall, chaplains, to claim and receive clerks accused before the king's justices of gaol delivery in Carlisle; and keep them securely until order is made by ecclesiastical judgment. Rose, 6 Aug. 1354.

Note of similar commission to the vicars of St. Michael's and St. Lawrence's, Appleby, for gaol delivery at Appleby. [Same date.]

543* [Fo.56; p.111] Mandate to the subprior of Carlisle. William de Hakne-showe was excommunicated for violating the liberty of the church and causing bloodshed in the churchyard of Carlisle cathedral.[401] The bishop absolved him, ordering that for penance he was to go at the head of the procession into the cathedral, without shoes or cap, carrying a candle of one pound, on the next and following Sundays. [The subprior] is to ensure this penance is performed and announce William's absolution, certifying the bishop. n.d.

544 Letters patent of Lambert, abbot of the monastery of the valley of the Blessed Mary Magdalene, Shap,[402] and its convent, and Bro. Nicholas de Preston, vicar of Warcop. A dispute recently arose between the abbey, which appropriated the church long ago (paying £4 p.a. to the bishop of Carlisle), and Bro. Nicholas, to whom was due the altarage with buildings and land belonging to the church.[403] Sterility of the soil impoverished the abbey's portion, and the pension to the bishop fell into arrears. By the mediation of friends, an agreement was made, *viz.* that while Nicholas was vicar, he would receive and use all the revenues of the church and pay 12 marks p.a. to the abbey, at Martinmas and Whitsun, the pension to the bishop and all charges on the church; he will be assisted by a canon of Shap or secular priest having board and lodging at the

---

[401] See **65***.
[402] The previous abbot known was William, in 1343. The only canon known named Lambert was L. de Morland, ordained deacon, 1345 (*Reg. Kirkby*, I.156, no.748; 164); fully named as abbot, 1379 (*VCH Cumberland*, II.146; Reg. Appleby, fo.105; p.314).
[403] For the terms of the appropriation, 1307, see *Reg. Halton*, I.292–4.

abbey; he is to pay £4 of the arrears to the bishop, and the abbey the remainder;[404] and the abbey will repair the chancel of Warcop church this time, but the vicar will do so in future.

The abbot, convent and vicar submitted to Bishop Gilbert's award, which they swore to accept in the principal chamber at Rose, in the presence of M. John de Welton, M. John de Hakethorp, Thomas de Salkeld and Richard de Aslakby, priests. Under the seals of the abbot and convent and of the vicar, Shap, 5 Sept. 1354.

Memorandum that this undertaking was given by the abbot and vicar in the presence of the above witnesses at Rose on the Thursday before their joint signature (*consignacionem*) [28 Aug. 1354].

545 [Fo.56ᵛ; p.112] Letters patent of the bishop, confirming the above document, which he has inspected, forbidding any attempt to invalidate it. If any complaint of non-compliance is made to the bishop, it must be remedied within 15 days under pains of excommunication, suspension of the abbey and interdict on the churches of Shap and Warcop; saving the appropriation of the church to the abbey and whatever rights this gave the bishop, his successors and their jurisdiction. Rose, 9 Sept. 1354.

[With this postscript] Approbation of the above by the abbot, convent and Bro. Nicholas; it had not been their intention to derogate from the appropriation of Warcop church. Under the common seal and vicar's seal, Shap, 15 Sept. 1354.

546 Letters patent granting an indulgence of 40 days for contributions to the repair of the place (*locus*) called Wragmire (*Wragmyre*), between Carlisle and Penrith, and support of Bro. John de Corbrig', a poor hermit working on its repair, and saying prayers for peace, the stability of the church and the welfare of the king and realm of England, with the *salutacio angelica*. Rose, 17 Sept. 1354.

547 Letters patent appointing M. John de Welton as attorney to prosecute pleas for the bishop and bishopric before the king's and other justices, show charters concerning their liberties, seek their award, and do whatever else [Fo.57; p.113] is necessary. Rose, 30 Sept. 1354.

548 Indenture between the bishop and Thomas de Lucy, lord of Cockermouth. The bishop had claimed for himself and his tenants of his barony of Dalston common pasture in Westward (*le Westwarde*) in Allerdale, as previous bishops had from time immemorial. Thomas had claimed that the place was his own: neither the bishop nor his tenants had seisin unless by sufferance of the lords [of Cockermouth]; their ministers had sometimes prevented John de Kirkeby, the previous bishop, and his tenants from using the common pasture. On the intervention of friends, the parties had come to terms, *viz.* while Gilbert was bishop, he and his tenants would be allowed common pasture there without hindrance by Thomas and his heirs; escapes of their beasts in Westward will be judged as in olden times. After Gilbert's death or departure from his church, however, the position will revert to what it was in Bishop Kirkby's time. In the meantime, if Bishop Gilbert finds proof of seisin by earlier bishops and their

[404] See **279**.

tenants and shows it to Thomas and his heirs, it will be lawful for them to have common pasturage as if this indenture had not been made. Should Thomas die before Gilbert, his heirs will observe the agreement for Gilbert's life. Both sealed a part of the indenture and exchanged copies, at Thursby, Cumberland, 23 Oct. 1354.

549 Letters patent of Nicholas son of Alexander de Caldebek', Adam de Bolton, Thomas de Raynyngton, Richard Fox, Thomas son of Rayncok'. John Dobson of Langholm,[405] John Redheved, John Clerk' of Sowerby, John Whitcheved, William son of Simon, John son of Nicholas and John de Holgill, acknowledging that they are bound to pay the bishop £100 (which he lent them) at Rose next Whitsun [1355]. Under their seals, Rose, 26 Oct. 1354.

DEFESANTIA. Letters patent of the bishop. This bond will be void if Nicholas son of Alexander, Adam de Bolton, and the others above, or one of them, return the body of John del Vikers, for whom they have mainperned to the bishop, to the bishop's prison at Rose in the presence of bailiffs of his liberty [Fo.57ᵛ; p.114] two days before the day appointed for the king's justices to take assises and deliver Carlisle gaol; and that all Englishmen in England will be safe in their bodies and goods from the said John, unless he is defending himself, and that John neither in person nor at his bidding will interfere with the bishop's bailiffs in their administration of goods which were John's at the time he escaped from arrest and so forfeited them. Rose, 27 Oct. 1354.

550 Letters patent acknowledging receipt of 20 marks from the abbot and convent of Selby (dioc. York), due to the bishop for the term of St. Andrew 1354, in part payment of an annual pension of 40 marks by their written undertaking and condemnation before William [Zouche], archbishop of York. York, 30 Nov. 1354.[406]

551 Writ *dedimus potestatem* of Edward III for the bishop to receive the oath of William de Legh as sheriff and escheator of the county of Carlisle, to which and the custody of Carlisle castle he has been appointed (during pleasure) by letters patent, which are enclosed. Westminster, 10 Nov. 1354.[407]

Return. The writ and commissions were received at Rose, 24 Dec. 1354. As it has been known that William has been seriously ill for some time, the bishop sent to him in haste and has now been informed that his illness is so serious that he is incapable and his recovery unlikely.[408] The writ could thus not be executed and both commissions are returned. 26 Dec. [1354].

552 Similar writ for the oath of William Threlkeld, appointed sheriff of Cumberland, keeper of Carlisle castle and escheator of Cumberland and Westmorland during pleasure. Westminster, 16 Jan. 1355.[409]

Form of oath (in French) as sheriff and escheator [as in **292**, with addition,

---

[405] In Sebergham, now lost (*EPNS Cumberland*, I.151).

[406] Cf. dating of **63–6**.

[407] *CFR*, VI.409,410.

[408] William's will is dated 17 Nov. 1354 (**91**).

[409] *CFR*, VI.409,410.

after clause on writs: Fo.58; p.115] He will personally take and return escheats and inquests [as in 530].

Return. William's oath was received and the king's letters delivered. 4 Feb. [1355].

553   Note of licence for one year to Robert Jardyn of Corby (*Corteby*), senior, to make a quest for the fabric of Durham cathedral. 20 Feb. 1355.

554   Memorandum that William de Croft', Carmelite friar of Appleby,[410] presented by the prior-provincial of the order, was admitted to the office of preaching and hearing confessions in place of John de Haytefeld. 24 Feb. [1355].

555*   Mandate to the dean of Westmorland. Christopher de Lancastre was lately admonished(?)[411] before the bishop in Rose chapel to treat Joan as his lawful wife. Scorning these monitions, however, he has left her for frivolous and fictitious reasons. He is to be ordered to return to her within 12 days, treating her with marital affection, under pain of excommunication. If he persists in his wickedness, he is to be cited to explain his reasons before the bishop (or his commissary or commissaries) in Rose chapel on the next law day after 10 Feb., when the dean is to certify. Rose, 20 Jan. 1355.[412]

HIC INCIPIT ANNUS DOMINI MILLESIMUS CCC^mus QUINQUAGESIMUS QUINTUS ETC.

556   Note of licence for one year to Robert de Hull, proctor of the hospital of St. Lazarus, Jerusalem, to make a quest. 28 Mar. 1355.

557   Note of renewal for one year of the letters for William Bell, proctor for the fabric of the choir of Carlisle cathedral, as in the preceding folio [534]. Rose, 3 Apr. 1355.

558   The like for Hugh de Jar' for the hospital of St. Thomas of Acon, London, until 2 February, in the form of his letters for the quest for St. Anthony [535]. Rose, 11 July 1355.

559   Note of licence to Walter de Swetehopp, rector of Scaleby, to be absent for one year, farming his church. Rose, 12 May 1355.

560   The like to M. Henry de Sandford, rector of Crosby Garrett. Rose, 3 Sept. 1355.

561   [Fo.58ᵛ; p.116] (i) Commission of Thomas [Hatfield], bishop of Durham, for an exchange of benefices between Peter de Morland, rector of [Low] Dinsdale (*Dittensall*), and Thomas Roland, vicar of Torpenhow

---

[410] Ordained subdeacon, 1345 (*Reg. Kirkby*, I.164).
[411] Verb omitted.
[412] Another medieval hand has commented in the margin *Memorandum de bona littera*.

(*Torpennowe*),[413] sending the report of an enquiry by the archdeacon of Durham's official. Auckland (*Aukland*) castle, 24 Aug. 1355. (ii) Certificate to the bishop of Durham, returning the sealed inquisition. (iii) Institution of Thomas Roland of Appleby, chaplain, to Low Dinsdale church; presented by the prior and convent of Durham. Rose, 30 Aug. 1355.

562 Resignation by Robert Merk' of Crosby on Eden vicarage,[414] under his seal. Rose, 6 Sept. 1355.

563 (i) Collation to Peter de Morland, chaplain, of Torpenhow vicarage, in the exchange [**561**]. (ii) Archdeacon to induct. Rose, 30 Aug. 1355.

564 [Fo.59; p.117] (i) Dispensation to John de Schorton, clerk (dioc. Carlisle), as the son of unmarried parents, to be promoted to all orders and hold a benefice with cure of souls if he resides; quoting letters of Stephen [Aubert], cardinal priest of SS. John and Paul, penitentiary of Pope [Clement VI], dated Avignon, 8 Oct. 1351. After enquiring into his life and character, the bishop accordingly dispenses him. (ii) Note of grant to John of letters dimissory to all orders. Rose, 6 Sept. 1355.

565 (i) Collation to Roger de Ledys, chaplain, of Crosby on Eden vicarage, vacant by the resignation of Robert Merk'. (ii) Archdeacon to induct. Rose, 12 Sept. 1355.

566 (i) Resignation by Robert de Merton of Newbiggin church,[415] under his seal. Newbiggin, 13 Sept. 1355. (ii) Institution of Robert de Appilby, clerk, to the same church; presented by William de Crakanthorpp. (iii) Archdeacon to induct. Rose, 20 Sept. 1355.

567 Note of licence to Hugh de Jar' for the quest for the hospital of Saint-Antoine-de-Viennois; until Whitsun [1356]. 30 Sept. 1355.

568 ADMISSIO FRATRUM AD PREDICANDI OFFICIUM JUXTA FORMAM CONSTITUCIONIS. Note that the bishop admitted Richard de Swynesheved, guardian of the convent of friars minor, Carlisle, William de Kirkeby and Adam de Waldyngfeld of the same, [as preachers] in place of Robert de Shirewod, Thomas Fannell and John de Dalton, in accordance with the constitution *Super cathedram*.[416] n.d.

569 Writ of Edward III summoning the bishop to a parliament at Westminster on 12 Nov. 1355; [Fo.59ᵛ; p.118] also the prior of Carlisle and archdeacons (*sic*)

---

[413] Ordained acolyte as Thomas son of Roland de Appelby, 1332. The previous known institution to Torpenhow was of Thomas de Whytefeld, 1345 (*Reg. Kirkby*, I.15,162, no.782).

[414] His institution, since March 1354 (see **30**), is not recorded.

[415] The previous known institution was of M. William de Cundale, 1342, who died in 1350 (*Reg. Kirkby*, I.143, no.709; *BRUO*, I.528). See also **111**, **112**, **176**.

[416] See D. Knowles, *The Religious Orders in England* (Cambridge, 1948–59), 3 vols., I.186–7.

in person, and the cathedral chapter and diocesan clergy by proctors. Portsmouth, 20 Sept. 1355.[417]

570   Mandate to the official of Carlisle to execute this writ (received 31 October), certifying the bishop by 6 November. Rose, 31 Oct. 1355.

571   To the king. The bishop is unable to attend the parliament because he is engaged in business about the west march towards Scotland.[418] He therefore appoints Henry de Ingelby, canon of York, William de Burgh and M. John de Welton, clerks, as his proctors, with powers to treat with the prelates, magnates and proctors of the realm about its condition and defence, and to explain his absence. Rose, 1 Nov. 1355.

572*   Licence, at the request of William de Bolton, for him to marry Ellen daughter of Alexander de Moubray, kt., in any parish church and by any chaplain of his choice in the diocese, after banns have been called three times before eight or six men on Sundays and festivals of his choice.[419] Rose, 14 Nov. 1355.

573   Indulgence of 40 days for those contributing to, or assisting, the upkeep of Kirkby Thore bridge. Rose, 27 Jan. 1356.

574   Note that the bishop admitted Fr. Thomas de Skipwyth to the office of preacher, to hear confessions, etc., at the request of Robert de Deyncourt, of the friars preachers, Carlisle, who came with him. 24 Feb. 1356.

575   Licence (until next Easter) to William de Dacre, reader of the friars minor, Carlisle, as confessor and penitentiary.[420] Rose, 21 Feb. 1356.

576   [Fo.60; p.119] Letters patent appointing John de Dalston the bishop's attorney to collect fruits, tithes, rents, farms and debts in Northumberland, issuing receipts at need. Rose, 6 Mar. 1356.

577   Commission to the prior of Carlisle to deputise for the bishop in the cathedral on Ash Wednesday [9 March. As in **87**]. Rose, 8 Mar. 1356.

578   Note of licence to John, vicar of Penrith, to hear confessions by his parishioners until Easter [24 April], except in reserved cases, as in the letter for Fr. William de Dacre in the last folio [**575**]. 8 Mar. 1356.

---

[417] As in *CCR 1354–60*, 233; but on 22 Oct. this parliament was prorogued to 23 Nov. (ibid., 234).
[418] On 18 July and 23 Nov. 1355 he was appointed to commissions to defend the marches against an expected Scottish invasion (*Rot. Scot.*, I.779, 782). His licence to crenellate Rose was granted 25 June 1355 (*CPR 1354–8*, 252).
[419] This entry invites speculation. After Alexander, the lordship of Bolton was held by John Neville of Raby (Nicolson & Burn, II.148).
[420] As in **20** but omitting usury.

579 Commission to M. William [de Salkeld], rector of a mediety of Aikton, John Boon and John Maresshall, chaplains, to claim and receive clerks accused before the king's justices of gaol delivery in Carlisle. Rose, 13 Mar. 1356.

580 Letters patent. Nicholas son of Alexander de Caldebek', Adam de Bolton, Thomas de Raynyngton, Richard Fox, Thomas son of Rayncok', John Dobsone of Langholm, John Redeheved, John Clerk' of Sowerby, John Whiteheved, William son of Simon, John son of Nicholas and John de Holgill are bound to pay the bishop £100 for a loan, as in their bond [549]. The bishop has granted that if they pay him or his attorney £10 at Rose, half on 27 March next and half on 3 May, the bond for £100 will be cancelled. Rose, 16 Mar. 1356.

581 Note of licence to Richard [de Askeby], rector of Uldale, to hear the confessions of his parishioners until Easter [etc., as in **575**]. 23 Mar. 1356.

582* Mandate to the deans, rectors, vicars and parish chaplains of the diocese. Many goods and sums of money have been bequeathed to the ruinous fabric of Eden bridge between Carlisle and Stanwix, but concealed by unknown persons careless of their souls and the danger to inhabitants of Carlisle and surrounding villages. The bishop has appointed Henry Martyn, rector of Stapleton, as receiver of these bequests; he has given surety to render true accounts. Monitions are to be published, as he requires, ordering delivery to him of these sums, under pain of excommunication. Enquiries are to be made for the names of offenders and the bishop informed. Rose, 12 May 1356.

583 [Fo.60ᵛ; p.120] Letters patent granting indulgence of 40 days for contributions to the upkeep of Eden bridge between Carlisle and Stanwix. Rose, 12 May 1356.

584 To John [Thoresby], archbishop of York. The bishop is unable to attend the provincial council on 3 June.[421] He therefore appoints Masters John de Heriz, Adam de Caldebek' and William de Ragenhill, clerks, as his proctors, with powers to take his part in business about ecclesiastical liberty and the defence of the realm, and to explain his absence. Rose, 28 May 1356.

585 Note of letters dimissory for Richard Clerk' of Warcop to be ordained priest. 6 June 1356.

586 Similar note for William Ryngrose of Crosthwaite to be ordained deacon and priest. 8 June 1356.

587* Mandate to the dean of Carlisle and parish chaplains of St. Mary's and St. Cuthbert's, Carlisle. Richard de Ragarth, clerk, was defamed before Sir Thomas de Seton and his fellow justices of the king at Carlisle of stealing a steer price 4s. from Richard Doste of Middlesceugh at Middlesceugh on 6 Nov. 1353, and was delivered to the bishop's prison. He humbly claimed before the bishop that he was innocent and sued for canonical purgation. The bishop has ordered

[421] See **125**.

an enquiry to learn his character and reputation in his neighbourhood and whether he was guilty. Proclamations are to be made in the churches of St. Mary's, St. Cuthbert's and Dalston, Carlisle market place and other public places, that any objectors to his purgation are to appear before the bishop or his commissaries in Dalston church on 11 June; a report is required in good time. Rose, 15 May 1356.

588 [Fo.61; p.121] Letters patent. Richard de Ragarth, clerk, was accused before Thomas de Seton and other justices of gaol delivery (as above). Proclamations were made for objectors to appear on 11 June. None came. He was then purged, in the bishop's presence in Dalston church, with [the oaths of] twelve rectors, vicars, priests and clerks, and his good name restored. Rose, 11 June 1356.

589 Note of letters dimissory for John de Crosseby to be ordained deacon and priest. 16 June 1356.

590 Bond of John de Dalston[422] that he owes the bishop £17 17s. 8d., received as a loan, to be paid to the bishop or his attorney at Rose on 8 September. Rose, 15 June 1356.
  Defeasance. This bond will be void if John pays £8 18s. 10d. on 8 September. Rose, 16 June 1356.
  Note that John was bound to the bishop in £18 6s. 8d. to be paid in halves on 15 August and 25 December next. Same date.
  Note that the bishop granted that the bond will be void if John pays £9 3s. 4d. at the same terms. 16 June 1356.

591 INDICTAMENTUM RICARDI DE RAGARTH CLERICI.[423] Richard de Ragarth was indicted before Sir Thomas de Seton and his fellow justices of assise[424] at Carlisle of stealing a steer (price 4s.) of Richard Doste of Middlesceugh on Wednesday *ut supra anno ut supra* [i.e. 6 Nov. 1353].

592 Note that Ivo de Derlyngton, of the friars minor, Carlisle, was admitted to the office of preacher in place of Richard Hawan. Rose, 8 Oct. 1356.

593 Note of licence for one year to Robert Jardyn for the quest for the fabric of Durham cathedral. 20 Dec. 1356.

594 [Fo.61ᵛ; p.122] Letter of Edward III under the privy seal (in French). According to a petition of the people of Carlisle (*Cardoil*) presented by the mayor, their walls, gates and other *forces* are dilapidated. The king has therefore granted them twelve oaks from Inglewood Forest and 100 marks to help with repairs. These good people have asked the king's council to reinforce the city.[425]

---

[422] See **576**.
[423] This is probably a copy from the court's record.
[424] The date of the offence is given here but underlined to cancel.
[425] An apparent reference to a petition to the chancellor, which gives credence to Thomas de Alanby, the mayor (*Calendar of Documents relating to Scotland*, ed. J. Bain (1881–8), 4

As it is in the march near the king's enemies, he is anxious that it should be secure. He trusts the bishop's judgment (*sen*) and advice, and orders him to call a meeting of the prior, mayor and leading people of Carlisle (*Kardoill*). They are to appoint two or three suitable persons to survey the progress of these works and ensure that this money and other assistance are well used, without delay. The bishop is to receive oaths of these deputies for good and prompt performance. Westminster, 7 Mar. 1354.

595 Memorandum that on 3 Apr. 1354, in the chapter house of Carlisle cathedral,[426] deputies were elected to survey the defects of walls and gates, as follow: Thomas Maleman and John Maresshall, from the first ward (*custodia*), *viz.* Botchergate (*Bochardgate*); Robert Groute and John de Musgrave, from the second ward, *viz.* Caldewgate; and Robert de Tybay and Gilbert Peper, from the third ward, *viz.* Rickergate (*Ricardgate*). Each swore on the Gospels to act faithfully.

Afterwards, on 30 Dec. [1354], in the chamber of the prior of Carlisle, the bishop appointed Thomas de Alanby and William de Arthuret to supervise [the deputies], replacing any who were insufficiently diligent with others more useful, as and when need arose; on which Thomas and William were sworn on the Gospels.

596 Letter of Edward III under the privy seal (in French). The sheriff of Cumberland was ordered to pay, from the issues of the county, for repair of the gateway of Carlisle castle and its brattices, and other defects inside the castle, under the supervision of the bishop or his deputy. The bishop is asked to survey these defects and give advice on their repair and their least cost, and testify whether the sheriff's expenses are reasonable. Westminster, 12 July 1356.

597 Writ *dedimus potestatem* of Edward III for the bishop to receive the oath of Robert Tilliol as sheriff and escheator of Cumberland,[427] to which he has been appointed (during pleasure) by letters patent. Westminster, 10 Nov. 1356.

Memorandum that Robert took this oath before the bishop in the chapter house of Carlisle cathedral on 10 December (quoting the form of the oath). [Fo.62; p.123] Return. The oath was taken and letters delivered. 10 Dec. 1356.

598 Letter of Edward III under the privy seal (in French) to the bishop and prior of Carlisle. He recently ordered William de Threlkeld, the former sheriff of Cumberland, to pay £40 from the issues of the county to repair the gates, walls and brattices of Carlisle castle, as in his letter [**596**]. He has left office without spending the money or attending to the works. Order to examine his account for this business and his reasonable costs in it. If any of the sum of £40 remains, he is to be required to deliver it to Robert Tilliol, now sheriff, for these repairs. Report what William has spent on them and whether he can be allowed for these

vols., III.290, no.1590). Dr. Summerson intends to print the above text (see note to **90**).

[426] For the bishop's presence, see **530**.

[427] Also of Westmorland, according to the margin; as in *CFR*, VII.20.

costs in his account at the Exchequer for his term as sheriff. Westminster, 16 Nov. 1356.

599 Licence[428] for John Boone, John de Brounfeld, Robert de Bolton and Thomas de Suthayk', chaplains, proctors of the prior and chapter of Carlisle, to collect alms for building the choir; with an indulgence for 40 days; valid for one year. Rose, 18 Jan. 1357.

600 Memorandum that John del Blamyre and Thomas del Cote mainperned for John Reson that he would [surrender to?] the bishop's prison whenever he was called before 1 August, under penalty of 40s., so that he will answer in the bishop's court to what is charged against him. They were both judicially condemned to this effect by M. John de Welton, in the chapel at Rose, 14 Mar. 1357.

601 [Fo.62ᵛ; p.124] Writ of Edward III. He had ordered the bishop to appoint a collector of the first part of a tenth [as in **149**]. The bishop has not yet reported the collector's name to the Exchequer, and is ordered to certify it by 17 April, as he values the king's honour and would save himself from harm. Wilford by Westminster, 2 Mar. 1357.

602 Letters patent. As the bishop is unable to attend the provincial council called by John [Thoresby], archbishop of York, in York cathedral on 19 May,[429] he appoints Masters John Heriz, advocate of the court of York, Adam de Caldebek', official of Carlisle, and William de Ragenhill, his familiar clerk, as proctors in business of the estate and liberty of the church, diocese and province of York, and defence of the realm, as expounded by the archbishop, and to agree to the council's ordinances, and also explain his absence. His inn, London, 12 May 1357.

603 ACQUIETANCIA SUPER SOLUCCIONE EXPENSARUM CARDINALIUM. Letters patent of William de Swafeld', canon of the chapel of St. Mary and Holy Angels, York, appointed by the archbishop to receive payments in Carlisle diocese for expenses of John [Jofrevi], bishop of Elne [*Elnen'*], and Androin [de la Roche], abbot of Cluny, nuncios to England from the Holy See;[430] these are due from benefices assessed for the tenth at the rate of one farthing in a mark. He has received 15s. ½d. from Bishop Gilbert, including his own portion. Under the seal of the official of the court of York, with his consent, York, 3 Sept. 1355.

604* Letters patent. William atte Hall, rector of Bowness, former rector of Kirkconnel, in Glasgow diocese, was charged before the bishop in that he had usurped and received revenues of Kirkconnel church before his institution and

---

[428] In similar terms to **534***; variations in **599** are shown in the Appendix.
[429] See **167**. The bishop was then attending parliament (see **155, 164, 167**).
[430] See *CPL*, III.616; Lunt, *Financial Relations*, 648–9, which gives the sum as '£5 15s. ½d'.

induction. He denied the charge, and from witnesses and information the bishop was convinced of his innocence and dismissed him from further impeachment.[431] Rose, 8 Aug. 1357.[432]

[431] This accusation may explain why William, although instituted to Bowness in 1354 (**36**), sought confirmation by provision (by the legate, Cardinal Talleyrand) to the same church (*CPP*, I.306; *Accounts*, ed. Lunt, 139). See also **325**.

[432] This is the last folio of the quire from Fo.53 (**518**). The last entry above ends leaving a lower margin of the usual depth. **604** is the last entry in Welton's register shown in the table of contents (Fo.vii^v).

605 [Fo.63; p.125][433] Dalston church, 8 March 1354.

Acolytes
Fr. Thomas Waryn of York, hermit, by letters dimissory of M. Robert de
Beverlaco, canon of York, vicar-general of John [Thoresby], archbishop of York
Richard de Walcote, Austin friar, Penrith
Adam de Dunsford, friar minor, Carlisle
William Cort', friar preacher, Carlisle
Richard de Langrik' ⎫
Alan de Midelham   ⎬ monks of Holm Cultram
Henry de Neuton   ⎭
John de Kyrkby, canon of Shap
Henry de Karghowe
Robert de Burgham
Stephen de Melborne
John de Cleveland
Adam Armestrang'
John de Holme
Adam Broune of Carlisle

Subdeacons
William de Ebor', rector of Bolton
Thomas de Whynfell, title of patrimony
Robert de Aplesthorp, York diocese, by letters dimissory of M. Robert de
Beverl', canon of York, vicar-general of Archbishop [Thoresby], title of papal
provision (*ad titulum provisionis et gracie per sedem apostolicam sibi factarum*)
Thomas son of John Tailor (*Cissor*) of Appleby, title of patrimony
John de Lythom, York diocese, by letters dimissory of said vicar-general, title of
chapter of York
John Strako', title of patrimony
John de Brounfeld, York diocese, by letters dimissory of archbishop, title
[omitted]
Thomas de Esyngwald ⎫ friars preachers, Carlisle
Thomas de Skelton   ⎭

Deacons
Richard de Norton by Campsall (*Campsale*), York diocese, by letters of said
vicar-general with the registrar (*remantes penes registrum*), title of prior and convent
of Monk Bretton (*Munkbreton*)
John Rose of Dalston, title of patrimony
John son of John Whitstones of Thornhill, York diocese, by letters of said vicar-
general, title of prioress and nuns of Kirklees (*Kirklyghes*) with the registrar
William de Wyrkesworth, Coventry and Lichfield diocese, by letters dimissory,
title of abbot[434] and convent of Felley (*Sallay*) with the registrar

---

[433] These lists are in two columns.
[434] *Recte* prior.

William de Askrigg', York diocese, by letters of said vicar-general, title [omitted]
John de Abbotesle, Lincoln diocese, by letters dimissory, title of prior and convent of St. Andrew's by York
Thomas de Wateby, title of patrimony
John de Graystok ⎫
William de Dalston ⎬ canons of Carlisle
John de Crauncewyk', Carmelite friar, Appleby
Robert de Grisley, friar minor, Carlisle
John de Hames, friar preacher, Carlisle

Priests
Roger de Ripon, York diocese, by letters of said vicar-general, title of a chantry in Ripon
John de Normanton, York diocese, by letters of said vicar-general, title of prior and convent of St. Andrew's by York
William de Wyntryngham, Lincoln diocese, by letters dimissory, title of abbot and convent of Whalley (*Whallay*)
Robert de Thirlkeld', title of patrimony
William de Morland, canon of Shap
William de Wynyhard, canon of Lanercost

606 Rose chapel, 29 March 1354.

Subdeacons
M. Richard de Wysebech, vicar of Kirkby Lonsdale, York diocese, by letters dimissory of M. Robert de Beverlaco, vicar-general of Archbishop [Thoresby]
Richard Short', York diocese, by letters as above, title 5 marks from abbot and convent of Furness (*Furneys*)
Thomas Waryn, hermit, York diocese, by letters as above, title of prior and convent of Kirkham

Deacons [sic]
Thomas de Whynfell, title of patrimony

Priests
John son of John Whitstones [as in **605**]
John Roose of Dalston, title of patrimony
Richard de Boulton, canon of Conishead
John de Crauncewyk', Carmelite friar, Appleby

607 Rose chapel, 12 April 1354.

[Subdeacons]
Alan de Midelham, monk of Holm Cultram
Richard de Langrig', monk [of the same]

608   [Fo.63ᵛ; p.126] Dalston church, 20 December 1354.

Acolytes
Richard son of William, son of Richard de Warthecopp'
Robert de Levyngton
John Baron of Bolton
John de Regle
John de Dighton, York diocese, by letters dimissory

Subdeacons
John de Clifland, sufficient title (*de quo reputavit se contentum*)
Thomas de Kirkandres, [title as above]
Adam Broune, [title as above]
Henry de Neuton, monk of Holm Cultram

Deacons
Thomas son of John Taillor of Appleby, sufficient title
John Strakor', [title as above]
Richard Short, York diocese, by letters of Robert de Beverl' etc. as above, title of annual pension of 5 marks from abbot and convent of Furness
John de Brounfeld, York diocese, by letters dimissory, title of prior and chapter of Carlisle
Richard de Langrik' ⎱ [monks] of Holm Cultram
Alan de Midelham ⎰
Thomas de Skelton ⎫
William de Cliff ⎬ friars minor[435]
Thomas de Esyngwald ⎭

Priests
William de Dalston ⎱ canons of Carlisle
John de Graystok' ⎰
Henry de Muskham, friar minor
Thomas de Whynfell, sufficient title
Thomas de Wateby, title of annual pension of 5 marks from Adam Parvyng'

609   Dalston church, 19 March 1356.[436]

Acolytes
M. Walter de Helton
Richard de Thirneby
Thomas de Louthre
Richard de Crosseby Ravenswath
John de Crosseby
Thomas de Penreth
Thomas Morell of Dacre
William son of John de Crosthwayt

[435] Cf. **605**.
[436] Fear of a Scottish invasion doubtless explains why there were no ordinations in 1355 (Summerson, *Medieval Carlisle*, I.310; see also **571**).

Subdeacons
Gerlac called de Clave, vicar of Gilling (*Gillyng*), archdeaconry of Richmond, by
letters dimissory of M. Thomas de Bucton, canon of Wells, vicar-general of John
[Thoresby], archbishop of York
M. Walter de Helton, title of annual rent of 5 marks from abbot and convent
of Shap
Richard de Thirneby, title of papal provision[437]
Richard Clerk of Warcop, title of annual rent of 5 marks from William de
Warthcopp'
John de Revegill, title of annual rent of 5 marks from William de Threlkeld, kt.

Deacons
William de Tyndale, friar minor, Carlisle
John de Holme, title of annual rent of 5 marks from Sir Robert Tylioll

Priests
Richard de les Lathes[438] ⎱
Alan de Midelham   ⎰ monks of Holm Cultram
John de Dighton, York diocese, by letters dimissory, title of annual rent of 5
marks from John de Orreton, kt.
John de Crosseby in Allerdale, title of annual rent of 5 marks from Thomas
Hardegill

610 Rose chapel, 9 April 1356.

Subdeacons
William Ryngrose, title of annual rent of 5 marks from Sir John de Orreton
John de Crosseby, title of annual rent of 5 marks from Sir R[ichard] de Denton

Deacons
M. Walter de Helton, title of abbot and convent of Shap
Richard de Thirneby, title of papal provision
Richard de Warthecop, title of William de Warthecopp'
John de Revegill, title of 5 marks from Sir W[illiam] de Threlkeld

611 [Fo.64; p.127] Rose chapel, 25 June 1356.

Deacons
Gerlac called de Clave, vicar of Gilling [etc. as in **609**]
William Ryngerose, title of John de Orreton, kt.

Priest
M. Walter de Helton, title of abbot and convent of Shap

[437] See **110**.
[438] Cf. Langrik previously.

612   Rose chapel, 24 September 1356.

Subdeacons
John de Kendall, Austin friar, Penrith
Thomas de Penreth, title of prior and convent of Warter

Priests
Ralph de Fethirstanhalgh, Austin friar, Penrith
Hugh de Yarum, by letters dimissory of archbishop of York, title of Robert de Tibay
William Ryngros, title of Sir John de Orreton

613   Rose chapel, 23 September 1357.

Acolytes
Henry de Preston   } friars preachers
Stephen de Acclom }

Subdeacon
Henry de Preston, friar preacher

Deacon
John de Grandon, vicar of Crosby on Eden

614   Memorandum that on 31 December 1357, *viz.* the Sunday after Christmas, on the festival of St. Silvester the pope, the bishop ordained the following as acolytes in Rose chapel:[439]
Richard de Hoton, rector of Greystoke
William de Sandford
William Gray

615   Rose chapel, 17 March 1358.

Subdeacons [sic]
Richard de Hoton Roef, rector of Greystoke

Priests [sic]
John de Grandon, vicar of Crosby on Eden

616   Rose chapel, 26 May 1358.

Deacons [sic]
Richard de Hoton, rector of Greystoke

617   Memorandum that on 15 September 1352, Thomas de Kirkpatrik' of Glasgow diocese was ordained priest by John de Kirkeby, late bishop of Carlisle, in Dalston church, with title from Richard de Berwys, as is sufficiently proved.[440]

---

[439] This heading is decorated on both sides, with a drawing of 2 vine leaves in the margin.
[440] Kirkby's register after June 1347 has not survived; he died by 3 Dec.1352.

618 [Fo.64ᵛ; p.128] Rose chapel, 22 September 1358.

Subdeacon
Stephen de Meborn, title of abbot and convent of Shap

Priests
Richard de Hoton, rector of Greystoke
John de Tanfeld, friar minor

619 Memorandum that on 19 September 1360, in Rose chapel, the bishop ordained Robert Paye, rector of Applegarthtown (*Appilgarth*), Glasgow diocese, showing letters dimissory, as acolyte and subdeacon to the title of his church.

620 The like for John de Souleby, rector of [Great] Musgrave, as priest. Rose chapel, 27 March 1361.

621 The like for Thomas Goldesmyth of Carlisle as acolyte, and Robert Pay, rector of Applegarthtown [etc. as in **619**] as deacon. Rose chapel, 22 May 1361.

622 Dalston church, 18 December 1361.

Acolytes
John de Overton ⎫
Adam del Gill ⎪
William de Karlo'⁴⁴¹ ⎬ canons of Carlisle
Thomas de Slegill ⎪
Robert de Parco ⎪
Robert de Edenhale ⎭
John de Hextildesham, canon of Lanercost
Henry Bosevill ⎫ friars preachers, Carlisle
Adam de Brigham ⎭
John Whyteheved of Aspatria
Walter de Eston
John de Arthureth
Thomas de Anandia
Nicholas Lambe of Dalston
Henry Best', canon of Shap

Subdeacons
Thomas de Karlo'⁴⁴² [and the other six above canons of Carlisle]
William de Sutton ⎫
William de Stokesley ⎬ canons of Shap
Henry le Best' ⎭
John de Hextildesham, canon of Lanercost

---

⁴⁴¹ Reappears as William Colt when ordained deacon, 1363, and at visitation, 1366 (Reg. Appleby, fos.13, 78; *VCH Cumberland*, II.146).
⁴⁴² Probably the Thomas Goldesmyth of **621**: a bracket links him to the six canons. He reappears as Thomas Orfeuer when ordained deacon, 1363; also at visitation, 1366 (Reg. Appleby, fos.13, 78).

Henry Bosevill   }
Adam de Brigham   } friars preachers
Robert de Louthre of Crosby, title of 5 marks from William de Arthureth
Thomas de Louthre, title of 5 marks from William Lenglis, kt.

Deacons
William del Lynehouse of Aspatria, title of 100s. from Thomas de Hardegill, junior
John de Stokdale, title of 5 marks from Thomas de Alanby
John de Golbergh, title of 5 marks from Thomas Lenglys, kt.

Priests
Henry Scarlett' of Penrith, title of prioress and convent of Wilberfoss (*Wilberfosse*), York diocese
Adam Maresshall of Aspatria, title of 5 marks of John de Dalston[443]

---

[443] This list may have continued on a folio now lost; but it is unlikely that there were ordinations in 1362 because of the plague.

APPENDIX OF TEXTS

Here follow original texts of the entries with asterisks following their numbers in the calendar. Additional information supplied in footnotes to the calendar is not repeated here, where footnotes concern only textual matters. Some of the texts have been reduced with references to preceding texts in the appendix.

Transcripts are preceded by references to folio and page numbers of the manuscript, followed by marginal titles in capital letters. All words except proper names have been extended as they are spelt in classical Latin; the manuscript's preference for other spellings, most regularly in the use of 'c' in place of the classical 't', has been followed where it occurs; but when 'i' and 'j' are consonants they are rendered as 'j' and 'v'. The editor is also responsible for capital letters and punctuation.

7

[Fo.1; p. 1] COMMISSIO VICARII GENERALIS. Universis Christi fidelibus ad quos presentes littere pervenerint Gilbertus permissione divina Karliolii' episcopus salutem in omnium salvatore. Nostrum siquidem pastorale officium salubrius excercere dinoscimur si viros fidedignos litterarum sciencia preditos ac in agendis providos et expertos in parte nostre solicitudinis assumamus. Hinc est quod nos quibusdam arduis prepediti extra nostram diocesim Karl' in remotis agentes, venerabilem et religiosum virum dominum abbatem monasterii de Holmecoltran nostre diocesis, de cujus fidelitate et industria plenam in domino fiduciam obtinemus, ordinamus facimus et constituimus nostrum in spiritualibus vicarium generalem, dantes et concedentes eidem specialem potestatem presentaciones ad ecclesias vicarias hospitalia capellas cantarias seu alia beneficia ecclesiastica quecumque dicte nostre diocesis vacancia seu vacatura factas vel faciendas admittendi et super eisdem ut est moris inquirendi, inquisicionesque hujusmodi examinandi ac presentatos hujusmodi in ipsis ecclesiis vicariis hospitalibus capellis cantariis ac aliis beneficiis ecclesiasticis quibuscumque instituendi et institutos hujusmodi in corporalem possessionem inducendi inducive faciendi, necnon decanos et alios ministros pro excercicio et conservacione jurisdictionis nostre ecclesiastice nobis necessarios ordinandi et preficiendi, ipsosque sic ordinatos et prefectos prout expedire videbitur amovendi, ceteraque omnia et singula faciendi et expediendi que ad hujusmodi vicariatus officium pertinent quovismodo; collationibus beneficiorum quorumcumque vacancium seu vacaturorum ad nostram collationem presentacionem seu provisionem nostram spectancium exceptis et nobis specialiter reservatis. Ad que omnia et singula facienda expedienda et exequenda eidem vicario nostro tenore presencium concedimus vices nostras cum cujuslibet cohercionis canonice potestate. In quorum omnium testimonium atque fidem presentes litteras nostras fieri fecimus has patentes, quas nostri sigilli appensione fecimus communiri. Datum Ebor' decimo die mensis Julii anno domini Millesimo CCC^mo liii° et nostre consecracionis primo.

11

PRO FRUCTIBUS ECCLESIE DE BOLTON SEQUESTRANDIS POST EJUSDEM RECTORIS INGRESSUM IN RELIGIONE. Salutem graciam et benedictionem. Carissime, de immensa vestrarum benevolencie ac diligencie affluencia quas in negociis nostris hactenus impendistis et impenditis hiis diebus vobis regraciamur et merito toto corde. Et eas in hiis que suplere sufficimus parati sumus et erimus votis vestris. Ceterum quia rector ecclesie de Bolton nostre diocesis religionem ingredi in proximo se disponit, cujus ecclesie custodia et regimen post ipsius ingressum in omnibus jure ordinario ad nos dinoscitur pertinere, vos rogamus quatinus quamcicius super prefati rectoris ingressu hujusmodi cerciorari poteritis, fructus et proventus ejusdem ecclesie ex officio vestro et vice nostra sequestrari faciatis et arcius custodiri, aliquem capellanum ydoneum ibidem deputantes qui dicte ecclesie et ipsius parochianis deservire valeat in divinis. In Christo diucius valeatis. Scriptum Ebor' quarto die Septembris.

12

ITEM. ALIA LITTERA DE EADEM MATERIA. Precarisime domine et amice, exactam diligenciam et solicitam quam nostris impenditis in agendis ut convenit recensentes, non solummodo et merito contentamur set vobis acciones referimus graciarum. Verumquia rector ecclesie de Bolton nostre diocesis curam animarum per se vel alium excercendam jam per nonnulla tempora dereliquit nec ad eandem sic regimine desolatam se disponitur amodo reversurum, sicuti vestrarum litterarum series representat. Satagens nichilominus non absque consciencie scrupulo vellus percipere deserti gregis, sequestrum in fructibus et proventibus dicte ecclesie taliter desolate per vos auctoritate nostra interpositum ac deputacionem custodie [capellano qui?][1] eidem ecclesie et ipsius parochianis interim deservire habeat in diem rata inducere volumus et observari, quousque idem rector intencione et opere rectorem se exhibens dicte ecclesie faciat modo debito deserviri. Processu insuper quem contra occupantes animalia vasa instrumenta et alia utensilia que ad nos pertinent et debeant pertinere hactenus inchoastis, continuare velitis viis et modis quibus consulcius vobis videbitur expedire. In prosperitate diutina arrideat vobis salus. Scriptum etc.

14

[Fo.1; p. 1] COMMISSIO AD CONVOCANDUM CLERUM DIOCESIS KARLII' PRO SUBSIDIO DOMINO EPISCOPO CONCEDENDO ETC. G. etc. venerabili et religioso viro domino .. abbati de Holmecoltran nostre diocesis ac magistro Johanni de Welton clerico juris perito salutem in auctore salutis. Quia super quibusdam urgentibus et

[1] MS. faded.

arduis negociis nos statum nostrum ac ecclesie nostre Karleolii concernentibus cum priore et capitulo dicte ecclesie nostre ac abbatibus et prioribus tam exemptis quam non exemptis, necnon archidiacono nostro Karlii' rectoribus vicariis et ceteris personis beneficia[2] ecclesiastica infra dictam diocesim nostram obtinentibus habere decrevimus colloquium et tractatum; nosque variis et arduis negociis prepediti quominus expedicioni premissorum interesse personaliter valeamus, ac de vestra industria circumspecta plenius confidentes, ad convocandum dictos priorem capitulum abbates priores archidiaconum rectores vicarios et ceteras personas ecclesiasticas ad certos dies et loca coram vobis et vestrum alterutro, ac presidendum et interessendum pro nobis et nomine nostro diebus et locis in convocacione per vos hac occasione citacione nostro nomine facienda, ac ad exponendum eisdem personis sic convocatis negocia hujusmodi ipsarumque deliberacionem providam et consensum in et super premissis requirendos audiendos et admittendos, ceteraque omnia et singula facienda et expedienda que premissa concernunt seu concernere poterunt quovismodo, vobis conjunctim et divisim committimus vices nostras cum cohercionis canonice potestate. Valete. Datum apud Eton ultimo die mensis Novembris anno domini [MCCC] liii°; et nostre consecracionis primo.

20

[Fo.2; p. 3] LICENCIA PRO FRATRE ROBERTO DEYN[COURT] AD AUDIENDUM CONFESSIONES. G. etc. dilecto filio fratri Roberto Deyncourt ordinis fratrum predicatorum Karlii' sacre theologie professori salutem graciam et benedictionem. Animarum saluti subditorum nostrorum quantum cum deo poterimus prospicere cupientes, vobis de cujus consciencie puritate plenam in domino fiduciam obtinemus, ad audiendum confessiones quorumcumque parochianorum nostrorum vobis in foro penitencie confiteri volencium et eosdem a peccatis que vobis confessi fuerint absolvendos et ad injungendum eisdem pro modo culparum penitencias salutares eciam in casibus nobis a jure specialiter reservatis, jurum et libertatum nostrorum ac ecclesie nostre beate Marie Karlii' violatoribus ac jurisdictionem nostram eciam impedientibus,[3] sanctimoniales rapientibus vel cum eis carnaliter commiscentibus, perjuris eciam in assisis et indictamentis in causis matrimonialibus et divorcii necnon ubi de exheredacione agitur vel amissione vite vel membrorum sive majoris partis substantie hominis, ac crimine usurarie utentibus dumtaxat exceptis, licenciam tenore presencium concedimus specialem, quam ultra octabas instantis festi Pasche nolumus perdurare. Valete. Datum in manerio nostro de Rosa tercio die mensis Marcii anno domini supradicto.

23

[Fo.2; p. 3] PREFECTIO OFFICIALIS IN DIOCESI KARLII'. G. etc. dilecto nobis in Christo magistro Nicholao de Whiteby clerico juris perito salutem in autore

---

[2] MS. *personis ecclesiasticis* (cancelled) *beneficia*
[3] Interlined from *ac jurisdictionem*

salutis. De vestris fidelitate et industria circumspecta plenius confidentes, ad cognoscendum procedendum statuendum diffiniendum et exequendum in omnibus causis et negociis inter quoscumque subditos nostros nostre diocesis qualitercumque introducendis vel ad presens pendentibus indecisis, ac ad inquirendum corrigendum et puniendum quorumcumque subditorum dicte nostre diocesis crimina et excessus, ceteraque omnia et singula expedienda facienda et excercenda que in premissis et circa ea necessaria fuerint seu eciam oportuna, vos officialem nostrum in dicta nostra diocesi preficimus et tenore presencium deputamus vobisque vices nostras in hac parte committimus cum cujuslibet cohercionis canonice potestate. Valete. Datum [Rose, 1 Mar. 1354].

25

[Fo.2; p. 3] LICENCIA CONCESSA INCOLIS ET INHABITATORIBUS VILLE DE KIRKLE-VYNGTON DIRIMENDI EXTERIORES ECCLESIE DE KIRKELEVYNGTON ET IN LOCO INTERIORI AD FORTIFICACIONEM DICTE ECCLESIE CONSTRUENDAM ETC.[4] G. etc. dilectis filiis incolis et inhabitatoribus ville de Kirklevyngton nostre diocesis salutem [*etc.*]. Plurimorum relacione nuper nobis innotuit fidedigna quod ecclesia vestra parochialis de Kirklevyngton antedicta magnam minuatur ruinam et periculosam propter ejus latitudinem hiis diebus et de majori verisimiliter indies[5] formidatur nisi hujusmodi ruine congruis remediis celerius objicitur, fuimusque ex parte vestra cum instancia requisiti ut ad parietes alarum exteriorum dicte ecclesie dirimendos et in loco interiori ad fortificacionem ejusdem ecclesie construendam vobis licenciam concedere dignaremur. Nos igitur peticiones vestras hujusmodi tanquam justas et legitimas amplectentes et eo presertim quod reparacio hujusmodi ad majorem securitatem conveniencium in dicta ecclesia cedere dinoscitur evidenter, vobis ad premissa facienda prout ad laudem et honorem dei ac utilitatem et soliditatem dicte ecclesie magis videbitur expedire licenciam tenore presencium concedimus specialem. In cujus rei etc. Datum [Rose, 13 Mar. 1354].

32

[Fo.3; p. 5] COMMISSIO AD PETENDUM SUBSIDIUM A CLERO DECANATUS KARLII' DOMINO EPISCOPO CONCESSUM PRO PRIMO TERMINO SOLUCIONIS EJUSDEM. G. etc. dilecto filio decano nostro Karl' salutem [*etc.*]. Cum nuper prior et capitulum ecclesie nostre Karlii' necnon abbates priores rectores vicarii cetereque persone ecclesiastice tam exempte quam non exempte beneficia ecclesiastica infra nostram diocesim obtinentes in supportacionem onerum nobis et ecclesie nostre Karlii' predicte multipliciter incumbencium eisdem personis ecclesiasticis ex parte nostra nuper plenius expositorum certum subsidium bonorum suorum spiritualium et temporalium solvendum ad certos futuros terminos concesserant graciose; nos de tuis fidelitate et industria circumspecta plenius

---

[4] Much of this summary is indistinct, but is supplied from the table of contents (fo.ii).
[5] Interlined.

confidentes, ad petendum exigendum colligendum recipiendum et fideliter conservandum totam pecuniam de dicto subsidio infra decanatum tuum pro primo termino solucionis ejusdem, videlicet ad festum Pasche proximo jam futurum vel ad ultimum infra octavas ejusdem, qualitercumque provenientem et nobis debitam tibi tenore presencium vices nostras committimus cum cujuslibet cohercionis canonice potestate; proviso quod de pecunia racione subsidii hujusmodi per te recipienda nobis fidele ratiocinium reddas nobisque singillatim de nominibus solvencium in hac parte ac non solvencium, si qui fuerint in eventum, ac omni eo quod feceris et inveneris in premissis infra quindecim dies dictum festum Pasche proximo secuturos distincte et aperte constare facias litteris tuis patentibus habentibus hunc tenorem. Vale. Datum [Rose, 29 Mar. 1354].

33

[Fo.3; p. 5] CITACIO CONTRA PRIOREM ET CAPITULUM KARL' AD ALLEGANDUM ET PROPONENDUM SIQUOD CANONICUM HABUERINT CONTRA ROBERTUM THIRNBEY PAUPERUM PRESBITERUM ET GRACIAM PER SEDEM APOSTOLICAM SIBI FACTAM. G. etc. executor seu provisor gracie Roberto Thirnbey pauperi presbitero de beneficio ecclesiastico spectante communiter vel divisim ad collationem vel presentacionem dilectorum filiorum prioris et capituli ecclesie nostre Karl' per sedem apostolicam nuper facte specialiter deputatus dilecto filio decano nostro Karlii' salutem [*etc.*]. Litteras sanctissimi in Christo patris et domini nostri domini Innocencii divina providencia pape sexti ejus vera bulla plumbea et filo canapis more Romane curie bullatas nobis per eundem Robertum humiliter presentatas recepimus prout decuit reverenter. Nos volentes eidem Roberto super premissis ut tenemur ac aliis quorum interest in hac parte facere justicie complementum, tibi mandamus quatinus cites peremptorie prefatos priorem et capitulum quod compareant coram nobis in capella manerii nostri de Rosa die Lune proximo post dominicam qua cantatur officium *Quasimodo geniti* proximo futuram si sua viderint expedire allegaturi proposituri ac eciam ostensuri siquod canonicum allegare proponere et ostendere voluerint contra personam dicti Roberti graciamve hujusmodi sibi factam quare ad execucionem litterarum apostolicarum hujusmodi juxta vim formam et effectum earundem minime procedere debeamus. Et ad probacionem citacionis inde facte nobis citra dictum diem remittas presentes sigillo tuo pendenti signatas. Vale. Datum [Rose, 29 Mar. 1354].

34

[Fo.3; p. 5] AD INQUIRENDUM DE ECCLESIIS ET CAPELLIS AC MAJORIBUS ALTARIBUS NON CONSECRATIS, ET DE NOMINIBUS DECEDENCIUM SIVE TESTAMENTO CONDITO SIVE NON, AC ALIIS UT IN LITTERA. G. etc. dilecto filio magistro Willelmo de Ragenhill clerico nostro familiari salutem in auctore salutis. Cum nonnulli nostre diocesis subditi bona defunctorum infra dictam nostram diocesim a diu est tam ab intestato quam testamento condito decedencium absque administracione eisdem commissa legitima in grave suarum animarum periculum, jurisdictionis ecclesiastice enervacionem ac contra sic decedencium ultimam voluntatem occupaverunt et occupant in presenti; sintque nonnulle ecclesie et capelle infra eandem nostram diocesim a quarum constructione biennii spacium et amplius est effluxum que nondum munere consecracionis sunt ut recepimus insignite, et nichilominus in eisdem contra sanctiones canonicas divina officia cotidie celebrantur; nos igitur super premissis volentes ex officii nostri debito effici certiores, ad inquirendum de ecclesiis et capellis hujusmodi ac majoribus altaribus nondum consecracionis munere dedicatis, et de quibuscumque infra dictam nostram diocesim ab anno domini Millesimo CCC^{mo} quadragesimo septimo hactenus testamento condito vel ab intestato decedentibus et ad quorum manus bona defunctorum hujusmodi et qualiter pervenerunt, an eciam aliqua legata ad reparacionem pontis ultra aquam de Eden juxta Karl' relicta extiterint ac que et qualia, necnon de ecclesiis sanguinis aut seminis effusione aliterve pollutis, ac omnibus aliis et singulis per quem et super premissis poterimus uberius informari, tibi tenore presencium vices nostras committimus cum cujuslibet cohercionis canonice potestate, certificans nos de omni eo quod feceris in premissis negocio hujusmodi expedito. Datum apud manerium nostrum de Rosa xxv die [Fo.3^v; p. 6] mensis Aprilis anno domini supradicto.

35

[Fo.3^v; p. 6] ADMISSIO FRATRIS WILLELMI DE TANFELD AD PRIORATUM DE WEDERHALE. Gilbertus etc. dilecto filio fratri Willelmo de Tanfeld commonacho monasterii beate Marie Ebor' ad prioratum de Wederhale nostre diocesis per religiosum virum abbatem monasterii supradicti nobis presentato salutem [*etc.*]. Ad prioratum de Wederhale predictum ac regimen ecclesiarum prefato prioratui de Wederhale pertinencium et ad curam animarum parochianorum earundem, juribus nostris episcopalibus et Karlii' ecclesie dignitate causisque litibus et processibus quibuscumque in quacumque causa inter prefatum abbatem monasteriique ejusdem conventum et predecessores nostros seu nostrum immediate predecessorem eisque aut ei adherentes et coram judicibus ordinariis vel delegatis quibuscumque et ubicumque inchoatis et adhuc pendentibus indecisis, quibus causis litibus et processibus sic pendentibus nomine nostro et Karlii' ecclesie supradicte adheremus et volumus effectualiter adherere, nobis et ecclesie Karlii' et successoribus nostris in omnibus semper salvis, te prestita nobis a te canonica obediencia juratoria et corporali admittimus et canonice instituimus in eisdem intuitu caritatis. Vale. Datum [Rose, 21 June 1354].

42

[Fo.4; p. 7] PRONUNCIACIO SUPER LEGITIMA ETATE DOMINI WILLELMI DEL HALL PRESBITERI AD ECCLESIAM DE BOUNES CANONICE PRESENTATI. Universis sancte matris ecclesie filiis ad quos pervenerit hec scriptura G. permissione divina Karlii' episcopus salutem in amplexibus salvatoris. Universitati vestre notum facimus per presentes quod cum in certificatorio inquisicionis super presentacione domini Willelmi del Hall presbiteri ad ecclesiam de Bounes nostre diocesis de mandato nostro nuper facte in ea parte, an videlicet dictus dominus Willelmus legitime etatis extiterat, difficultas continebatur aliqualis prout prima facie apparebat; idem dominus Willelmus ad certos diem et locum sibi in hac parte assignatos coram nobis personaliter comparens, se fuisse et esse legitime etatis tempore presentacionis hujusmodi de se facte per testes quamplures juratos ac per nos secreto et singillatim diligenter examinatos sufficienter docuit et probavit, unde predictum dominum Willelmum sic fuisse et esse etatis legitime ut prefertur pronunciavimus per decretum justicia exigente. Et hec omnibus et singulis quorum interest vel interesse poterit innotescimus per presentes, quibus sigillum nostrum apposuimus in testimonio presencium. Datum [Rose, 22 July 1354].

47

[Fo.4^v; p. 8] MONICIO PRO DECIMIS ET PRECIPUE GARBARUM EXSOLVENDIS UT PATET. G. etc. dilecto filio decano nostro Karliol' salutem [*etc.*]. Sanctorum patrum instituta canonica et sacrosancte ecclesie observancias presertim in decimis exsolvendis immutare nolentes quinpocius juxta doctrinam evangelicam adimplere, tibi mandamus firmiter injungentes quatinus omnes et singulos subditos nostros tui decanatus diebus dominicis et festivis intra missarum solempnia moneas efficaciter et inducas quod decimas deo et ecclesie debitas et hactenus solvi consuetas et precipue garbas decimales de terris suis provenientes que in campis dimitti solebant ibidem dimittant, illas vero que ad hostia horreorum^6 suorum cariari consueverant ab antiquo solvant ibidem integraliter et dimittant sub pena excommunicacionis majoris, quam in omnes et singulos monicionibus tuis hujusmodi non parentes ac alio modo vel loco decimantes quam fieri consuevit, fulminare decrevimus justicia id poscente. De die vero recepcionis presencium et quid feceris in premissis nos citra festum sancti Dionisii proximo futurum distincte et aperte certifices per litteras tuas patentes harum seriem continentes. Datum [Rose, 15 Sept. 1354].

53

[Fo.5; p. 9] MONICIO NE BLADA SEU FENA IN ECCLESIIS SEU CAPELLIS REPONANTUR PRO TEMPORE CONSERVANDA. G. etc. dilecto filio priori de Wederhale nostre diocesis salutem [*etc.*]. Licet tam veteris quam novi nobis insinuet auctoritas testamenti quod in dierum longitudinem deceat domum domini sanctitudo, nonnulli tamen ut recepimus filii degeneres almam matrem ecclesiam ausu molliuntur nephario indies prophanare dum in quampluribus ecclesiis et capellis deo et divinis cultubus dedicatis blada fena ac bruta inferentes animalia, ipsam domum domini ad inhonestos usus et forinsecos utpote ad horrea secularia ac insolencium speluncam messis temporibus ut plurimum contra instituta canonica redigere se disponant. Nolentes igitur tante temeritatis excessum sub neglectu conniviencie sicuti nec valentes improvide pertransire,

---

^{6} MS. *orriorum*

vos monemus in domino exhortantes ne in ecclesiis de Wederhale aut Warthewyk' ipsarumve capellis aut aliis ecclesiis seu capellis infra dictam nostram diocesim ad vos et prioratum vestrum spectantibus blada vel fena eciam conservanda pro tempore inferatis nec ab aliis cujuscumque status vel condicionis extiterit inferri aliqualiter permittatis, monentes insuper et inhibentes palam et publice per vos seu alios in dictis ecclesiis et capellis diebus dominicis et festivis omnibus et singulis nostris subditis ne in ipsis ecclesiis vel capellis seu earundem aliqua blada fena vel alia ad prophanos usus spectancia inferant vel recondant eciam ut premisimus pro tempore conservanda inferrive faciant aut reponi sub pena majoris excommunicacionis in contravenientes monicionibus et inhibicionibus vestris quin verius nostris fulminanda. De die recepcionis presencium et quid feceritis in premissis nos citra festum sancti Michaelis proximo futurum certificetis litteris vestris patentibus habentibus hunc tenorem. Valete. Datum [Rose, 13 Sept. 1354].

57

[Fo.5ᵛ; p. 10] COMMISSIO AD PRESIDENDUM ET INTERESSENDUM IN SYNODO APUD KARLIOL' CELEBRANDA. G. etc. dilecto filio priori ecclesie nostre cathedralis beate Marie Karl' salutem [*etc.*]. Quia in instanti synodo nostra proxima post festum sancti Luce Evangeliste in dicta nostra ecclesia celebranda interesse personaliter non valemus arduis domini nostri regis Anglie negociis prepediti, vobis de cujus industria circumspecta fiduciam gerimus pleniorem, ad presidendum et interessendum pro nobis et nomine nostro in dicta synodo nostra ut premittitur celebranda ceteraque omnia et singula facienda que in synodis celebrandis hujusmodi quomodolibet requiruntur tenore presencium committimus vices nostras cum cujuslibet cohercionis canonice potestate, proviso quod nos de omni eo quod feceritis in hac parte curetis per vestras litteras reddere cerciores. Valete. Datum [Rose, 18 Oct. 1354].

59

LICENCIA A PERSONALI COMPARICIONE IN SYNODIS PRO PRIORE DE WARTR' PRO TOTO TEMPORE SUO. G. etc. dilecto filio fratri Ricardo priori prioratus de Wartr' salutem [*etc.*]. Solicitudines et labores quos circa curam et regimen ejusdem prioratus vos habere novimus hiis diebus nos excitant et inducant ut vos a laboribus exteris et remotis quantum poterimus relevemus. Vos igitur a personali comparicione in synodis nostris apud Karliol' celebrandis racione ecclesiarum de Ascom et Barton nostre diocesis vobis conventui vestro dictoque prioratui appropriatarum debita et consueta quamdiu regimen dicti prioratus prefueritis in priorem exoneramus et absolvimus per presentes, ita tamen quod per procuratorem sufficientem et idoneum compareatis prout convenit in eisdem. Valete. Datum [Rose, 12 Oct. 1354].

61

[Fo.5ᵛ; p. 10] LICENCIA PRO RECTORE DE ULNEDALE AD CELEBRANDUM IN CAPELLA. Gilbertus etc. dilecto filio domino Ricardo rectori ecclesie de Ulnedale nostre diocesis salutem [etc.]. Ex injuncta nobis solicitudine pastorali exhibere nos credimus obsequium deo gratum cum utilitati subditorum nostrorum prospicimus pariter et quieti. Cum igitur parochiani tui ab ecclesia tua parochiali tantum distent quod propter distanciam hujusmodi nequeunt congruo tempore ecclesiasticis officiis interesse, ut in capella infra villam de Ulnedale predicta notorie situata divina cum placuerit celebrare et per capellanum idoneum facere valeas licite celebrari absque tamen aliquali prejudicio dicte ecclesie tue licenciam tenore presencium concedimus specialem per unum annum datam presencium proximo secuturum tantummodo duraturam. Vale. Datum [Rose, 27 Oct. 1354].

65

[Fo.6; p. 11] INHIBICIO NE ALIQUIS DE PAROCHIA ECCLESIE BEATE MARIE KARL' AD SEPULTURAM ADMITTATUR QUOUSQUE ETC. DICTUM CIMITERIUM ETC. G. etc. dilecto filio decano nostro Karl' salutem [etc.]. Cum cimiterium ecclesie nostre cathedralis beate Marie Karl' fuerit et sit occasione injectionis manuum violentarum facte nuperrime in eodem suppositum interdicto, nec curent ejusdem ecclesie parochiani reconciliacionem dicti cimiterii procurare; tibi mandamus firmiter injungentes quatinus priori ejusdem ecclesie nostre capellano parochiali ecclesie sancti Cuthberti Karl' rectoribus vicariis et capellanis parochialibus ecclesiarum eidem ecclesie nostre circumvicinarum ac omnibus aliis quibus expedit in hac parte inhibeas firmiter vice nostra ne quemquam parochianum dicte ecclesie nostre qualitercumque decedentem sub pena districcionis canonice ad sepulturam admittant, nec eorum aliquis admittat, sine nostra licencia speciali quousque dictum cimiterium reconciliacionis munere fuerit insignitum, inquirens de nominibus prefatam nostram inhibicionem contravenientibus, de quibus cum tibi constiterit nobis constare facias de eisdem. Datum [Rose, 30 Nov. 1354].

66

LITTERA AD INQUIRENDUM DE IMPOTENCIA VICARII DE DERHAM ET AN EGEAT CURATORE VEL NON. G. etc. dilecto filio .. officiali nostro Karl' salutem [etc.]. Ad nostrum deduxit auditum relacio fidedigna quod dominus Johannes perpetuus vicarius⁷ ecclesie de Derham nostre diocesis adeo existit senio confractus ac viribus corporis destitutus, ab eo eciam loquela quasi totaliter est exempta, quod curam et regimen in dicta ecclesia sibi commissa quod dolenter referimus per se non poterit excercere nec eciam sibi aut suis comode prospicere ut deberet. Volentes igitur super suggestis hujusmodi effici plenius

⁷ *vicarius* repeated.

cerciores, vobis committimus et mandamus quatinus de statu dicti vicarii ejus impotencia et utrum egeat curatore vel non, et si sic quam personam sibi in curatorem dari et assignari magis affectaret, ac de ceteris articulis et circumstanciis universis que nos magis informare poterunt in hoc casu inquiratis diligencius veritatem. Et quid per inquisicionem eandem inveneritis, nobis expedito hujusmodi inquisicionis negocio distincte et aperte constare faciatis litteris vestris patentibus habentibus hunc tenorem. Datum [Rose, 30 Nov. 1354].

70 (ii)

[Fo.6ᵛ; p. 12] INSTRUMENTUM PER IPSUM PRESTITUM DE QUIBUSDAM INJUNCTIONIBUS OBSERVANDIS. Et memorandum quod eodem [die] coram dicto venerabili patre in camera sua principali dicti manerii sui prefatus frater Thomas prior ad observandum infrascriptas injunctiones sibi per eundem venerabilem patrem factas juramentum ad sancta dei Evangelia prestitit corporale, videlicet quod caritatem fovebit et nutriet inter fratres; quod mitis erit[8] prout status suus exigit omnibus de conventu; quod majora negocia statum dicti prioratus concernencia sine consensu conventus minime pertractabit; quod sigillum commune sub custodia trium canonicorum dicti conventus vel duorum ad minus fideliter conservetur; quod canes non teneat nisi paucos; quod communibus venacionibus non intersit nec se immisceat de eisdem; quod nullus religiosus vel secularis dicti prioratus canes teneat quoquomodo; quod priori immediato predecessori suo faciet de hiis que per dictum venerabilem patrem inferius ordinantur modo congruo deserviri.

71

CESSIO PRIORIS PREDECESSORIS SUI ET ORDINACIO SUPER VITE NECESSARIIS EJUSDEM CEDENTIS. Universis [as in 42 – salvatoris]. Nuper ad prioratum de Lanercost nostre diocesis pro quibusdam statum et regimen ipsius prioratus concernentibus declinantibus, frater Johannes de Bothecastre prior dicti prioratus tunc coram nobis in domo capitulari ejusdem personaliter constitutus, presentibus eciam tunc ibidem omnibus et singulis dicti loci canonicis et [Fo.7; p. 13] conventum facientibus, adeo senio confractum se asserens ac imbecillitate corporis pregravatum quod cure et regimini ejusdem prioratus ulterius preesse non sufficit et prodesse, a nobis cum instancia postulavit ut cessionem suam de eodem prioratu admittere dignaremur. Nos igitur informacione super premissa habita pleniori, ne sic languente pastore grex quod absit insidiatoris laniandus dentibus exponatur ecclesieve utilitas ipsius depereat, ejusdem cessionem ex causis hujusmodi duximus admittendum.

Cumque eundem senectutis necessitas non labes criminis ab execucione suscepti regiminis impedit et abducit, nos institutis inherentes canonicis de consensu omnium et singulorum canonicorum dicti loci tunc ibidem ut premittitur presencium expresso et unanimi pro ipsius fratris Johannis vite

[8] *erit* repeated.

necessariis porcionem infrascriptam decrevimus ordinandum, videlicet quod idem frater Johannes ad tempus vite sue pro inhabitacione sua domus competentes habeat et honestas infra septa dicti prioratus situatas. Habeat eciam et percipiat diebus singulis dum vixerit de priore dicti prioratus qui pro tempore fuerit et ejusdem loci conventu duas liberatas canonicales in esculentis et poculentis, ac duo paria botarum novarum et duo paria caligarum novarum pro calciamentis annis singulis percipiendas illis temporibus quo bote et calige hujusmodi consueverant liberari, necnon quadraginta sex solidos et octo denarios pro indumentis suis laneis et lineis ac aliis sibi necessariis annis singulis dum vixerit percipiendos ad tres anni terminos, festa videlicet Natalis domini xiii s. iv d., Pentecostes xx s. et sancti Michaelis xiii s. iv d., prima solucione incipiente in festo Natalis domini proximo jam futuro; quodque eidem fratri Johanni focalia et candele sufficienter de tempore in tempus quoad vixerit ministrentur.[9] Insuper quia dictus frater Johannes sine ministro sibi ipsi prospicere nequeat ut deceret, idem frater Johannes providebit sibi de ministro hujusmodi; cui siquidem ministro quem ipsum fratrem Johannem habere contigerit, iidem prior et conventus quamdiu frater Johannes predictus vixerit unam liberatam qualem liberi servientes videlicet *yhomen* in dicto prioratu diebus singulis facient liberari, necnon stipendium tantum et tale eidem ministro una cum roba competenti annis singulis quale et qualem hujusmodi recipiunt servientes in dicto loco facient ministrari vel dimidiam marcam sterlingorum pro roba hujusmodi in festo sancti Nicholai,[10] illo videlicet anno dumtaxat quo robas suis servientibus non dederint in eventum.

Et ad premissa omnia et singula observanda et fideliter perimplenda priorem subpriorem celerarium sacristam ac singulos canonicos dicti prioratus qui pro tempore fuerint ac omnes alios et singulos de conventu per censuras ecclesiasticas quascumque fore decrevimus compellendos. Et nichilominus suppriorem celerarium sacristam ac singulos canonicos dicti prioratus monemus primo secundo tercio et peremptorio et sub pena excommunicacionis majoris in personas suas et eorum cujuslibet ferende quatinus premissa omnia et singula per nos ut predicitur ordinata observent fideliter et faciant observari. In quorum omnium testimonium atque fidem presentes litteras nostras nostri sigilli appensione fecimus communiri. Data et acta in domo capitulari dicti prioratus [2 Dec. 1354].

77

[Fo.7ᵛ; p. 14] COMMISSIO GENERALIS IN OMNIBUS CAUSIS SEU NEGOCIIS ETC. G. etc. dilectis nobis in Christo domino Johanni de Shupton rectori medietatis ecclesie de Lynton in Craven Ebor' diocesis ac magistro Willelmo de Ragenhill clericis nostris familiaribus salutem in auctore salutis. De vestre circumspeccionis

---

[9] This is the last word in its line. To its right, in the outer margin, this clause begins: *de quibus omnibus disponat idem frater Johannes in eventu prout sibi videbitur expedire.* It is in the same hand as the rest of the page. There does not appear to be an insertion mark; it could reasonably have followed *ministrentur.* The clause is enclosed in a box of lines, like marginal headings, and it has been copied as if it were one in the list of contents (fo.iiᵛ).

[10] Interlined from *in*

industria et consciencie puritate plenius confidentes, ad cognoscendum procedendum statuendum diffiniendum et exequendum in omnibus causis et negociis ad nostram specialem audienciam ex officio vel ad quamcumque partis instanciam deductis vel deducendis et ea fine debito terminanda, vobis et alteri vestrum per se et insolidum committimus vices nostras cum cujuslibet cohercionis canonice potestate donec eas ad nos duxerimus revocandas, proviso quod nos de omni eo quod feceritis reddatis in eventum[11] plenius cerciores. In cujus rei testimonium sigillum nostrum presentibus est appensum. Datum [Rose, 15 Jan. 1355].

79

[Fo.7ᵛ; p. 14] CONFIRMACIO SUPER SENTENCIA LATA PER OFFICIALEM KARL' IN CAUSA DIVORCII INTER THOMAM FILIUM DOMINI THOME DE ROKEBY ET ELIZABETHAM FILIAM DOMINI PETRI DE TYLIOLL MILITIS DEFUNCTI. Universis [as in 42- salvatoris]. Noverit universitas vestra nos infrascriptum processum sive publicum instrumentum per officialem nostrum Karl' nuper factum sigilloque ejusdem officialis ac signo et subscripcione magistri Willelmi de Fenton clerici notarii publici communita per omnia diligencius inspexisse, cujus tenor sequitur in hec verba:

Noverint universi quod nos .. officialis Karl' nuper in causa divorcii que coram nobis vertebatur inter Elizabetham filiam domini Petri de Tylioll militis defuncti partem actricem ex parte una et Thomam filium domini Thome de Rokeby militis junioris partem ream ex altera sentenciam diffinitivam tulimus in hunc modum:

In dei nomine amen. Auditis et intellectis meritis cause matrimonialis et divorcii que coram nobis officiale Karl' vertitur inter Elizabetham filiam domini Petri de Tylioll militis defuncti partem actricem ex parte una et Thomam filium domini Thome de Rokeby militis junioris partem ream ex altera, oblato coram nobis per partem dicte Elizabethe parti dicto Thome libello, qui talis est:

In dei nomine amen. Coram vobis, domine judex, dicit et in jure proponit procurator Elizabethe de Tylioll nomine procuratorio pro eadem contra Thomam filium domini Thome de Rokeby militis junioris et contra quemlibet legitime comparentem in judicio pro eodem quod licet predicti Thomas et Elizabeth matrimonium adinvicem in facie ecclesie de facto contraxerint, dictum tamen matrimonium de jure validum non subsistebat nec subsistit, pro eo quod tempore matrimonii contracti inter eos idem Thomas fuit impubes non proximus pubertati nec pubes factus consensit matrimonialiter in eandem, et pro eo quod ipsa renitens et reclamans ad contrahendum matrimonium cum eodem Thoma compulsa et coacta fuerit per metum qui cadere poterit in constantem mulierem, nec unquam libere consensit in eundem quovis modo, que offert se dictus procurator in forma juris probaturus.

Quare petit probatis in hac parte probandis matrimonium inter predictos Thomam et Elizabetham sic contractum nullum et irritum de jure fuisse et esse sentencialiter declarari, et quatenus de facto processit revocari, ac ulterius in premissis et ea contigentibus utrique parti fieri justicie complementum. Hec dicit et petit dictus procurator nomine quo supra conjunctim et divisim, juris

---

[11] Repeated from *reddatis*

beneficio addendi mutandi minuendi declarandi ac aliis omnibus semper sibi salvo. Lite ad eundem per partem dicti Thome affirmative contestata, dicendo narrata prout narrantur vere esse et petita prout petivit fieri debere, juramento de calumpnia et de veritate dicenda per partes predictas hinc inde prestito. Testibus per partem dicte Elizabethe productis rite receptis juratis et examinatis et eorum attestacionibus publicatis, factisque interrogacionibus per nos dictis partibus ad uberiorem informacionem nostram et responsionibus datis ad easdem, demum de consensu dictarum parcium in causa concluso et ad audiendum sentenciam diffinitivam certo termino per nos assignato, nos .. officialis antedictus omnipotentis dei nomine invocato ad sentenciam diffiniti-vam in dicta causa procedimus in hunc modum:

Quia invenimus prefatam Elizabetham intencionem suam coram nobis in judicio deductam sufficienter et legitime probavisse, matrimonium inter ipsam Elizabetham et prefatum Thomam contractum de jure non posse[12] subsistere nec subsistere debere set nullum irritum et inane fuisse et esse pronunciamus decernimus et declaramus, [Fo.8; p. 15] idemque matrimonium quatenus de facto processit adnullamus et dissolvimus et divorciamus sentencialiter et diffinitive in hiis scriptis. In cujus rei testimonium presentes litteras sive presens publicum instrumentum signo et subscripcione notarii publici infrascripti ac sigilli nostri appensione fecimus communiri. Lecta et lata fuit dicta sentencia in ecclesia sancti Cuthberti Karl' anno ab incarnacione domini secundum cursum et computacionem ecclesie Angl' Millesimo CCC[mo] quinquagesimo quarto indiccione septima, pontificatus sanctissimi in Christo patris et domini nostri domini Innocencii divina providencia pape sexti anno secundo, mensis Maii die vicesimo quarto; presentibus discretis viris magistris Ada de Caldebek' Waltero de Helton juris peritis Willelmo de Ragenhill notario publico Ebor' et Karlii' diocesium ac aliis testibus ad premissa vocatis specialiter et rogatis.

Et ego Willelmus de Fenton clericus Karlii' diocesis auctoritate apostolica notarius publicus prolatione dicte sentencie per magistrum Nicholaum de Whiteby officialem Karl' facte anno indiccione pontificatu mense die et loco prenotatis una cum testibus suprascriptis personaliter presens interfui et eam sic fieri vidi et audivi, et de mandato dicti domini .. officialis in hanc publicam formam redegi signoque meo consueto signavi rogatus in fidem et testimonium premissorum.

Quem quidem processum sive publicum instrumentum nos .. Gilbertus Karl' episcopus memoratus ac omnia et singula in eodem contenta ratificamus confirmamus et eciam approbamus. In quorum omnium et singulorum fidem et testimonium premissorum sigillum nostrum fecimus hiis apponi. Datum [Rose, 10 Dec. 1354].

84

[Fo.8; p. 15] DIMISSIO VICARII ECCLESIE DE KIRKBYSTEPHAN SUPER LAPSU CARNIS CUM M[ARGARETA] WYVILL. Universis pateat per presentes quod cum coram nobis G. etc. dominus Johannes de Boghes vicarius ecclesie de Kirkby Steffan nostre diocesis super lapsu carnis et incontinencia cum Margareta Wyvill et aliis,

---

[12] Interlined.

ac quod idem Johannes contra tenorem constitucionis legati super hoc edite dictam Margaretam publice tenuit concubinam, penam dicte constitucionis dampnabiliter incurrendo, fuisset ex officio nostro impetitus; auditis et intellectis responsionibus et defensionibus dicti domini Johannis ac probacionibus coram nobis factis, [quia] invenimus et sufficienter comperimus dictum dominum Johannem penam dicte constitucionis nullatenus incurrisse, prefatum dominum Johannem occasione premissa nullatenus inquietari debere nec in penam constitucionis predicte incidisse sentencialiter et diffinitive pronunciamus et declaramus, ipsumque dominum Johannem de lapsu carnis et incontinencia cum dicta Margareta et aliis quibuscumque usque ad diem confeccionis presencium qualitercumque per ipsum comissis debite et sufficienter correximus, et ipsum sic plene correctum ab impeticione et inquietacione [Fo.8ᵛ; p. 16] officii nostri et successorum nostrorum dimittimus per presentes, ac cum prefato domino Johanne super premissis omnibus et singulis si et quatenus dispensacione nostra indigeat aut indiget aliquod premissorum ex certis sciencia et causis legitimis nos ad id moventibus auctoritate nostra pontificali dispensamus. In cujus rei testimonium sigillum nostrum presentibus est appensum. Datum [Rose, 5 Feb. 1355].

87

[Fo.8ᵛ; p. 16] COMMISSIO AD RECIPIENDUM PENITENTES IN ECCLESIA KARL'. G. etc. dilecto filio priori ecclesie nostre cathedralis beate Marie Karl' salutem [*etc.*]. Variis negociis prepediti quominus in ecclesia nostra predicta hac instanti die Mercurii cinerum interesse personaliter valeamus, ad recipiendum quoscumque penitentes dicte¹³ nostre diocesis ad dictam ecclesiam nostram prout moris est confluentes ceteraque facienda que necessaria fuerint in hoc casu vobis tenore presencium committimus vices nostras. Valete. Datum [Rose, 16 Feb. 1355].

93

[Fo.9ᵛ; p. 18] EXECUCIO CONTRA NON SOLVENTES PROCURACIONES ARCHIDIACONI. G. etc. dilecto filio decano nostro Karl' salutem [*etc.*]. Licet nonnulli rectores et vicarios, quorum nomina in cedula presentibus annexa plenarie conscribuntur, archidiacono nostro Karl' in diversis pecuniarum summis pro suis procuracionibus racione visitacionum nuper in ecclesiis suis factarum ut recepimus teneantur, fuerintque sufficienter auctoritate legitime moniti quod eidem archidiacono de procuracionibus sibi ex causa premissa debitis infra certum terminum a diu est effluxum, prout ipsos et ipsorum quemlibet particulariter concernabat, sub penis gravibus et censuris satisfacerent ut tenentur; iidem tamen rectores et vicarii de eisdem procuracionibus sic ut premittitur debitis et a retro existentibus prefato archidiacono hactenus satisfacere non curarunt nec curavit aliquis eorundem, prout per dictum archidiaconum nobis extitit querelatum. Nolentes igitur eidem in sua deesse justicia sicuti nec debemus,

---

¹³ Underdotted.

tibi mandamus firmiter injungentes quatinus omnes et singulas personas hujusmodi efficaciter moneas et inducas quod infra quindecim dierum spacium a tempore monicionis tue eis et eorum cuilibet facte continue numerandarum eidem archidiacono nostro de procuracionibus sibi debitis et a retro existentibus ut prefertur, prout ipsas et ipsarum quamlibet particulariter concernit, integraliter satisfaciant ut tenentur sub penis suspensionis et excommunicacionis in personas non solventes ac interdicti in earum ecclesias, quas quidem censuras in personas omnium et singulorum ac beneficiorum suorum tuis monicionibus quin verius nostris non parencium in hac parte ipsorum mora et culpa precedentibus tenore presencium promulgamus, ac per te contra hujusmodi personas et beneficia sua mandamus et volumus extunc de diebus in dies solempniter publicari. De die vero recepcionis presencium monicionis et execucionis inde factarum ac de omni eo quod feceris in premissis nobis, cum ex parte dicti archidiaconi fueris congrue requisitus, distincte et aperte constare facias per litteras tuas patentes harum seriem et nomina non solvencium in hac parte plenius continentes. Vale. Datum etc.

114

[Fo.12ᵛ; p. 24] CASSACIO CONTRACTUS MATRIMONIALIS INTER WILLELMUM DEL PARK DE KARLIOLO ET ELENAM BOGHER DE EADEM. Universis sancte matris ecclesie filiis ad quos presentes littere pervenerint G. etc. salutem in amplexibus salvatoris. Noverit universitas vestra quod cum nuper ad nostram audienciam delatum fuisse quod Willelmus del Park' de Karlo' et Elena Bogher de eadem matrimonium per verba de presenti mutuo contraxerunt, quodque procurare solempnizari in facie ecclesie prout moris est nullatenus curaverunt, eosdem Willelmum et Elenam coram nobis ad certos diem et locum comparentes ad ostendendum et proponendum causam racionabilem si quam haberent quare ad solempnizacionem matrimonii hujusmodi procurandam minime compelli deberent fecimus evocari. Quibus die et loco eis in hac parte assignatis coram nobis in audiencia nostra personaliter comparentibus, propositoque per eosdem tunc ibidem et judicialiter allegato ipsos ad hujusmodi solempnizacionem matrimonii inter eosdem ut premittitur sic contracti compelli non debere, pro eo quod idem Willelmus tanta frigiditate detentus ipsam Elenam seu aliam mulierem carnaliter cognoscere non poterat quoquo modo licet iidem Willelmus et Elena ipsis solis in lectis nudis diversis vicibus existentibus pluries hoc temptassent, prout iidem Willelmus et Elena in hac parte tunc ibidem jurati judicialiter fatebantur. Unde ad probandum hujusmodi impedimentum in personam dicti Willelmi sic propositum et allegatum, assignavimus eisdem Willelmo et Elene certos locum et terminum competentes. Quibus die et loco dictis Willelmo et Elena coram nobis in dicta audiencia nostra personaliter comparentibus, productisque ex parte eorumdem nonnullis testibus, quibus admissis juratis et secrete et singillatim examinatis eorumque attestacionibus publicatis diligencius et rimatis. Quia per probaciones hujusmodi testium in hac parte productorum nobis evidenter constabat quod impedimentum per dictos Willelmum et Elenam ut premittitur propositum et allegatum veritatem per omnia continebat, nos Gilbertus Karlii' episcopus supradictus, habita super premissa deliberacione pleniori invocatoque dei nomine, ad solempnizandum hujusmodi matrimonium inter dictos Willelmum et Elenam ut premittitur sic contractum ipsos compelli nequaquam debere necnon matrimonium hujusmodi sic contractum quatenus inter eosdem de facto processit cassavimus irritavimus et adnullavimus, ac cassum irritum et adnullatum fore decrevimus justicia exigente, quod omnibus et singulis quorum interest innotescimus per presentes quibus sigillum nostrum apposuimus in testimonium premissorum. Datum [Rose, 27 Feb. 1356].

115

[Fo.12ᵛ; p. 24] MONICIO CONTRA EOS QUI CONFREGERUNT ET AMMOVERUNT QUAMDAM SEMITAM IN CIMITERIO ECCLESIE DE PENRETH DE LAPIDIBUS CONFECTAM CUM CLA[USULA] EX[COMMUNICACIONIS] IN FINE. G. etc. dilectis filiis dominis Thome rectori ecclesie de Burgham nostre diocesis ac Johanni de Dokwra capellano salutem [etc.]. Cum laicis disponendi de rebus ecclesie ac locis deo consecratis consistentibus absque locorum ordinariorum licencia nulla potestas fuerit attributa quin verius interdicta, sintque omnes et singuli qui immunitatem sancte matris ecclesie quam sancti Romani pontifices et principes seculares numer[os]is privilegiis munierunt impugnant violant seu perturbant majoris excommunicacionis sentenciis sacrarum auctoritate constitucionum dampnabiliter involuti; ad nostras tamen aures noviter jam pervenit quod quidam parochiani ecclesie nostre peculiaris de Penreth nostre diocesis ingratitudinis filii manus nescientes a vetitis cohibere sentenciam excommunicacionis hujusmodi non verentes, quorum ignorantur nomina et persone, quamdam semitam de lapidibus et terra in cimiterio dicte ecclesie nostre confectam eo videlicet ut ministri dicte ecclesie ad eandem ecclesiam et chorum ejusdem pro divinis officiis inibi peragendis incedere possent honestius et redire, non attendentes quodque religiosis adherent religiosa sunt et debeant indicari, quod die feriato dum missa in eadem celebratur ecclesia quo quidem tempore divine contemplari ut veri Christiani debuerant vacavisse, temeritate propria confregerunt et eciam ammoverunt, et hiis delictis non contenti lapides in dicta semita collocatos et ex eadem extractos ad edificia et muros mansi vicarie dicte ecclesie nostre cimiterio ejusdem contigui dei timore postposito impetu nephario temere projecerunt ac cooperturam mansi hujusmodi ac muros et hostia ejusdem cum eisdem lapidibus sic corr[u]entibus nequiter dampnificarunt, ecclesiasticam libertatem notorie violantes in dei et sancte matris ecclesie ignominiam et contemptum, dicte nostre jurisdiccionis prejudicium, animarum sic delinquencium grave periculum et exemplum pessimum plurimorum. Ne igitur tante temeritatis audacia transeat aliis presumptoribus in exemplum, vobis et alteri vestrum per se et insolidum in virtute sancte obediencie et sub pena excommunicacionis majoris mandamus firmiter injungentes quatinus omnes et singulos qui ad semitam hujusmodi ammovendam nostra irrequisita licencia manus temerarias apposuerunt ac confregerunt ammoverunt et destruxerunt, libertates ecclesie in hac parte temere infringendo, hac instanti die dominica in dicta ecclesia nostra de Penreth ac aliis diebus dominicis et festivis intra missarum solempnia dum major affuerit populi multitudo moneatis et efficaciter inducatis seu alter vestrum moneat efficaciter et inducat quod infra decem dies a tempore monicionis vestre seu alterius vestrum sic facte continue numerandorum deo et ecclesie ac nobis de hujusmodi temeraria presumpcione satisfaciant competenter, alioquin lapsis dictis decem diebus ipsos omnes et singulos temeritatis hujusmodi perpetratores monitis vestris quin verius nostris legitimis non parentes in majoris excommunicacionis sentenciam contra hujusmodi presumptores proinde promulgatam dampnabiliter incidisse ac excommunicatos fuisse et esse occasione premissa in ecclesia nostra predicta diebus quibus magis videbitur expedire adhibita solempnitate qua decet publicetis et publicet alter vestrum, a publicacione hujusmodi non cessantes nec alter vestrum cessans donec hujusmodi temeritatis perpetratores quorum absolucionem nobis specialiter reservamus ad gremium sancte matris ecclesie redierint et beneficium absolucionis in forma juris meruerint obtinere; inquirentes nihilominus seu alter vestrum inquirens de nominibus malefactorum hujusmodi, de quibus [Fo.13; p. 25] cum vobis seu alteri vestrum constiterit, nobis constare faciatis seu alter vestrum faciat de eisdem per vestras aut suas patentes litteras harum seriem et nomina hujusmodi continentes aliquo sigillo auctentico consignatas. Datum [Rose, 28 Jan. 1356].

116

[Fo.13; p. 25] MEMORANDUM DE ABSOLUCIONE IMPENSA HIIS QUI CONFREGERUNT SEMITAM IN CIMITERIO ECCLESIE DE PENRITH, de qua in proximo precedenti littera memoratur etc. Et memorandum quod xiiii°; die Februarii anno predicto coram venerabili patre domino G. dei gracia Karlii' .. episcopo in capella manerii sui de Rosa comparuerunt Johannes de Wilton Johannes Taverner Robertus de Thresk' de Penreth et alii ecclesie de Penreth parochiani, et fatebantur se una cum nonnullis aliis ejusdem ecclesie parochianis semitam de qua in proximo precedenti littera memoratur confregisse et ammovisse, super quo ab eidem venerabile patre beneficium absolucionis a sentencia excommunicacionis majoris si quam ea occasione incurrerant sibi impendendi humiliter postularunt. Unde dictus venerabilis pater habita super hujusmodi facto deliberacione eorum precibus misericorditer annuens, contemplacioneque Rogeri de Salkeld qui venerat cum eisdem, ipsos qui tunc ibidem presentes extiterant in forma juris absolvit, committens vicario dicte ecclesie tunc ibidem presencialiter existenti vices suas omnes alios et singulos dicte ecclesie parochialis hujusmodi facti participes absolvendi. Quibus omnibus et singulis tam absentibus quam presentibus penitenciam injunxit infrascriptam, videlicet quod offerant unanimiter unum cereum iii librarum cere in ecclesia de Penreth coram ymagine beate virginis Marie die dominica proximo tunc futura.

125

[Fo.13ᵛ; p. 26] MANDATUM ARCHIEPISCOPI EBOR' PRO CONCILIO CELEBRANDO. Johannes permissione divina Ebor' archiepiscopus et apostolice sedis legatus venerabili fratri nostro domino .. Gilberto dei gracia Karl' episcopo salutem et fraternam in domino caritatem. Ob quedam ardua et urgencia negocia tam statum et libertatem ecclesie Anglicane et cleri ejusdem quam defensionem regni necessariam concernencia prelatis et aliis in parliamento nuper apud

Westmonasterium celebrato convenientibus publice exposita inter nos et dictos prelatos, consensum fuerat et condictum quod in Cantuar' et Ebor' provinciis celebrarentur concilia provincialia in quibus divina assistente clemencia super hiis communi consilio ordinari possit remedium salutare. Nos vero volentes que sic condicta fuerant quantum ad nos attinet in omnibus observare, vos tenore presencium peremptorie citamus et per vos omnes et singulos abbates et priores electivos abbates proprios non habentes tam exemptos quam non exemptos, saltim quorum monasteria ecclesiastica beneficia infra nostram provinciam habuerint non exempta, necnon decanos et prepositos ecclesiarum collegiatarum et archidiaconos vestre diocesis quoscumque totumque clerum ejusdem diocesis citari volumus et mandamus, quatinus vos predictique abbates et priores decani prepositi et archidiaconi personaliter, singula vero capitula seu collegia locorum hujusmodi per unum totusque clerus vestre diocesis per duos procuratores sufficientes et idoneos, tercio die mensis Junii videlicet die Veneris in crastino Ascensionis dominice proximo futuro cum continuacione et prorogacione dierum sequencium quatenus opus fuerit coram nobis in ecclesia nostra cathedrali beati Petri Ebor' compareatis, et sitis presentes concilium tunc ibidem nobiscum juxta sacrorum exigenciam canonum celebraturi, ac super hiis que ecclesiasticam libertatem et utilitatem ac regni Anglie defensionem necessariam concernunt vobis in eventu plenius exponendis, consilium vestrum providum impensuri facturi et recepturi quod ipsum sacrum concilium divina cooperante clemencia duxerit ordinandum; vobis prefatoque clero vestro expressius intimantes quod contra absentes in forma canonica procedemus, nullius sic absentis excusacionem admissuri nisi quatenus ad hoc nos arteverint canonice cauciones. Denuncietis itaque seu denunciari faciatis in genere omnibus et singulis vestre diocesis qui se gravatos senserint, quod in casibus illis quorum correccio seu reformacio ad concilium hujusmodi pertinere dinoscitur, audiencia efficax per divinam clemenciam eis in forma debita concedetur et fiet in omnibus justicie complementum. De die vero recepcionis presencium et quid feceritis in premissis necnon de modo et forma quibus presens mandatum nostrum executi fueritis nos dictis die et loco distincte et aperte certificetis per vestras litteras patentes harum seriem et nomina per vos citatorum in hac parte plenius continentes. Valeat diutissime vestra cara fraternitas in domino Jesu Christo. Datum in manerio nostro juxta Westmonasterium xii° die mensis Marcii anno domini Millesimo CCC^{mo} quinquagesimo quinto et nostre translacionis quarto.

135

[Fo.14; p. 27] COMMISSIO AD INQUIRENDUM[14] AN ECCLESIA SIVE CAPELLA SANCTI ALBANI KARLI' SIT CONSECRACIONIS MUNERE INSIGNITA. G. etc. dilectis filiis priori ecclesie nostre beate Marie Karli' necnon magistris Willelmo de Routhbury archidiacono nostro Karli' et Johanni de Welton clericis nostris familiaribus ac officiali nostro Karli' salutem [etc.]. Licet in locis preterquam deo dedicatis non debeant divina ministeria celebrari nec corpora mortuorum in Christo decedencium sepelliri juxta canonicas sanctiones, ad nostras tamen aures noviter

---

[14] MS. *inquirendo*

jam pervenit quod in ecclesia sive capella [Fo.14ᵛ; p. 28] sancti Albani infra civitatem nostram Karli' situata divina ministeria assidue celebrantur ac mortuorum corpora in eadem et ejus cimiterio tumulantur, et an dicta ecclesia sive capella fuerit et sit dedicacionis munere insignita ac pro loco sacro et deo dedicato communiter reputata, an eciam dictus locus ecclesia parochialis ab antiquo fuerat vel capella penitus ignoramus. Quocirca vobis committimus et mandamus quatinus vos vel duo vestrum per viros fidedignos clericos et laicos tam dicte nostre civitatis quam locorum aliorum adjacencium premissorum noticiam plenius obtinentes super omnibus et singulis articulis superius expressatis inquiratis vel inquirant diligencius veritatem. Et nos de omni eo quod feceritis et inveneritis in premissis reddatis seu duo vestrum reddant qui premissa fuerint executi expedito hujusmodi negocio cerciores. Datum [Rose, 20 Oct. 1356].

161

[Fo.16ᵛ; p. 32] COMMISSIO AD LEVANDUM SUBSIDIUM DOMINO .. EPISCOPO CONCESSUM PRO PRIMO TERMINO SOLUCIONIS EJUSDEM. G. etc. dilectis filiis magistro Ade de Caldebek' officiali nostro Karli' ac domino Thome de Salkeld rectori ecclesie de Clifton clerico nostro familiari salutem [etc.]. Cum nuper prior et capitulum ecclesie nostre cathedralis beate Marie Karlioli necnon abbates priores rectores et vicarii cetereque persone ecclesiastice tam exempte quam non exempte beneficia ecclesiastica infra nostram diocesim obtinentes quoddam subsidium ducentarum marcarum de bonis suis spiritualibus et temporalibus solvendum ad festa Pasche et nativitatis sancti Johannis Baptiste proximo futura per equales porciones ex certis causis ex parte nostra coram eisdem expositis et per eosdem admissis et approbatis nobis concesserant mera et spontanea voluntate, quodque ipsi sic concedentes ad solucionem dicti subsidii supradictis terminis faciendam per censuras compelli possint ecclesiasticas et eciam coherciri; nos volentes de hujusmodi subsidio terminis superius expressatis prout justum fuerit responderi, vobis et alteri vestrum de quorum fidelitate fiduciam in domino gerimus pleniorem ad petendum exigendum colligendum recipiendum et levandum totam pecunie summam nobis de dicto subsidio pro primo termino solucionis ejusdem debitam ac hujusmodi solventes acquietandos si necesse fuerit in hac parte, necnon omnes et singulos qui ad solucionem hujusmodi pro dicto primo termino tenentur per suspensionis excommunicacionis et interdicti sentencias compellendos, vices nostras committimus per presentes; proviso quod de pecunia hujusmodi sic recepta nobis fidele raciocinium reddatis et alter vestrum reddat cum super hoc fueritis requisiti, certificantes nos oportuno tempore de omni eo quod feceritis in premissis per litteras vestras patentes harum seriem et nomina non solvencium in hac parte si qui fuerint continentes. Datum [Rose, 2 April 1357].

186

[Fo.20; p. 39] CERTIFICATORIUM DICTARUM LITTERARUM ET PROCESSUS UT PATET. Reverendissimo in Christo patri et domino suo domino Talairando dei gracia episcopo Albanen' sacrosancte Romane ecclesie cardinali et apostolice sedis nuncio suus humilis et devotus episcopus Karlii' obedienciam cum omnimodis reverencia et honore. Litteras vestras venerabiles xxiii° die Junii ultimo preterito recepimus tenorem qui sequitur continentes: Talairandus etc. ut scribatur totus tenor. Quibus quidem litteris reverenter parentes et parere volentes in omnibus ut tenemur, totum vestrum processum in eisdem contentum ad noticiam omnium et singulorum nostrarum civitatis et diocesis quos presens tangit negocium rite deduci ipsosque congrue et solicite requiri infra tempus in dictis vestris litteris nobis limitatum in forma fecimus demandata; ac per registra libros et scripturas distribucionum taxacionum imposicionum et solucionum et presertim per quasdam acquietancias dominorum cardinalium dudum in Anglia et Francia nunciorum et ipsorum procuratorium super similibus procuracionibus habitarum, que exactissime propter premissa scrutari fecimus, comperimus informati quod hujusmodi procuraciones dominorum cardinalium pro uno anno ad racionem quatuor denariorum sterlingorum de qualibet marca veri valoris omnium et singulorum beneficiorum reddituum fructuum et proventuum ecclesiasticorum tam mense nostre episcopali pertinencium quam aliorum quorumcumque dicte civitatis et diocesis Karli' in casibus similium procuracionum hactenus exactarum percepi consueverunt et non ad majorem summam solucionis faciendam hujusmodi procuraciones ascenderunt in toto, quam ad summam quadraginta trium marcarum quinque solidorum et novem denariorum sterlingorum ut premittitur, prout per acquietancias dominorum cardinalium supradictas vobis si libeat ostendendas poterit apparere. Et licet beneficia redditus et proventus ecclesiastica dictarum civitatis [Fo.20^v; p. 40] et diocesis in marchia Scocie contigue et notorie situata per invasiones depredaciones combustiones et varias destrucciones Scottorum a multis retroactis temporibus et presertim modernis plus solito invalescentes et indies assiduas contingentes adeo depauperentur, et ad tantam et talem exilitatem et insufficienciam devenerunt quod ad racionem quatuor denariorum pro qualibet marca veri valoris ipsorum omnium et singulorum beneficiorum reddituum fructuum et proventuum tam mense nostre episcopali quam aliorum quorumcumque verus valor ad summam quadraginta trium marcarum quinque solidorum et novem denariorum ascendere non poterit quovis modo; volentes nichilominus vestris mandatis parere et processibus exequentes sine indignacionis nota prout in similibus fieri consueverat ac hujusmodi beneficia redditus fructus et proventus ecclesiastica infra nostras civitatem et diocesim obtinentes ac nos a censurarum involucione ac intricacionis et dubietatis scrupulo in quantum possumus perseverare,[15] facta distribucione inter dicta beneficia fructus redditus et proventus et nos ut premittitur obtinentes nomine procuracionum vestrarum pro uno anno de quo in dictis vestris litteris fit mencio quadraginta tres marcas et quinque solidos et novem denarios non absque difficultate nimia[16] exigi fecimus et levari, quam siquidem pecunie summam una cum nominibus omnium et singulorum beneficiorum ecclesiasticorum dictarum civitatis et diocesis et in quantum ad decimam sunt taxata in rotulis sub nostro inclusis sigillo hiis nostris litteris annexis conscriptis vobis et vestris

---

[15] MS. *perservare*
[16] Followed by erasure of 1.5 cm.

procuratoribus et ipsorum cuilibet per exhibitorem presencium transmittimus liberandam. Datum [Carlisle, 12 Sept. 1357].

203

[Fo.22; p. 43] CITACIO CONTRA RECTOREM ECCLESIE DE CASTELKAYROK' AD DICENDUM QUARE COADJUTOR NON DEBEAT SIBI DARI ETC. G. etc. dilecto filio decano nostro Karli' salutem [*etc.*]. Quia dominus Adam rector ecclesie de Castelkayrok' nostre diocesis quod dolenter referimus lepre macula sicuti plurimorum relacione didicimus est respersus, adeo quod propter ejusdem morbi deformitatem et horrorem parochianis suis sacramenta et sacramentalia ministrare nec sibi aut suis comode prospicere poterit; tibi mandamus quatinus cites peremptorie dictum dominum Adam quod die Jovis proximo post instans festum Epiphanie domini in capella manerii nostri de Rosa compareat si poterit personaliter coram nobis, alioquin per procuratorem sufficienter instructum potestatem sufficientem in hac parte ab ipso rectore habentem, causam racionabilem si quam habeat quare sibi coadjutorem dare et assignare juxta sanctiones canonicas minime debeamus propositurus et ostensurus, facturus ulterius et recepturus quod justicia suadebit. Et qualiter presens mandatum nostrum fueris executus, nos ad dictos diem et locum distincte et aperte certifices per litteras tuas patentes hanc seriem continentes. Datum [Rose, 31 Dec. 1357].

206

[Fo.22; p. 43] CERTIFICATORIUM LITTERE OFFICIALIS CURIE EBOR' PRO ALICIA UXORE THOME DE NEUTON DIRECTUM ut patet in eadem littera. Carissime domine et amice, litteras vestras nuper recepimus infrascriptas:
Venerabili in Christo patri et domino domino Gilberto dei gracia Karlii' .. episcopo .. officialis curie Ebor' salutem cum reverencia et honore debitis tanto patri. Cum in causa divorcii quoad thorum et mutuam cohabitacionem et aliis causis inter Thomam de Neuton et Aliciam uxorem suam coram nobis motis et pendentibus, pars ipsius Alicie coram nobis in forma juris fidem fecerit quod nonnulla [Fo.22^v; p. 44] instrumenta et munimenta parti ipsius Alicie in dicta causa ad probacionem intencionis sue necessaria in archivis vestris remaneant et consistunt, vestram reverendam paternitatem requirimus quatinus scrutatis archivis vestris predictis ipsa instrumenta sive munimenta fideliter transsumpta nobis sub sigillo vestro cum celeritate clausa transmittere velitis quibus negocium hujusmodi poterit expediri. Ad regimen ecclesie sue conservet vos altissimus per tempora diuturna. Datum Ebor' xviii° die mensis Januarii anno domini Millesimo CCC^{mo} lvii°.
Quarum occasione scrutatis archivis nostris inter cetera comperimus in eisdem quod Thomas de Neuton ad promocionem Alicie uxoris sue ad diem Jovis proximo post dominicam in Passione domini anno domini Millesimo CCC^{mo} liiii^{too} fuerat evocatus, quo die in capella manerii nostri de Rosa idem Thomas coram nobis personaliter comparuit, cui per nos objectum fuerat quod ipse dictam Aliciam uxorem suam a se et cohabitacione conjugali afuit temere

ammoverat nec eidem uxori sue vite necessaria ministraverat ut deberet. Qui quidem Thomas fatebatur quod cum dicta uxore sua non cohabitaverat, et dixit se ere alieno pregravatum quod non sufficiebat ad ministrandum eidem uxori sue vite necessaria. Et tandem post aliquales altercaciones obtulit se paratum ad standum mandatis ecclesie, et ibidem coram nobis promisit et tactis sacrosanctis dei Evangeliis juravit quod infra octo dies proximo sequentes ipsam uxorem suam ad cohabitacionem conjugalem reacciperet et ipsam extunc pertractaret affeccione conjugali et eidem vite necessaria ministraret prout sue suppetunt facultates. Et nichilominus eundem Thomam tunc ibidem presentem monuimus primo secundo et tercio quod premissa adimpleret sub pena excommunicacionis majoris, quam in ipsum exnunc prout extunc si in observacione premissorum defecerit in scriptis protulimus tunc ibidem.

Item subsequenter ad diem Mercurii proximo post festum sancti Dionisii Martiris anno domini Millesimo CCC^{mo} lv^{to} ad promocionem dicte Alicie uxoris sue idem Thomas coram nobis fuerat evocatus, quo die in capella dicti manerii coram nobis dictus Thomas personaliter comparuit et eidem per nos objectum fuerat quod dictam uxorem suam ad cohabitacionem conjugalem nondum readmiserat nec eidem vite necessaria ministraverat contra juramentum suum alias coram nobis prestitum, reatum perjurii aceciam sentenciam excommunicacionis majoris in ipsum late si ipsam infra dictum terminum non reacciperet ut predicitur incurrendo. Qui siquidem Thomas fatebatur quod ipsam Aliciam uxorem suam nondum reacceperat ad cohabitacionem conjugalem nec eidem vite necessaria ministraverat, set dixit quod tractatus inter ipsum Thomam et dominum Willelmum de Dacre super certa porcione dicte uxori sue pro vite ejusdem necessaria annuatim assignanda pendebat, petens quod de benignitate nostra supersedere vellemus a processu et execucione ulteriori contra eum faciendis tractatu hujusmodi suspendente et quousque certificati essemus de exitu dicti tractatus per dominam de Dacre et dominum Willelmum de Dacre supradictum; quam supersessionem eidem concessimus illa vice, et extunc usque in presens nichil omnino fecimus in negocio suprascripto. Et alia instrumenta sive munimenta dictas partes concernencia in nostris archivis non invenimus de presenti. Datum apud manerium nostrum de Rosa xxii° die mensis Januarii anno etc. lvii° et nostre consecracionis v^{to}.

207

LITTERA RECOM[M]ENDATORIA PRO NEGOCIIS ALICIE UXORIS THOME DE NEUTON. Amantissime domine et amice, negocium Alicie uxoris Thome de Neuton que coram vobis pendere dinoscitur vobis specialiter commendamus, rogantes quatinus parti dicte Alicie super expedicione negocii supradicti favorem quem bono modo impendere poteritis exhibere dignemini, justicia inoffensa. Experimento namque didicimus cerciori quod dicta Alicia non modo debito pertractata fuerat temporibus retroactis. Et ecce in hiis que penes nos volueritis parati erimus votis vestris. Scriptum apud manerium nostrum de Rosa xxii° Januarii.

213

[Fo.23; p. 45] BULLA PAPALIS PRO VISITACIONE IN DIOCESI KARLII' AUCTORITATE
APOSTOLICA EXCERCENDA. Innocencius episcopus servus servorum dei venerabili
fratri .. episcopo Karlii' et dilectis filiis ejus vicario in spiritualibus ac officiali
Karlii' salutem et apostolicam benedictionem. Licet universis .. archiepiscopis et
episcopis indicat sacrorum auctoritas canonum inter cetera visitacionis officium
ut subditos eis clerum et populum reficiant pabulo verbi dei et in eis corrigenda
corrigant, indirecta dirigant, reformanda reforment et reservata eis ministrent
indigentibus ecclesiastica sacramenta; quia tamen propter dierum maliciam et
pericula temporum que peccatis exigentibus invalescunt, nonnulli ex archiepiscopis et episcopis ipsis pro ecclesiarum commissarum eis tuicione vel
recuperacione jurium ab ecclesiis ipsis abesse compulsi sunt et compelluntur
inviti, quidam vero in propriis ecclesiis residentes propter guerras quibus
ipsorum aut vicine dioceses agitantur eorum civitates exire formidarunt eciam
et formidant, et alii justis impedimentis diversis aliis que parit hujusmodi
malicia dierum et temporum prepediti in aliis necessario ecclesiarum suarum
negociis occupantur, hujusmodi visitationis officium sicut moleste percepimus
fere ubique diu siluit ac silet.

Quod nos anxie cogitantes ac dignum et congruum arbitrantes ut dicti ..
archiepiscopi et episcopi onera incumbencia eis que soli portare nequeunt
mandata celestia exequendo cum aliis parcientes, hujusmodi visitacionis
officium viris timoratis et potentibus opere ac sermone committant salubriter
exequendum, ac ex debito apostolice servitutis que indicit ecclesiarum omnium
generaliter nobis curam cupientes, sic te (frater episcope) tuis et ecclesie tue
imminere negociis aliis quod populos tue cure commissos destitui proinde
auxilio spiritualis alimonie non contingat, discrecioni vestre de fratrum nostrorum et archiepiscoporum et episcoporum aliorumque prelatorum apud
sedem[17] apostolicam presencium[18] consilio districte precipiendo mandamus
quatinus per aliquam vel aliquas personam seu personas zelum dei ejusque
timorem habentes per te (predicte episcope) vel te a civitate et diocesi tuis
absente, per vos (filii vicarie et officialis aut alterum vestrum) ad id auctoritate
apostolica specialiter deputandum seu deputandos ecclesias et monasteria
aliaque loca ecclesiastica necnon capitula collegia conventus et personas
eorum secularia et regularia civitatis et diocesis[19] Karleolii' non exempta in
quibus tibi (episcope predicte) competit visitacionis officium de consuetudine
[Fo.23ᵛ; p. 46] vel de jure semel tantum, statim receptis presentibus vel sequenti
immediate proximo anno, si hoc anno tu (predicte episcope) visitaveris forsitan[20]
visitantes corrigenda corrigatis, reformanda reformetis, indirecta dirigatis et
quemcumque emendacionis sarculo indigere cognoveritis solicite expurgetis,
ac omnia exequamini que ad visitacionis dinoscuntur officium pertinere, ab

---

[17] This word, in another hand, in margin before line beginning *apostolicam*.
[18] From *et archiepiscoporum* not in the first version of the mandate (see note to **213** in
calendar).
[19] *et diocesis* apparently underdotted, but by a smudge from underdotting of *Lanercost*,
the last word on the facing folio (see **211** and note).
[20] From *vel sequenti* is another insertion.

ecclesiis monasteriis locis capitulis collegiis conventibus et personis eisdem taliter procuraciones visitatis personaliter episcopo exhiberi solitas juxta formam constitucionis per felicis recordacionis Benedictum papam xii predecessorem nostrum super hoc edite in pecunia numerata racione visitacionis hujusmodi recepturi.

Ut autem visitacio hujusmodi absque mora longioris temporis compleatur,[21] eisdem personis unum duo tria vel plura ecclesias monasteria et loca capitula conventus et collegia una et eadem die visitandi et a singulis eorum recipiendi procuraciones exhiberi solitas ut premittitur episcopo personaliter visitanti, nichil tamen de hiis que circa hujusmodi visitacionis officium debent fieri omittendo, plenam concedimus tenore presencium potestatem; non obstantibus constitucionibus a felicis recordacionis Gregorio x et Innocencio iiij ac eodem Benedicto et quibuslibet aliis Romanis pontificibus predecessoribus nostris in contrarium editis, ac privilegiis et indulgenciis apostolicis quibuscumque generalibus vel specialibus, de quibus quorumque totis tenoribus de verbo ad verbum in nostris litteris specialem fieri oporteat mencionem et per que ipsis nostris litteris non expressa vel totaliter non inserta effectus earum impediri valeat quomodolibet vel differri, seu si eisdem capitulis collegiis conventibus ac personis communiter vel divisim a sede apostolica sit indultum quod interdici suspendi vel excommunicari non possint per litteras apostolicas non facientes plenam et expressam ac de verbo ad verbum de indulto hujusmodi mencionem, contradictores per censuram ecclesiasticam appellacione postposita compescendo.

Sic igitur fideles diligentes et sedulos exhibeatis vos in premissis quod ex operacionibus vestris uberes fructus proveniant ut speramus, vosque preter mercedis eterne premium et apostolice favoris graciam laudabilis fame attolli preconiis valeatis.[22] Nostre tamen intencionis existit quod hii quorum facultates ad integram solucionem hujusmodi procuracionis, supportatis aliis oneribus consuetis, non suppetunt ultra quam juxta suarum hujusmodi facultatum exigenciam comode possunt. Illi vero qui de dicta procuracione nichil solvere possunt, super cujus modi eorum impotencia vestras consciencias oneramus, ad solvendum aliquid pretextu mandati hujusmodi nullatenus compellantur. Datum apud Villamnovam Avinion' diocesis x kalendas Septembris pontificatus nostri anno tercio.

219

[Fo.24; p. 47] COMMISSIO AD CORRIGENDUM COMPERTA IN DICTA VISITACIONE. G. etc. dilecto filio magistro Johanni de Welton clerico nostro familiari juris perito salutem [etc.]. Cum in visitacione, quam nuper auctoritate apostolica nobis in hac parte commissa per certos commissarios nostros ad hoc specialiter deputatos in nostris civitate et diocesi Karlii' fecimus excerceri, nonnulli defectus excessus et crimina comperti fuerint et detecti; nos volentes super reformacione super hujusmodi defectuum excessuum et criminum procedere

---

[21] From *Ut autem* replacing *persone ipse per vos ad visitacionem hujusmodi ut premittitur deputande minus in ea exequenda graventur,* in first version.

[22] From *non obstantibus constitucionibus* (15 lines above) inserted in this second version.

prout de mandato apostolico nobis in hac parte directo nobis arcius est injunctum, set quia sumus ad presens arduis [negociis] prepediti quominus expedicioni premissorum[23] valeamus, ad corrigendum puniendum et canonice reformandum defectus excessus et crimina in dicta visitacione qualitercumque comperta, necnon ad cognoscendum procedendum statuendum diffiniendum et exequendum in premissis et ea contingentibus ac in omnibus et singulis articulis incidentibus vel emergentibus quovismodo si et quatenus judicialem indaginem seu cause cognicionem requirunt, aliaque omnia et singula facienda et expedienda que in premissis et circa ea necessaria fuerint seu eciam oportuna, tibi de cujus fidelitate et industria plene confidimus vices nostras committimus cum cujuslibet canonice potestate. In cujus rei testimonium sigillum nostrum est appensum. Datum [Rose, 13 May 1358].

247

[Fo.26ᵛ; p. 52] LITTERA GENERALIS SENTENCIE CONTRA OMNES QUI INJECERUNT MANUS VIOLENTAS IN WILLELMUM CAUDRYMAN APPARITOREM DECANATUS KARLIOLI. G. etc. dilectis filiis priori et suppriori ecclesie nostre Karl' .. archidiacono et .. officiali nostris Karl' .. prioribus de Lanercost' et Wederhale nostre diocesis ac omnibus et singulis decanis rectoribus et vicariis per nostras civitatem et diocesim constitutis salutem [*etc.*]. Etsi quorumdam delinquencium interdum pro tempore dissimularentur offense, illorum tamen proterviam tollerare non convenit qui emulacione livida almam matrem ecclesiam et ipsius ministris continuatis versuciis opprimunt et conculceant. Sane prothdolor rumor inplacidus cunctis Christi fidelibus perquam execrabilis prorumpens in publicum ad nostrum deduxit auditum quod cum Willelmus Caudryman decanatus Karlii' noster apparitor et pro apparitore nostro habito palam habitus et publice reputatus ad exequendum mandata nostra et officialium nostrorum licita et canonica nuper apud Brampton dicte nostre diocesis se contulerat die mercatus inibi observati et presertim ut propter subditorum nostrorum copiam ibidem affluencium sic sibi commissum posset officium execucioni uberius demandare, nonnulli siquidem Christiane religionis immemores ex precogitatis malicia et insidiis in ipsum Willelmum nostrum ut premittitur apparitorem circa execucionem sui officii insistentem ne nostra et officialium nostrorum mandata suumque ulterius exequeretur officium irruentes manusque inicientes temere violentas ipsum maliciose et inhumaniter pertractarunt et atrociter vulnerarunt, vociferantes prout refertur vulgariter 'quia coram ministris episcopi nos evocari fecisti, jam talia donaria reportabis', in omnipotentis dei sancteque juris ecclesie contumeliam juris injuriam libertatis et imunitatis ecclesiasticarum enervacionem nostreque jurisdictionis spiritualis et ecclesie Karlii' multiplicem et notoriam lesionem. Cumque contra tam nephanda perpetratores facinora sit majoris excommunicacionis sentencia non solum a canone quam eciam sanctorum patrum auctoritate proinde promulgata, nos considerantes quanta ex tam horrenda feritate sceleris perpetrati spiritualis jurisdictionis depressio libertatisque ecclesiastice subversio provenirent in cleroque et populo cismata pulularent facinoribus neglectis hujusmodi impunitis, vobis igitur et vestrum

[23] Here repeating *ad presens*

cuilibet conjunctim et divisim in virtute sancte obediencie et sub pena districcionis canonice firmiter injungentes committimus et mandamus quatinus omnes et singulos, qui in prefatum Willelmum apparitorem nostrum manus injecerunt temere violentas ipsumque ut premittitur vulnerarunt et nequiter pertractarunt hujusmodive maleficia fieri mandarunt procurarunt seu eisdem auxilium prestiterunt vel favorem, sic fuisse et esse majoris excommunicacionis sentencia dampnabiliter involutos in ecclesia nostra cathedrali Karlii' singulisque aliis ecclesiis nostrarum civitatis et diocesis singulis diebus dominicis et festivis, assumptis ad hoc vobiscumque omnibus capellanis et aliis in ecclesiis hujusmodi divina ministrantibus albis indutis, intra missarum solempnia cum major aderit populi multitudo, pulsatis campanis etc., a denunciacione hujusmodi non cessantes quousque etc., inquirentes insuper de nominibus etc., de quibus cum vobis etc.[24] Datum [Rose, 28 Apr. 1359].

254

[Fo.27ᵛ; p. 54] DIMISSIO MAGISTRI HENRICI DE ROSSE RECTORIS ECCLESIE DE CLYBORNE SUPER NON RESIDENCIA ET TERMINO SUSCEPCIONIS SACRORUM ORDINUM. Universis [as in 71 – salvatoris.] Noverit universitas vestra quod nos nuper nostram diocesim jure nostro diocesano visitantes, invenerimus quod magister Henricus dictus Heynes de Rosse rector ecclesie de Clyborne dicte nostre diocesis a tempore institucionis et induccionis sue in ecclesia antedicta se ab eadem ecclesia sua contra instituta canonica pluries absentavit, curam et regimen dicte ecclesie et parochianorum ejusdem sibi commissa deseruit, et in locis aliis a dicta ecclesia sua distantibus et remotis temeritate propria moram traxit, bona ad eandem ecclesiam spectancia improvide dispensando, in anime sue periculum et exemplum pessimum aliorum, ac eciam quod idem magister Henricus se non fecerat infra annum a tempore promocionis sue ad dictam ecclesiam et pacifice possessionis ejusdem ad sacerdocium juxta s[c]ita canonum promoveri; eundem magistrum Henricum ad certos dies et loca super premissis fecimus coram nobis ad judicium evocari. Quibus diebus et locis dictus magister Henricus comparuit coram nobis et diversas litteras dispensacionum de insistendo studio litterarum juxta capitulum *Cum ex eo* ac legitime super non residencia sua in dicta ecclesia predecessorum nostrorum episcoporum Karlii' sigillis suis signatas nobis satis notis retroactis facta temporibus, quodque non teneretur ad ulteriorem ordinum suscepcionem preterquam ad ordinem subdiaconatus durantibus dispensacionibus et licenciis supradictis, coram nobis exhibuit et ostendit, necnon quod hujusmodi licenciis et dispensacionibus juxta vim formam et effectum earumdem usus est nos sufficienter et ad plenum docuit et eciam informavit, propter quod ipsum magistrum Henricum habita super premissis deliberacione pleniori ab ulteriori impeticione officii nostri quoad premissa dimittimus et absolv[i]mus per decretum. In cujus rei testimonium litteras nostras sibi fieri fecimus has patentes, quas nostri sigilli appensione fecimus communiri. Datum [Rose, 1 May 1357].

---

[24] Cf. **284*** for complete version.

265

[Fo.29; p. 57] INSTRUMENTUM SUPER PERCEPCIONE OBLACIONUM PER VENERABILEM
PATREM G. KARLII' EPISCOPUM DIE SEPULTURE DOMINI WILLELMI BARONIS DE
CRAYSTOK IN ECCLESIA DE CRAYSTOK EIDEM VENERABILI PATRI FACTARUM RACIONE
PERSONALIS PERACTIONIS OFFICII DICTE SEPULTURE PER EUNDEM PATREM ETC. UT
INFRA. In dei nomine amen. Per presens publicum instrumentum cunctis
appareat evidenter quod anno domini ab incarnacione ejusdem secundum
cursum et computacionem ecclesie Anglicane Millesimo CCC^mo lix°, indiccione
duodecima et pontificatus sanctissimi in Christo patris et domini nostri domini
Innocencii divina providencia pape vj anno septimo mensis Augusti die octavo,
videlicet die Jovis proximo post festum sancti Petri quod dicitur Ad vincula, in
ecclesia parochiali de Craystok Karlii' diocesis venerabilis in Christo pater et
dominus dominus Gilbertus dei gracia Karlii' episcopus presencialiter constitutus, missam pro anima nobilis viri domini Willelmi baronis de Craystok
defuncti que pro defunctis celebrari solet in eadem ecclesia celebravit, intra
cujus misse solempnia tempore oblacionis ut moris est faciende idem venerabilis
pater omnes et singulas oblaciones in dicta ecclesia (videlicet duas cassides,
unam pro pace et alteram pro guerra; duos gladios, unum pro pace et alterum
pro guerra; duo scuta, unum pro pace et alterum pro guerra; duas lanceas,
unam pro pace et alteram pro guerra; duos equos armatos, unum pro pace et
alterum pro guerra; duos homines armatos, unum pro pace et alterum pro
guerra in armis dicti defuncti armatum, prout moris est) ac pecuniam in denariis
numeratis per diversos nobiles milites et alios ibidem congregatos sibi factas
recepit personaliter et admisit, ac suis familiaribus ibidem astantibus tradidit
conservanda. Qua siquidem missa celebrata officioque sepulture per eundem
venerabilem patrem peracto, corporeque ipsius domini Willelmi tradito sepulture, prefatus venerabilis pater dictos nobiles viros prelatos et alios ibidem
congregatos coram eo in dicta ecclesia fecerat evocari, et contemplacione
dominorum et prelatorum tunc ibidem astancium omnia et singula sibi in
dicta missa oblata, que ad eum ut dicebat de jure et consuetudine racione
celebracionis personalis dicte misse et peractionis hujusmodi officii pertinebant,
domine Johanne nuper consorti ipsius domini Willelmi et jam relicte contulit et
donavit et sibi fecit eidem realiter liberari, pecuniam tamen in denariis sibi ut
premittitur oblatam clericis de capella sua tantummodo reservando.

Acta sunt hec in nobilium et venerabilium virorum dominorum Radulphi de
Nevill, Thome de Lucy domini de Cokerm', Rogeri domini de Clifford, Henrici
Lescropp, Thome de Musgrave senioris, militum, fratrum Johannis prioris
Karli', Roberti abbatis de Holmcoltram', Lamberti abbatis de Hepp, ac
magistrorum Willelmi de Routhbury archidiaconi Karli', Thome de Salkeld
rectoris ecclesie de Clifton notarii publici, domini Ricardi de Aslakby vicarii
ecclesie de Staynwigges, meique notarii publici infrascripti presencia et aliorum
in multitudine copiosa.

Et ego Willelmus de Ragenhill clericus Ebor' diocesis publicus auctoritate
apostolica notarius premissis omnibus et singulis dum sic ut premittitur
agerentur et fierent sub anno indiccione pontificatu die mense et loco superius
annotatis una cum predictis testibus presens interfui, eaque sic fieri vidi et audivi
ac de mandato dicti venerabilis patris et domini mei domini Karlii' episcopi

scripsi et in hanc publicam formam redegi signoque meo et nomine consuetis signavi in fidem et testimonium premissorum.

283

[Fo.31; p. 61] DIMISSIO PRIORIS ET CONVENTUS DE WARTR' QUOAD RETENCIONEM ECCLESIARUM DE BARTON ET ASCOM ET ALIA SUPRADICTA IN EADEM DIMISSA. Universis [as in 114 – salutem] in domino sempiternam. Nobis nuper ecclesiam et diocesim nostram Karlii' jure diocesano visitantibus, inter ceteros vocatos ad visitacionem predictam specialiter vocari fecimus ad eandem religiosos viros priorem et conventum monasterii sancti Jacobi de Wartria Ebor' diocesis ad ostendendum nobis quo jure pretendunt se tenere et possidere ecclesias de Ascom et de Barton parochiales et unam marcam nomine pensionis annue in ecclesia de Clifton, necnon decimas parciales de Sokbred et Tyrerga; item tam de superiori quam inferiori Wynderga infra fines et limites ecclesie de Barton parochialis antedicte. Dicti religiosi per procuratorem sufficientem dictis die et loco per nos sibi assignatis legitime coram nobis comparentes, primo quantum ad ecclesiam de Ascom; item quoad pensionem i marce de ecclesia de Clifton, necnon quoad parciales decimas supradictas, tam per legitima documenta episcoporum Karli' predecessorum nostrorum ac ceterorum Christi fidelium quam ex cursu tanti temporis cujus contrarii memoria hominum non existit se sufficienter munitos, ac omnia et singula premissa absque interpellacione interrupcione seu turbacione qualibet continue et pacifice possedisse et in presenti possidere legitime ostenderunt. Quantum vero ad ecclesiam de Barton eis similiter appropriatam, exhibuerunt coram nobis tam appropriacionem bone memorie Johannis predecessoris nostri quam confirmacionem prioris et capituli nostre ecclesie Karlii' predicte, continentes causas motivas et probabiles quare facta fuit eis appropriacio antedicta. Verum licet assercioni tanti patris in hiis que in sua appropriacione predicta expressit[25] merito fidem deberemus, nos tamen ut veritas lucidius patefiat omniumque opinio salva fiat in premissis, ad probandum causas in dicta appropriacione contentas veras esse tam testium fidedignorum in magno numero quam aliorum documentorum informacionem plenam recepimus in predictis, propter quod visis et intellectis supradictis, dicimus pronunciamus et declaramus in hiis scriptis quoad omnia tam ad duas ecclesias antedictas et ad pensionem ipsam quam ad decimas parciales predictas prefatos priorem et conventum sufficienter munitos fuisse et esse, ac eosdem tanquam canonicos possessores illorum ab officio nostro absolvimus et pro futuris temporibus in pace dimittimus absolutos. In cujus rei [*etc.* Rose, 1 Sept. 1359].

284

[Fo.31; p. 61] MANDATUM AD PUBLICANDUM OMNES EXCOMMUNICATOS QUI CEPERUNT ET ABSTULERUNT QUEMDAM BOVEM NIGRUM EPISCOPI KARLII'. G. etc. dilecto filio vicario ecclesie de Penreth nostre diocesis salutem [*etc.*]. Cum sanctorum

[25] MS. *expremit*

patrum pia devocio circa immunitatem et conservacionem ecclesiastice libertatis et rerum ecclesiasticarum laudabiliter laboraverat, inter cetera statuendo quod si quis de domibus maneriis grangiis vel aliis locis ad archiepiscopos episcopos vel aliquas personas ecclesiasticas vel ad ipsas ecclesias pertinentibus quicquam preter voluntatem aut permissionem dominorum vel eorum quo sunt hujusmodi rerum custodiis deputati consumere vel auferre aut contrectare vel liberta[te]s ecclesiasticas violare perturbare aut infringere presumpserit, sit ipso facto majoris excommunicacionis sentencia involutus, a qua donec satisfecerit absolucionis graciam minime consequatur; quidam tamen iniquitatis filii sue salutis immemores manus suas nescientes a vetitis cohibere nuper post festum sancti Michaelis proximo preteritum quemdam bovem nostrum nigrum de locis et pasturis ad nos et episcopatum nostrum pertinentibus et infra parochiam ecclesie nostre de Penreth predicta situatis ceperunt abstulerunt et ad loca remota et extera abduxerunt, in animarum suarum grave periculum, libertatis et immunitatis ecclesiastice violacionem, dampnum nostrum non modicum et gravamen, dictam majoris excommunicacionis sentenciam contra hujusmodi delinquentes proinde promulgatam dampnabiliter incurrendo. Quocirca tibi mandamus firmiter injungentes quatinus omnes et singulos qui dictum bovem nostrum ut premittitur ceperunt abstulerunt et abduxerunt, seu qui eisdem in premissis consilium dederunt auxilium vel favorem, in dictam majoris excommunicacionis sentenciam incidisse ac excommunicatos fuisse et esse occasione premissa in ecclesia nostra de Penreth predicta hac instanti die omnium sanctorum ac extunc singulis diebus dominicis et festivis intra missarum solempnia, dum in ea major fuerit populi multitudo, pulsatis campanis, candelis accensis et extinctis, cruceque erecta et alia solempnitate qua decet adhibita publice solempniter et in genere denuncies et facias nunciari, a denunciacione hujusmodi non cessans quousque super hoc aliud a nobis habueris in mandatis; inquirens nichilominus de nominibus hujusmodi delinquencium, de quibus cum tibi constiterit nobis constare facias de eisdem una cum omni eo quod feceris in premissis citra instans festum sancti Edmundi regis per litteras tuas patentes harum seriem et nomina malefactorum hujusmodi continentes. Datum [Rose, 28 Oct. 1359].

291

[Fo.31ᵛ; p. 62] LITTERA CONTINENS PROCESSUM FACTUM CONTRA ABBATEM ET CONVENTUM MONASTERII BEATE MARIE EBOR' IN VISITATIONE AUCTORITATE APOSTOLICA EXCERCITA RATIONE ECCLESIARUM ETC. NOTIFICATIONEM OFFICIALI CURIE EBOR' ETC. UT INFRA. Gilbertus permissione divina Karlii' episcopus sub infrascripta forma auctoritate apostolica delegatus venerabili viro .. officiali curie Ebor' ipsius commissario seu vices ejus gerentibus quibuscumque pluribus aut uno²⁶ ac omnibus et singulis quos infrascripta tangunt seu tangere poterunt in futurum salutem in omnium salvatore. Litteras apostolicas xixᵒ die mensis Junii anno domini Millesimo CCCᵐᵒ quinquagesimo septimo recepimus in hec verba: Innocencius episcopus servus servorum dei venerabili fratri .. episcopo Karli' et dilectis filiis vicario ejus in spiritualibus ac officiali Karli'

---

²⁶ Interlined from *pluribus*

salutem et apostolicam benedictionem. Licet universis[27] .. archiepiscopis et
episcopis indicat sacrorum auctoritas canonum inter cetera visitacionis officium
etc. ut supra in ix° folio proximo precedenti.[28] Quarum auctoritate litterarum in
quibus inter alia continetur nichil de hiis que circa hujusmodi visitacionis
officium debent fieri omittendo, nos nuper nostram diocesim Karlii' per certum
deputatum nostrum virum utique providum et discretum secundum formam
dictis litteris traditam visitantes, nonnulli religiosi viri beneficia ecclesiastica
decimas parciales ac pensiones infra dictam nostram diocesim in usus proprios
se habere pretendentes ad ostendendum et producendum jus et titulum quod et
quem super pretensione et occupacione beneficiorum ecclesiasticorum decimarum parcialium et pensionum hujusmodi habuerunt et habere noscuntur
coram nostro deputato hujusmodi ad certos dies et loca eis assignata fuerant
evocati. Inter quos siquidem religiosos viros venerabiles viri abbas et conventus
monasterii beate Marie Ebor' ecclesias parochiales de Kirkebystephan, Morland, Brounfeld, sanctorum Michaelis et Laurencii de Appelby, Wederhale et
Warthewyk', una cum quibusdam decimis parcialibus et pensionibus infra
Karlii' diocesim, sibi et ipso monasterio unitas fore pretendentes pariter et
annexas, ad certos diem et locum eis assignatos per quemdam Adam de Burton
procuratorem suum sufficienter et litteratorie constitutum coram dicto nostro
deputato comparuerunt. Idemque procurator nomine dominorum suorum
predictorum pro jure et titulo quod et quem super unione annexione et
occupacione predictarum ecclesiarum parochialium decimarum parcialium et
pensionum hujusmodi memorati religiosi domini sui se habere dicebant
quamplura litteras instrumenta et munimenta tam Romanorum pontificum
quam episcoporum Karli' predecessorum nostrorum, capituli ecclesie Karlii' ac
diversorum dominorum temporalium, necnon quamdam proposicionem in
scriptis redactam dictis die et loco coram supradicto deputato exhibuit produxit
et proposuit, ac eidem deputato tunc ibidem veram omnium sic exhibitorum
productorum et propositorum copiam una cum copia sui procuratorii liberavit.

Subsequenterque dictus deputatus volens dicta exhibita producta et proposita
per partem dictorum religiosorum ut prefertur examinare ac super sufficiencia
et insufficiencia pertinencia et admissibilitate eorundem juxta juris exigenciam
informari, partique dictorum religiosorum super premissis exhibere justicie
complementum, supradicti religiosi domini abbas et conventus ad comparen-
dum et faciendum super sic exhibitis productis et propositis in visitacione
auctoritate apostolica excercita ut prefertur et ipsorum examinacioni interessendum ad certos diem et locum ac terminum sufficientem coram nobis
deputatis nostris pluribus aut uno citati fuerant legitime et premuniti, prout
per certificatorium citacionis hujusmodi inde transmissum liquere dinoscitur
evidenter. Quibus vero die et loco prefati religiosi palam et publice ac successivis
vicibus et repetitis preconizati et diucius exspectati, per se vel procuratorem
minime comparuerunt unde reputati fuerunt et merito contumaces, adjecto
tamen tunc ibidem quod iterato dicti religiosi coram deputatis nostris pluribus
aut uno pro loco et tempore oportunis evocari et premuniri deberent ad
faciendum et recipiendum super productis propositis et exhibitis memoratis
prout superius memoratur ac natura negocii hujusmodi exigit et requirit.

---

[27] Interlined.
[28] Cf. **213***.

Vobis igitur, domine .. officialis curie Ebor', vestris commissariis vicesve gerentibus quibuscumque et ipsorum cuilibet ac omnibus et singulis quos suprascripta negocia tangunt seu tangere poterunt communiter vel divisim auctoritatem a sede apostolica nobis episcopo Karli' delegatam visitacionemque nostre diocesis Karlii' dicte sedis auctoritate et processus in ea parte factos ut premittitur et indecisos pendentes notificamus et intimamus, ac ad vestram, domine officialis predicte, vestrorum commissariorum vicesve gerencium et ipsorum cujuscumque communiter et divisim ac omnium aliorum quos presens tangit negocium seu tangere poterit noticiam deducimus per presentes, auctoritate apostolica qua fungimur in hac parte mandantes firmiterque inhibentes ne vos, domine officialis predicte, quicquam attemptetis seu attemptari faciatis vestrive commissarii aut vices gerentes attemptent vel faciant attemptari eorumve aliquis attemptet vel faciat attemptari per quod memorati visitacio et processus in ea parte facti et pendentes ut premittitur impediri valeant quomodolibet vel differri. Et ne presidentes dicte curie Ebor' qui sunt et erunt pro tempore ipsorum vel aliquis aut quamvis alius cujuscumque dignitatis preeminencie vel condicionis extiterit quicquam usurpent vel attemptent usurpet vel attemptet per quod visitacio et processus auctoritate apostolica habiti ut predicitur et pendentes impediri valeant vel differri, vel quod in prejudicium seu derogacionem juris et jurisdiccionis sedis apostolice cedere poterit quovis modo, ad quam immediate solum et insolidum reformacio et reparacio minus legitime gestorum et exercitorum in visitacione hujusmodi vel ipsius occasione sique sunt vel erunt pro tempore dinoscitur pertinere, sacrosanctam sedem apostolicam provocamus et provocando pariter appellamus in hiis scriptis. In quorum omnium et singulorum premissorum sigillum nostrum fecimus hiis apponi. Datum [Rose, 4 Jan. 1360].

301

[Fo.32ᵛ; p. 64] PROVOCACIO PRO DOMINO GILBERTO KARLII' EPISCOPO GENERALIS. In dei nomine amen. Cum nos Gilbertus permissione divina Karlii' .. episcopus fuerimus et simus episcopatum Karli' canonice assecuti ipsumque episcopatum sic assecutum cum suis juribus et pertinenciis universis possederimus per nonnulla tempora et possideamus in presenti pacifice et quiete, fuissemusque et simus integri status et bone fame nullis suspensionis vel excommunicacionis sentenciis involuti; metuentes tamen et conicientes ex quibusdam probabilibus causis ac aliis verisimilibus conjecturis nobis circa statum nostrum jus et possessionem quod et quam in dicto episcopatu obtinere dinoscimur grave posse de facto in futurum prejudicium gravari, ne quis vel qui cujuscumque dignitatis preeminencie status vel condicionis extiterit quicquam in prejudicium nostrum vel status nostri juris et possessionis nostrorum predictorum attemptet vel attemptent faciat vel faciant aliqualiter attemptari citando monendo suspendendo excommunicando excommunicatum vel suspensum denunciando vel denunciari mandando interdicendo jura nostra et ecclesie nostre Karlii' usurpando spoliando spoliarive mandando molestando inquietando perturbando seu quovis alio modo gravando, sacrosanctam sedem apostolicam directe et curiam Ebor' tuitorio in hiis scriptis provocamus et provocando appellamus et apostolos instanter instancius et instantissime ac iterum quatenus in hoc casu de jure sunt petendum petimus, subicientes nos jus nostrum statumque et possessionem nostros predictos proteccioni et defensioni sedis et curie predictarum.

Memorandum quod xxvii° die Januarii anno domini ab incarnacione ejusdem secundum cursum et computacionem ecclesie Angl' millesimo CCC^{mo} lix° indictione xiii^a et pontificatus sanctissimi in Christo patris et domini nostri domini Innocencii divina providencia pape vi anno octavo, dictus venerabilis pater in deambulatorio coram hostio capelle manerii sui de Rosa Karlii' diocesis presencialiter constitutus dictam provocacionem in scriptis redactam fecit et legit, presentibus discretis viris dominis Petro de Morland vicario ecclesie de Torpenhowe, Ricardo de Aslacby vicario ecclesie de Wygton et Ada[29] de Foresta rectori ecclesie de Cambok', Karlii' diocesis, et me Willelmo de Ragenhill notario publico etc. —— Ragen'.

316

[Fo.34; p. 67] PRONUNCIACIO ET DECLARACIO FACTA PER DOMINUM KARLII' EPISCOPUM PRO ARCHIDIACONO KARL'. In primis fiat pronunciacio et declaracio pro archidiacono Karli' quod liceat sibi habere clericum in capitulis nostris per totam diocesim nostram per officialem et ministros nostros celebrandis ad assistendum eisdem officiali et ministris nostris capitula hujusmodi sic celebrantibus in omnibus correccionibus inibi faciendis et ad contrarotulandum super correccionibus sic factis. Item quod liceat eidem archidiacono subditis sue visitacioni per suas litteras ad subeundum visitacionem suam convocare. Item quod contra non comparentes sic vocatos procedere possit per censuras ecclesiasticas. Item quod contra non solventes procuraciones sibi debitas racione visitacionis sue impense et excercite et eorum beneficia similiter procedere possit per censuras ecclesiasticas quascumque. Item quod liceat sibi quociens decani nostri dicte nostre diocesis compotum reddiderint coram ministris nostris ad audiendum hujusmodi compotum deputatis, porcionem correccionum omnium in dictis capitulis nostris per dictos ministros nostros factarum, videlicet tercium denarium correccionum hujusmodi, ac porcionem synodalium, videlicet tercium denarium sibi debitum, per manus dictorum decanorum nostrorum recipere et habere, ac contra decanos hujusmodi porciones non solventes servato processu debito procedere per censuras ecclesiasticas.

Memorandum quod secundo die Maii anno domini Millesimo CCC^{mo} lx^{mo} facta fuit pronunciacio et declaracio premissorum per venerabilem patrem et dominum dominum Gilbertum dei gracia Karlii' episcopum in camera principali manerii sui de Rosa, presentibus magistro Willelmo de Routhbury archidiacono Karli' et me W. de Rag' clerico.

320

[Fo.34^v; p. 68] LITTERA TESTIMONIALIS SUPER DIVORCIACIONE MATRIMONII INTER WILLELMUM DE STAPELTON ET ALICIAM FILIAM RICARDI DE WHYTEFELD ILLEGITIME

---

[29] MS. *Adam*

CONTRACTI. Universis ad quos presentes littere pervenerint Gilbertus permissione divina Karlii' .. episcopus salutem in omnium salvatore. Noverit universitas vestra quod cum Willelmus de Stapelton et Alicia filia Ricardi de Whytefeld fuissent nuper coram nobis ex officio nostro super matrimonio in casu a jure non permisso, ac eciam clandestine inter eosdem ut dicebatur celebrato contra canonicas sancciones, judicialiter impetiti; iidem Willelmus et Alicia ad certos dies et loca eis in hac parte assignatos coram nobis legitime comparentes, impetita et sic eis opposita, hujusmodi matrimonium fuisse inter eosdem dictis subsistentibus causis et obstantibus illegitime contractum et celebratum judicialiter sunt confessi. Super quibus necnon oppositis ut premittitur et impetitis, tam per testes coram nobis productos et examinatos quam alias informaciones legitimas sufficienter et ad plenum recepimus veritatem. Et quia per hujusmodi testimonium deposiciones ac alias informaciones legitimas coram nobis in hac parte productas evidenter comperimus matrimonium inter ipsos Willelmum et Aliciam illegitime et de facto ut premittitur contractum de jure non posse subsistere nec debere, ipsum matrimonium quatenus de facto processit divorciavimus adnullavimus dissolvimus et irritum nunciavimus sentencialiter et diffinitive, quod omnibus et singulis quorum interest innotescimus per presentes quibus sigillum nostrum apposuimus in fidem et testimonium premissorum. Datum [Rose, 1 June 1360].

324

COMMISSIO AD INQUIRENDUM SUPER PROSTRACIONEM QUORUNDAM ARCUUM IN ECCLESIA DE BURGO SUPER SABUL'. G. etc. dilectis filiis magistro Willelmo de Ragenhill clerico nostro familiari ac decano nostro Karli' salutem [etc.]. Quia nuper relacione nobis innotuit plurimorum quod quidam parochiani ecclesie parochialis de Burgo super Sabulon' nostre diocesis nuper quemdam arcum operi novi campanilis adherentem in dicta ecclesia antiquitus situatum, irrequisito consensu et assensu nostri loci ordinario, ipsius ecclesie parochianorum temeritate propria circumfoderunt, lapides et cementa inde amoventes, cujus occasione non tam arcus hujusmodi set alii dicte ecclesie arcus prefato arcui contigui corruerunt in deformitatem ecclesie, sancte libertatis ecclesie prejudicium ac parochianorum dicte ecclesie dampnum non modicum et gravamen; nos volentes super hujumodi facto effici cerciores, vobis et alteri vestrum committimus et mandamus quatinus ad dictam ecclesiam personaliter declinantes, per viros fidedignos dicte ecclesie parochianos juratos et diligenter examinatos, quis hujusmodi arcuum ruinam fecerat at occasionem ruine hujusmodi prestiterat, et an de consensu parochianorum dicte ecclesie hec facta fuerant vel non, et an prostracio arcuum hujusmodi prefate ecclesie sit dampnosa et si sic in quantum, an eciam ille vel illi qui arcus corruere fecerant hujusmodi potentes sint ad satisfaciendum deo et ecclesie ac parochianis ejusdem de dampnis hujusmodi sic illatis, necnon de ceteris circumstanciis in hac parte requisitis at de nominibus eorum qui arcus corruere fecerunt hujusmodi, inquiratis et alter vestrum inquirat diligencius veritatem. Et nos de omni eo quod feceritis et inveniritis seu alter vestrum fecerit et inveniret in premissis, ac de nominibus per quos hujusmodi inquisicio capta fuerit, certificetis seu alter vestrum certificet hujusmodi negocio expedito per litteras vestras aut suas patentes harum seriem continentes sigillo tuo decane signatas. In cujus rei testimonium sigillum nostrum est appensum. Datum [Rose, 15 July 1360].

325

DIMISSIO DOMINI WILLELMI DEL HALL RECTORIS DE BOUNESSE. In dei nomine amen. Nuper nos Gilbertus permissione divina Karlii' .. episcopus ex officii nostri debito nostram diocesim visitantes, dominum Willelmum del Hall rectorem ecclesie de Bounesse dicte nostre diocesis se pretendentem[30] inter alios rectores et vicarios nostre diocesis ad producendum et exhibendum titulum et jus si quem vel quod super assecucione occupacione et retencione ecclesie de Bounesse memorate se habere pretendit ad certos diem et locum ad judicium coram nobis fecimus evocari; qui siquidem dominus Willelmus rectorem ecclesie de Bounesse ut premittitur se pretendens dictis die et loco personaliter comparuit coram nobis, allegans et quemdam articulum in scriptis redactum exhibens et proponens infrascriptum seriem continentem:

In dei nomine amen. Coram vobis venerabili in Christo patre et domino domino Gilberto dei gracia Karlii' episcopo diocesim vestram actualiter visitanti,[31] dico allego et propono ego Willelmus del Hall rector ecclesie de Bounesse dicte vestre Karlii' diocesis quod ipsam ecclesiam meam de Bounesse fueram a diu est et sum in presenti titulo canonico et legitimo assecutus ac in corporalem possessionem ejusdem ecclesie rite et legitime auctoritate sufficienti inductus, quodque a tempore assecucionis et induccionis hujusmodi memoratam ecclesiam de Bounesse possedi occupavi et tenui, possideo occupo et teneo hiis diebus. Quare probatis premissis seu aliqua via juris detectis vel declaratis, peto a vobis, reverendo in Christo patre et domino, quod vos me Willelmum predictum predictam ecclesiam de Bounesse fuisse et esse canonice et legitime assecutum ipsamque possedisse occupasse et tenuisse ac possidere occupare et tenere canonice et legitime vestra sentencia diffinitiva pronuncietis judicialiter et declaretis, meque tanquam sufficienter et plene munitum in et super premissis ab ulteriori impeticione quoad premissa totaliter dimittentes. Hec dico allego et propono conjunctim et divisim, juris beneficio michi semper salvo.

Quo namque articulo sic proposito et per nos admisso, liteque contestata ad eundem ac de calumpnia et veritate dicenda prestitis juramentis, assignatisque eidem domino Willelmo certis die et loco competentibus ad exhibendum et producendum coram nobis pro se quicquid voluerit super assecucione et retencione ecclesie memorate.

Quibus [Fo.35; p. 69] vero die et loco idem dominus Willelmus comparens judicialiter coram nobis, quamplura et diversa litteras et instrumenta auctentica exhibuit et produxit, quibus de consensu ipsius domini Willelmi dictis die et loco apertis et publicatis, renunciacionem eciam factam[32] per partem dicti domini Willelmi super ulteriori produccione et proposicione

---

[30] MS. *pretendens*
[31] MS. *visitante*
[32] Interlined.

facienda coram nobis in causa memorata; nos de consensu ipsius domini Willelmi personaliter coram nobis in judicio constituti, ad audiendum pronunciacionem nostram in et de premissis certos diem et locum eidem assignavimus coram nobis.

Quibus siquidem die et loco dicto domino Willelmo coram nobis personaliter comparente, producta et exhibita presentialiter coram nobis super assecucione et retencione ecclesie supradicte per nos et juris peritos nobis assidentes recenseri examinari et rimari fecimus diligenter. Et quia premissa cause cognicione hujusmodi invenimus dictum Willelmum articulum memoratum coram nobis ut premittitur propositum et contenta in eodem plene et sufficienter probasse, prefatum dominum Willelmum supradictam ecclesiam de Bounesse canonice rite et legitime fuisse et esse assecutum ac possedisse et tenuisse possidereque et tenere canonice et legitime per nostram sentenciam diffinitivam pronunciamus et declaramus in hiis scriptis, ipsumque dominum Willelmum rectorem de Bounesse predictum ab ulteriori impeticione quoad premissa totaliter dimittentes. In cujus rei testimonium atque fidem nos Gilbertus Karlii' episcopus antedictus sigillum nostrum fecimus hiis apponi. Datum [Rose, 20 May 1359].

328

LITTERA TESTIMONIALIS SUPER DIVORCIO MATRIMONII INTER JOHANNEM DE GAYTES- CALES ET ALICIAM FILIAM RICARDI DE WHYTEFELD DE KARLO'. Universis [as in 320 – salutem]. Noverit universitas vestra quod licet Willelmus de Stapelton et Alicia filia Ricardi de Whytefeld de Karlo' dudum matrimonium per verba mutuum consensum exprimencia contraxerint et illud matrimonium sic contractum solempnizari fecerint, carnali copula subsecuta; eadem tamen Alicia, matrimo- nio inter dictum Willelmum et ipsam contracto ut premittitur constante et nullatenus divorciato, matrimonium cum quodam Johanne de Gaytescales de Karlo' per verbum mutuum consensum exprimencia de facto, cum de jure non posset, contraxit et illud in facie ecclesie solempnizari procuravit, carnali copula inter eosdem Johannem et Aliciam subsecuta. Super quibus ipsos Johannem et Aliciam coram nobis ad certos dies et loca successive fecimus ad judicium evocari. Quibus quidem Johanne et Alicia diebus et locis sic eis successive ut premittitur assignatis legitime comparentibus coram nobis, servato processu legitimo in hac parte requisito, quia evidenter comperimus matrimonium inter ipsos Johannem et Aliciam [as in 320 – premissorum]. Datum [Rose, 8 July 1360].

350

[Fo.36ᵛ; p. 72] COMMISSIO AD RECIPIENDUM PURGACIONEM ROBERTI WEROR ET ISABELLE UXORIS WILLELMI DE HELTON UT PATET. G. etc. dilecto filio decano nostro Westmerl' salutem [*etc.*]. Ad admittendum et recipiendum purgacionem Roberti Weror' et Isabelle uxoris Willelmi de Helton, utriusque videlicet eorumdem cum octava manu bonorum virorum et mulierum conversacionum suarum noticiam obtinencium, super adulterio inter eosdem ut dicitur commisso, et in eventu quo poterint[33] in hac parte canonice se purgare, ad restituendum ipsos bone fame sue; alioquin ad citandum eos quod compareant coram nobis in capella manerii nostri de Rosa aliquo certo die tuo arbitrio statuendo, penitenciam condignam pro suis demeritis humiliter recepturi, tibi tenore presencium committimus vices nostras, proviso quod de omni eo quod feceris et inveneris in premissis nos citra festum sancte Katerine virginis proximo futurum distincte et aperte certifices per litteras tuas patentes harum seriem continentes. Datum [Rose, 13 Nov. 1360].

357

[Fo.37; p. 73] INDULGENCIA PRO FRATRIBUS DE PENRETH UT PATET. Universis sancte matris ecclesie filiis ad quorum noticiam presentes littere pervenerint G. etc. salutem in sinceris amplexibus salvatoris. Tenens impendere credimus obsequium deo gratum quociens mentes fidelium ad pie devocionis opera excitamus. Attendentes quod religiosi viri fratres ordinis sancti Augustini de Penreth nostre diocesis quoddam luminare in honore Nativitatis domini nostri Jesu Christi salvatoris nostri et beatissime Marie matris ejus in ecclesia sua conventuali de Penreth ad missam qua cantatur officium *Lux fulgebit* in festo Nativitatis ipsius Salvatoris nostri annis singulis accendendum noviter inchoarunt et continuare proponunt, ad quod diucius sustendandum et continuandum dicti religiosi nequaquam sufficiunt nisi eis in hac parte de fidelium elemosinis succuratur; nosque volentes ea que ad laudem et honorem ejusdem Salvatoris nostri et beatissime Marie matris ejus tendere dinoscuntur in quantum poterimus promovere, de ipsius Salvatoris nostri misericordia et genetricis sue ac beatorum apostolorum Petri et Pauli omniumque sanctorum meritis et intercessionibus confisi, omnibus parochianis nostris et aliis quorum diocesani hanc nostram indulgenciam ratam habuerint de peccatis suis vere contritis penitentibus et confessis qui causa devocionis ad ecclesiam conventualem predictam in festo Nativitatis ejusdem Salvatoris nostri accesserint [et] decantacioni predicte misse interfuerint, aut de bonis sibi a deo collatis ad sustentacionem luminaris predicti quicquam erogaverint vel in testamentis et ultimis voluntatibus suis legaverint et assignaverint, seu eciam inter vivos donaverint aliosve ad id induxerint, quadraginta dies de injuncta sibi penitencia deo propicio misericorditer relaxamus; indulgencias a venerabilibus patribus coepiscopis nostris catholicis graciam sedis apostolice et execucionem officii sui obtinentibus ad id rite concessas et imposterum concedendas ratas habentes pariter et acceptas. In cujus rei testimonium sigillum nostrum presentibus est appensum. Datum [Rose, 16 Dec. 1360].

361

[Fo.37ᵛ; p. 74] PRONUNCIACIO ET DECLARACIO SUPER CERTIS ARTICULIS ARCHIDIACONATUM KARLIOLI CONCERNENTIBUS UT PATET. In dei nomine amen. Nos Gilbertus permissione divina Karlii' episcopus ex frequenti querela venerabilis

---

[33] MS. *poterunt*

viri magistri Willelmi de Routhebury archidiaconus Karlii' recepimus conquerentis quod idem archidiaconus super visu et excercicio quamplurimum articulorum ad ipsum et archidiaconatum suum pertinencium per nos et ministros nostros aliquamdiu fuerat impeditus ut asseruit minus juste. Propterea nos volentes eidem archidiacono exhibere justicie complementum super hiis que ad ipsum et suum archdiaconatum pertineant et debeant pertinere, tam per testes juratos et examinatos quam alias informaciones inquiri fecimus diligenter, et inter cetera coram nobis compertum fore dinoscitur et detectum, videlicet quod ad dictum dominum archidiaconum et ejus archidiaconatum pertineat et pertinere solebat habere clericum in capitulis per officialem et decanos nostros ministros per totam nostram diocesim celebrandis ad assistendum eidem officiali et ministris nostris capitula hujusmodi celebrantibus in omnibus correccionibus inibi faciendis et ad contrarotulandum super correccionibus sic factis; item quod liceat eidem archidiacono subditos sue visitacioni per litteras suas ad subeundum visitacionem suam archidiaconalem convocare, et quod contra non comparentes sic vocatos procedere possit debite servato processu ecclesiasticas per censuras; quodque contra non solventes procuraciones sibi debitas racione sue visitacionis excercite impense et eorum beneficia procedere possit modo simili ut prefertur ecclesiasticas per censuras. Cum itaque articulos supradictos superius expressatos, informacione legitima et sufficienti prehabita ut prefertur, ad dictum dominum archidiaconum comperimus pertinuisse et pertinere debere, ad excercendum supradictos articulos omnes et singulos sub modo et forma quibus superius expressantur memoratum dominum archidiaconum admittendum fore et admitti debere judicialiter et in scriptis pronunciamus et eciam declaramus. Ipsum necnon dominum .. archidiaconum ab ulteriori impedimento et impeticione in et super premissis per nos vel ministros nostros decetero faciendis totaliter dimittimus per presentes, quibus sigillum nostrum apposuimus in testimonium premissorum. Datum [Rose, 4 May 1360].

378

[Fo.38ᵛ; p. 76] LITTERA TESTIMONIALIS SUPER DIMISSIONE WILLELMI WHYTEHEVED QUANTUM AD CONTRACTUM MATRIMONIALEM CUM GODYTHA FILIA NICHOLAI DE MOTHERBY UT IPSA ASSERUIT INITUM UT INFERIUS PATET. Universis [as in 357 — salvatoris]. Noverit universitas vestra quod cum Willelmus Whyteheved de Sourby fuisset coram nobis ex officio nostro per Godytham filiam Nicholai de Motherby de Sourby predicta promoto judicialiter impetitus quod idem Willelmus nuper matrimonium cum dicta [Godytha] per verba de presenti legitime contraxerat, carnali copula subsecuta, et nichilominus stante matrimonio hujusmodi et nullatenus divorciato, dictus Willelmus matrimonium cum Alicia relicta Johannis de Stokdale temere contraxit quam de facto tenet in uxorem; prefati Willelmus et Godytha coram nobis ad certos diem et locum eisdem in hac parte assignatos personaliter comparuerunt. Liteque ad eundem articulum per dictum Willelmum negative contestata, ac juramento de calumpnia et de veritate dicenda hinc inde prestito, productisque ex parte dicte Godythe tunc ibidem duobus testibus, videlicet Nicholao de Motherby et Alicia uxore Johannis Yholehorne de Sourby predicta, quibus receptis et in forma juris juratis et examinatis et eorum dictis in scriptis redactis ac de consensu dictorum

parcium publicatis, decreta dictis partibus copia attestacionum hujusmodi, dato
eciam termino ad dicendum in testes et eorum dicta. Quo quidem termino
adveniente, nichil dicto nec proposito in hac parte renunciacioneque ulteriori
productioni testium in hac parte per partes predictas facta, terminoque ad
proponendum omnia in facto consistencia et ad concludendum in dicta causa
dictis partibus assignato, ac demum in dicta causa concluso et ad audiendum
sentenciam diffinitivam assignato termino partibus supradictis. Nos Gilbertus
Karlii' episcopus supradictus, auditis et intellectis meritis dicte cause ac
deliberacione in hac parte habita pleniori, quia per dicta et deposiciones testium
predictorum invenimus dictam Godytham intencionem suam quoad contenta
in predicto articulo nullatenus probavisse set in hujusmodi probacione totaliter
defecisse, ipsum Willelmum ab ulteriori impeticione et inquietacione tam officii
nostri quam dicte Godythe quoad premissa dimittimus et absolvimus per
decretum. In cujus rei testimonium sigillum nostrum presentibus est appensum. Datum [Rose, 10 May 1361].

394

[Fo.40; p. 79] MEMORANDUM. Et memorandum quod dicto die Jovis, videlicet
secundo die Septembris anno etc. lxi°, prefati commissarii virtute commissionis
dicti venerabilis patris domini Karlii' episcopi ipsis ut premittitur directe, litteras
venerabilis patris domini Ebor' archiepiscopi mandata apostolica continentes
prout superius memoratur coram prelatis rectoribus et vicariis Karlii' diocesis in
domo capitulari ecclesie Karlii' juxta citacionem eis in hac parte factam
congregatis legi et publicari fecerunt, ac censuras in eisdem promulgatas
palam et publice intimari. Et ad satisfaciendum de expensis in litteris et
mandatis hujusmodi expressatis, videlicet de qualibet marca singulorum
beneficiorum civitatis et diocesis Karlii' tres quadrantes juxta taxam antiquam,
omnibus et singulis beneficia ecclesiastica infra dictam Karlii' diocesim
obtinentibus tam absentibus quam presentibus terminum triginta dierum
dictum diem Jovis proximo sequencium assignarunt, ita quod citra ultimum
diem dictorum triginta dierum de hujusmodi expensis sit integre satisfactum,
sub penis et censuris in litteris et mandatis hujusmodi plenius expressatis. Et ad
petendum colligendum et recipiendum hujusmodi expensa directa fuit commissio priori Karli' cujus tenor de verbo ad verbum inferius est insertus.

407

[Fo.41; p. 81] LICENCIA CONCESSA DOMINO ROBERTO DE BURGHAM CAPELLANO
TENENDI SCOLAS INFRA PAROCHIAM DE PENRETH. Universis ad quos presentes
littere pervenerint Gilbertus [*etc.*] salutem in omnium salvatore. Quia ad
utilitatem rei publice tendere novimus evidenter quod in locis diversis scole
pro informacione juvenum teneantur, noverit universitas vestra quod domino
Roberto de Burgham capellano, de cujus sciencia sumus plenius informati, ad
tenendum scolas in villa de Penreth nostre diocesis et ad informandum pueros et
juvenes super psalteriis Donato et cantu prout sua novit industria licenciam
tenore presencium concedimus specialem pro nostro beneplacito duraturam;

monentes et districcius inhibentes ne quis infra parochiam de Penreth predictam, in ecclesia videlicet ejusdem loci vel alibi, aliquas scolas preterquam
idem Robertus teneat absque nostra licencia speciali. Datum [Rose, 29 Oct.
1361].

412

[Fo.41ᵛ; p. 82] LITTERA MISSA DOMINO ARCHIEPISCOPO EBOR' RACIONE CUJUSDAM
SUBSIDII DOMINO PAPE CONCEDENDI[34] UT PATET. Reverende pater et domine, juxta
vestrarum litterarum missivarum et clausarum per magistrum [Robertum] de
Hakthorpp' nuper ante Natale nobis transmissarum ac ipsius Roberti credencie
per vos sibi commisse continenciam informati, supposuimus quod clerus nostre
diocesis in eventum absque ostensione commissionis vestre sub litteris patentibus effectualiter non pareret ut novistis, venerande pater, nec deberet. Nichilominus presente dicto magistro Roberto, in promocione negocii hujusmodi
quamplurima asserente, clerum nostre diocesis ad certum diem, videlicet
diem Lune in vigilia sancti Thome apostoli proximo tunc futura, apud Karlii'
ordinavimus convocare, quam autem vigiliam convocacioni illa occasione apud
Ebor' factam subsequi debere ut asseruit ad minus per quinque dies. Qui
siquidem Robertus nobis cercius verbis omissis superfluis expromisit quod ante
dictam vigiliam patentes litteras commissionis vestre nobis una cum hiis que in
convocacione cleri vestre diocesis Ebor' contigerit concedari paratas transmit-
teret in nostre diocesis convocacionem hujusmodi ostendendas. Quo vero die
convocacionis nostre diocesis ut premittitur facte vel ante, assertis et expromissis
per dictum Robertum ut premittitur expositis omnino frustrati, non absque
anxietate ex quo commissionem vestram non habuimus, cum ipso clero nostre
diocesis nobis tunc plurimum reluctante ac simplicitatem nobis quin verius
fatuitatem imponente tractavimus modo quo potuimus meliori. Demum tamen
sub infrascripta forma ipsum clerum obtinuimus concordari, quod ipse clerus
nostre diocesis in eventum quo de equali et racionabili proporcione oneris per[35]
provinciam Ebor' subeundi pro rata beneficiorum singulorum per vestras
patentes litteras cercioratus extiterit, quod extunc juxta modum et formam
videlicet novam taxam vel antiquam, pro eciam spiritualibus dumtaxat vel
spiritualibus et temporalibus, et ad eosdem terminos quos in subeundo
solucionis oneris hujusmodi faciendi, ipsi de diocesibus vestra Ebor' et
Dunelm' se teneri contribuendo agnoscerent; ipsi de diocese nostra Karlii' in
omnibus pro rata singulorum suorum beneficiorum tam quantitate quam
solucione faciendi in ea parte contribuere in eventum et non alio modo, super
quibus cum celeritate accomoda per litteras vestras nos et clerum dicte nostre
diocesis dignemini reddere cerciores, ut per hoc tam ipse clerus nostre diocesis
quam nos informati uberius deliberare poterimus et nos conformare super
execucioni conformi et provida premissorum. Ad ecclesie sue regimen et
munimen paternitatem vestram diucius conservet incolumem deitas increata.
Scriptum apud Rosam quarto die Januarii.

---

[34] MS. *concedendo*
[35] MS. *p[ro]*

429

[Fo.43; p. 85] CERTIFICATIO RESCRIPTI APPELLACIONIS CONTRA MAGISTRUM JOHAN-
NEM DE APPILBY UT PATET INFRA. Gilbertus [*etc.*] venerabili viro officiali curie
Ebor' obedienciam debitam cum honore. Mandatum vestrum decimo die
instantis mensis Februarii recepimus tenorem continens infrascriptum:
Reverendo in Christo patri et domino domino .. Gilberto dei gracia Karlii'
episcopo .. officialis curie Ebor' reverencias tanto patri debitas cum honore. Ex
parte Thome Olifant de Hilton', Alicia uxoris sue, Johannis Olifant, Emme
uxoris sue et Willelmi Olifant nobis extitit intimatum quod vos dominus
Gilbertus Karlii' episcopus absque processu legitimo precedente ipsos
Thomam Aliciam Johannem Emmam et Willelmum, cause cognicione que
requiritur in hoc casu pretermissa in omnibus et omissa, in sentenciam
excommunicacionis majoris propter violenciam manuum injectionem in quemdam Robertum de Appilby fratrem magistri Johannis de Appilby legum
doctoris a constitucione *Siquis suadente diabolo* latam et promulgatam incidisse
et ea occasione excommunicatos fuisse et esse reputastis pronunciastis et
declarastis, ac ipsos et eorum quemlibet fuisse et esse publicastis et publicari
fecistis per diocesim Karlii' in omnibus et singulis ecclesiis decanatus Westmerl', virtute cujusdam processus pretensi quem vos ut asseritur ad instigacio-
nem indebitam et injuriosam prosecucionem dicti magistri Johannis de
Appilby, ipsis Thoma Johanne Alicia Emma et Willelmo non legitime citatis
non vocatis nec debite premunitis absentibus et non per contumaciam fecistis
minus juste in ipsorum Thome Johannis Alicie Emme et Willelmi prejudicium
non modicum et gravamen. Unde ex parte dictorum Thome Johannis Alicie
Emme et Willelmi, senciencium se ex premissis gravibus et eorum alteri
indebite gravari, ab eisdem gravibus ad curiam Ebor' extitit ut asseritur legitime
appellatum. Quocirca vobis tenore presencium cum ea qua decet reverencia
inhibemus et per vos prefato magistro Johanni ac omnibus et singulis quibus jus
exigit inhiberi volumus et mandamus, ne pendente in dicta curia prefate
appellacionis causa quicquam ea occasione in dictis partis appellantis prejudicium attemptetis vel attemptent faciatis vel faciant quomodolibet attemptari,
quominus ipsa pars appellans liberam habeat appellacionis sue prosecucionem
prout fuerit justum. Citetis insuper seu citari faciatis peremptorie predictum
magistrum Johannem de Appilby partem ut premittitur appellatam quod
compareat coram nobis vel commissario nostro in majori ecclesia Ebor' die
Sabbati proximo post festum sancti Petri in Cathedra proximo futurum in[36]
[Fo.43ᵛ; p. 86] prefate appellacionis causa secundum ipsius cause qualitatem et
naturam et dicte curie consuetudinem processurum facturum ulterius et
recepturum quod justicia suadebit. Et vos agitacioni et defensioni dicte cause
ad dictos diem et locum intersitis si vestra videritis interesse; terminum vero
hujusmodi peremptorium, distancia locorum ac qualitate et natura negocii seu
cause hujusmodi debite consideratis, sic duximus moderandum. De diebus
recepcionis presencium inhibicionis et execucionis inde factarum modo et forma
earundem nos vel commissarium nostrum ad dictos diem et locum certificare

---

[36] MS. repeats *in* on verso.

curetis per vestras litteras patentes harum seriem continentes, scituri quod super porreccione presencium vobis in eventu facienda, latori earundem nuncio nostro in hac parte jurato plenam fidem volumus adhibere. Datum Ebor' quinto die mensis Februarii anno domini M° CCC^{mo} lxi°.

Cui quidem mandato parere volentes, dictum magistrum Johannem de Appilby inquiri fecimus diligentem, ipsum tamen eo quod inveniri non potuit, non citavimus nec eidem inhibuimus ista vice. In aliis tamen dicto mandato contentis paruimus et parebimus sicut decet. In cujus rei testimonium sigillum nostrum presentibus est appensum. Datum [Rose, 19 Feb. 1362].

439

[Fo.44^v; p. 88] LITTERA PRO ELENA FILIA RICARDI FILII ROBERTI DEL HALL. G. etc. dilecto filio nostro decano Westmerl' salutem [*etc.*]. Questa est nobis dilecta filia Elena filia Ricardi filii Roberti del Hall de Meborne Matillidis nostre diocesis quod cum ipsa sit ut dicit filia legitima et heres ipsius Ricardi, qui frater carnalis et heres cujusdam Stephani de Meborne quondam clerici de Banco domini nostri regis extiterat dum vivebat, ad ipsam jure hereditario descendere deberent omnia terre et tenementa de quibus idem Stephanus seisitus extitit tempore mortis sue; quidam tamen ipsius mulieris fame et comodo invidentes dictam Elenam nequaquam fuisse filiam legitimam et heredem predicti Ricardi nec ad ipsam descendere debere terre et tenementa de quibus dictus Stephanus, cujus heres ipsa est ut dicit, seisitus obiit asserunt publice predicando, unde dicta mulier a nobis cum instancia postulavit ut super hujusmodi suggestis inquirere ac super compertis in hac parte perhibere testimonium dignaremur. Nos igitur ipsius mulieris supplicacionibus inclinati, pium et meritorium reputantes testimonium veritati super hiis que revocantur in dubium perhibere, tibi mandamus quatinus cites seu citari facias sex vel quatuor homines fidedignos decanatus tui eandem mulierem in gradu consanguinitatis vel affinitatis nullatenus attingentes quod compareant coram nobis in capella manerii nostri de Rosa die Lune proximo post dominicam in Passione domini futuram, veritatem super suggestis hujusmodi deposituri [et] facturi ulterius quod justum fuerit in hac parte. Et qualiter presens mandatum nostrum fueris executus, nos ad dictos diem et locum distincte et aperte certifices per litteras tuas patentes harum seriem ac nomina propria et cognomina citatorum hujusmodi continentes. Datum [Rose, 18 Mar. 1362].

478

[Fo.48^v; p. 96] COMMISSIO AD ADMITTENDUM PROBACIONES TESTAMENTORUM PRO DECANATU KARL'. G. etc. dilecto filio domino Thome rectori ecclesie de Beaumont nostre diocesis salutem [*etc.*]. De tuis fidelitate et industria circumspecta plenius confidentes, ad admittendum et recipiendum insinuaciones et probaciones testamentorum quorumcumque subditorum nostrorum infra decanatum Karli' decedencium, et ad committendum administracionem bonorum sic decedencium executoribus in testamentis hujusmodi decedencium nominatis[37] si eam in eventum admittere voluerint juxta formam constitucionis legati edite in hoc casu. In cujus rei [*etc.*]. Datum [Rose, 29 July 1362].

487

[Fo.49ᵛ; p. 98] ELECCIO PRIORISSE DE ERMYTHWAYT. In dei nomine amen. Vacante nuper prioratu de Ermythwayt' Karlii' diocesis per mortem domine Isabelle ultime priorisse dicti prioratus, nos Cecilia Dryng' suppriorissa ac cetere moniales dicti loci volentes eidem prioratui de priorissa futura providere, in domo capitulari dicti loci die Jovis proximo post festum sancti Bartholomei ultimo preterito anno domini Millesimo CCCᵐᵒ lxiiᵒ conveniebamus, habito-que tractatu inter nos et dictas moniales de futura priorissa providenda, demum prehabito scrutinio consenciebamus unanimiter, domina Katerina de Lancastre dicte domus commoniali excepta, in dictam dominam Katerinam [Fo.50; p. 99] de Lancastre et ipsam eligimus in futuram priorissam domus supradicti. Et hoc significamus venerabili in Christo patri et domino domino Gilberto dei gracia Karlii' episcopo et aliis quorum interest in hac parte per presentes sigillo communi domus nostre predicte signatas. Datum in domo nostra capitulari die et anno domini supradicti.

CONFIRMACIO DICTE ELECCIONIS AC PREFECCIO DOMINE KATERINE DE LANCASTRE IN PRIORISSAM DICTI PRIORATUS UT PATET. Et memorandum quod secundo die Septembris, videlicet die Veneris proximo post festum Decollacionis sancti Johannis Baptiste, anno etc. lxii presentata fuit dicto venerabili patri in capella manerii sui de Rosa prefata eleccio, quam dictus pater examinavit, defectus in eadem existentes graciose suplens, et dictam dominam Katerinam ut premittitur sic electam prefecit in priorissam dicte domus, committendo sibi curam et administracionem in spiritualibus et temporalibus dicti loci, que sic prefacta obedienciam prestitit dicto patri,

ARCHIDIACONO KARLI' PRO INSTALLACIONE EJUSDEM DOMINE KATERINE. Et memor-andum quod dictis secundo die Septembris et anno domini supradictis scripta fuit archidiacono Karli' ad assignandum eidem domine Katerine stallum in choro et locum in capitulo dicti prioratus etc.

518

[Fo.53; p. 105] PROCURACIO PRO DOMINO AD PRESENTANDUM ET NOTIFICANDUM LITTERAS PROVISIONIS SUE AD DICTUM EPISCOPATUM AC ALIAS LITTERAS APOSTO-LICAS ETC. UT INFRA. In dei nomine amen. Anno a nativitate ejusdem secundum cursum et computacionem ecclesie Angl' Millesimo CCCᵐᵒ quinquagesimo tercio, indiccione sexta, pontificatus sanctissimi in Christo patris et domini nostri domini Innocencii divina providencia pape sexti anno primo, mensis Julii die decima octava, in mei notarii publici infrascripti et testium subscriptorum presencia, constitutus personaliter reverendus in Christo pater dominus Gilbertus dei gracia Karlii' .. episcopus, nuper tempore promocionis sue ad episcopatum Karlii' predictum ut asseruit canonicus

---

[37] Followed by *juxta formam*, cancelled.

ecclesie Ebor' et prebendarius prebende de Osbaldeswyk' in eadem sicuti adhuc est auctoritate cujusdam gracie specialis sanctissimi in Christo patris et domini nostri domini Innocencii divina providencia pape sexti supradicti de ipsis canonicatu et prebenda una cum episcopatu suo predicto eciam postquam munus consecracionis susceperit licite retinendis fructibusque redditibus et proventibus ac emolumentis eorundem usque ad certum tempus jam futurum percipiendis prout ante promocionem suam predictam percipere consuevit sibi concesse, sicuti in litteris apostolicis inde factis dicebatur plenius contineri, dilectos sibi in Christo venerabilem virum magistrum Simonem de Bekyngham dicte ecclesie Ebor' cancellarium, dominos Radulphum de Drayton, Robertum Swetemouth, Ricardum de Aslacby, Nicholaum de Bautre, presbiteros, Ricardum de Meaux, Johannem de Midelton', Johannem de Wyrkesop', Gerlacum dictum de Clave et Johannem de Piperharowe, clericos, conjunctim et divisim et quemlibet eorum insolidum ita quod non sit melior condicio occupantis set quod unus eorum inceperit aliis prosequi valeat et finire suos veros et legitimos procuratores fecit constituit et ordinavit, dans et concedens eisdem et eorum cuilibet potestatem specialem et mandatum generale et speciale nomine suo et ecclesie sue Karlii' predicte litteras provisionis sue ad episcopatum predictum et alias litteras apostolicas quascumque graciam seu justiciam continentes sibi concessas cujuscumque tenoris extiterint ecclesiarum cathedralium et collegiatarum prelatis et earum capitulis ac singulis personis capitulorum hujusmodi omnibusque quorum interest seu interesse poterit presentandi et notificandi, ipsasque in judicio et extra prosequendi ad omnem usum et effectum qui ex eisdem litteris sequi poterint seu poterit et haberi ac earum tenor exigit et requirit, nomineque suo et premissorum cujuslibet agendi articulandi defendendi excipiendi [et] replicandi, litem contestandi, juramentum de calumpnia et de veritate dicenda ac quodlibet aliud genus liciti sacramenti in animam suam prestandi ponendi [et] interrogandi, positionibus et interrogacionibus respondendi, crimina et defectus objiciendi et probandi et objectis respondendi, testes et instrumenta producendi et exhibendi et producta reprobandi, beneficium absolucionis et relaxacionis a quibusdam sentenciis excommunicacionis eciam majoris suspensionis et interdicti in ipsum et ecclesiam suam Karlii' a jure vel ab homine promulgatis seu promulgandis statusque sui et ecclesie sue predicte reformacionem ac in integrum restitucionis beneficium dampna eciam expensa et interesse petendi et recipiendi, decreta confessiones et sentencias audiendi provocandi et appellandi, provocaciones et appellaciones intimandi [et] notificandi, apostolos petendi et recipiendi, provocacionumque et appellacionum causas prosequendi, alium seu alios procuratorem seu procuratores loco suo et cujuslibet eorundem substituendi ac substitutum seu substitutos hujusmodi revocandi, procuratorisque officium reassumendi quociens et quando videbitur expedire, necnon omnia alia et singula faciendi expediendi et excercendi que in premissis et eorundem quolibet ac circa ea necessaria fuerint seu oportuna, eciam si mandatum exigant speciale. Pro eisdem vero procuratoribus suis et eorum quolibet ac substitutis vel substituendis ab ipsis et quolibet eorundem rem ratam haberi judicem sisti et indicatum solvi cum omnibus suis clausulis sub ypotheca et obligacione omnium bonorum suorum, idem dominus .. episcopus constituens michi notario publico infrascripto tanquam persone publice stipulanti vice et nomine omnium quorum interest promisit et exposuit cauciones. Acta fuerunt hec Ebor' in hospicio quod dictus venerabilis pater tunc infra clausum dicte ecclesie Ebor' habitavit sub anno indiccione pontificatu mense et die supradictis, presentibus ibidem discretis viris Johanne dicto Coke et Ricardo de Babelak' testibus ad premissa vocatis specialiter et rogatis.

Et ego Ricardus de Wysebech clericus Elien' diocesis publicus apostolica et imperiali auctoritate notarius premissa procuratorum constitucioni ac omnibus aliis et singulis suprascriptis dum sic ut premittitur agerentur et fierent una cum prenominatis testibus presens interfui, eaque sic fieri vidi et audivi scripsi et in hanc publicam formam redegi meoque signo solito signavi rogatus in testimonium premissorum.

519

COMMISSIO AD PETENDUM CAPELLAM EPISCOPALEM KARLEOLII' ETC. Noverint universi quod nos Gilbertus permissione divina Karleolii' .. episcopus ordinavimus et constituimus dilectum nobis in Christo magistrum Johannem de Welton clericum ad petendum et recipiendum nomine nostro de religiosis viris priore et conventu ecclesie nostre beate Marie Karl' capellam episcopalem nostre ecclesie antedicte ac omnia et singula ornamenta libros et vasa ac alia que ad dictam capellam nostram et execucionem officii pastoralis debeant pertinere, necnon registra omnia et singula predecessorum nostrorum acta rotulos et alia memoranda ad dicta registra pertinencia, ceteraque omnia et singula facienda et expedienda que in premissis et circa ea necessaria fuerint seu eciam oportuna. In cujus rei testimonium sigillum nostrum presentibus est appensum. Datum Ebor' duodecimo die mensis Julii anno domini Millesimo CCC^{mo} quinquagesimo tercio et nostre consecracionis primo.

520

LITTERA ATTORNATI AD PETENDUM ET RECIPIENDUM TEMPORALIA ET AD CONVOCANDUM TENENTES DOMINI ETC. Noverint universi quod nos Gilbertus etc. attornavimus et loco nostro posuimus dilectum nobis in Christo magistrum Johannem de Welton clericum ad petendum et recipiendum de escaetoribus comitatuum Cumbr' Westmerl' et Northumbr' temporalia nostra quecumque episcopatus predicti, necnon ad convocandum tenentes et subditos nostros quoscumque, curiasque et sessiones tenendas et faciendas, ac de hujusmodi tenentibus nostris recogniciones fidelitates redditus firmas et alia servicia quecumque necnon fructus decimas et proventus quoscumque tam de ecclesiis episcopatui nostro Karlii' et nobis assignatis et annexis quam alias de spiritualibus et temporalibus dicti episcopatus nostri eciam extra dictam diocesim nostram ubilibet provenientes et eosdem ad firmam dimittendos et tradendos ac alias de eisdem disponendos, prout ad utilitatem nostram videbitur expedire, ac omnia alia et singula facienda que in premissis fuerint oportuna, ratum habentes et habituri quicquid dictus Johannes fecerit in premissis vel aliquo premissorum. In cujus rei testimonium etc. Datum Ebor' die et anno domini supradictis.

521

[Fo.53; p. 105] LITTERA ATTORNATI AD PETENDUM ET CAPIENDUM SERVICIA ETC. A SUBDITIS. Pateat universis per presentes quod nos Gilbertus etc. attornavimus et loco nostro posuimus dilectum nostrum in Christo dilectum nobis in Christo magistrum Johannem de Welton clericum ad petendum exigendum et recipiendum a quibuscumque tenentibus et subditis nostris episcopatus nostri Karlii' predicti cujuscumque condicionis fuerint servicia fructus redditus et proventus quoscumque nobis debita et ad dictum episcopatum nostrum ubicumque pertinencia et pro eisdem distringendum, prout fuerit faciendum et fieri hactenus consuevit, ratum et gratum habituri quicquid idem Johannes ad utilitatem nostram fecerit in premissis. Datum Ebor' die loco et anno domini supradictis et nostre consecracionis primo.

525

[Fo.53ᵛ; p. 106] LITTERA DIRECTA PRIORI ET CONVENTUI ECCLESIE KARLEOL'. Carissimi, pridie cum vestris litteris ut plurimum credencie frater Thomas de Appelby vester concanonicus et nuncius ad nostram presenciam destinastis, cui exposita nobis sua credencia congruum responsum non tam racionabiliter quam benigne dedimus ad singula ut decebat; subsequenter tamen dictus Thomas latenter et subdole nobis inconsultis ad auditorem capituli Ebor' ecclesie se conferens, causam super assecucione cujusdam mortuarii de predecessore nostro immediato vobis ut asseruit debiti molitus est introducere, et super hoc litteras monitorias et citatorias nomine vestro vicario ecclesie de Masham jurisdiccionis immediate ipsius capituli directas sub sigillo dicti capituli sibi concedi obtinuit et liberari. Que siquidem littere non tam injuriose [vobis?] fore noscuntur set eciam ecclesie Karl', cujus esse deberetis proni et seduli defensores, ac nobis et jurisdiccioni ordinario necnon domino nostro archiepiscopo Ebor' loci metropolitano plurimum prejudicales, nam sedibus Ebor' et Karl' ecclesiarum plenis dictum capitulum in causis hujusmodi se nullatenus intromittet. Maximam insuper injuriam prelato vestro nuper defuncto et nobis ipsius successori inferre intuimur dum de bonis sic defuncti defensore ex testamento et ab intestato notorie carentibus legitimo presumpcione improvida contenditis disceptare. Etenim si nos per quam tepidos et remissos taliter pungere et excitare decreveritis, opus est ut evigilati contra sic adversantes nobis ipsis vice versa prospicere studeamus. Ceterum quia jam sumus certi per experienciam operis quod nuncius vester predictus nobis verba pacifica varia et in dolo vestro nomine ut dixerat est locutus, hesitamus nihilominus an que gesta sunt ut premisimus de intencione vestra processerant et assensu. Vobis mandamus hortantes in domino quatinus receptis presentibus cum celeritate accomoda super premissis nos vestris litteris reddatis plenius cerciores. In sancte religionis mundicia diucius vos conservet dominus Jesus Christus. Scriptum Ebor' xxvi die Augusti.

526

ALIA LITTERA SUPER EADEM MATERIA EISDEM PRIORI ET CAPITULO. Salutem graciam et benedictionem. Litteris vestris quos nobis insistis ac serie singularis excessus fratris Thome de Appelby vestri concanonici sue vive vocis modulo coram nobis exposita recensitis, vos super hiis que pridie vobis scripsimus habemus ut convenit excusatos, sequentes quod scribitur 'ibi esse penam ubi noxia repperitur'. Ceterum quamquam tanti excessus et presertim in ecclesiam propriam et pastorem presumpta temeritas non tam correspondentem quam celerem penam exigeret et condignam. Quam precipitare nolentes a reformacione in ea parte actualiter jam facienda supersedere decrevimus, quousque vobiscum[38] sit confrater vester deliberacionem habuerimus personalem. Quem siquidem fratrem Thomam contritum et humiliatum ad veniam amplectentes vobis sub expectacione reformacionis faciende hujusmodi remittimus commendatum. In Christo diucius arrideat vobis salus. Scriptum Ebor' quarto die Septembris.

534

[Fo.54^v; p. 108] PRO QUESTU FABRICE CHORI ECCLESIE BEATE MARIE KARLIOL'. G. etc. dilectis filiis abbatibus prioribus rectoribus vicariis capellanis parochialibus et aliis in ecclesiis et capellis divina celebrantibus tam exemptis quam non exemptis per nostram diocesim constitutis salutem graciam et benediccionem. Cum dilecti in Christo filii prior et capitulum ecclesie nostre cathedralis beate Marie Karl' chorum dicte ecclesie nostre ad decorem domus domini opere construere inceperint sumptuoso, ad quod novimus fidelium subsidium oportunum[39] devocionem vestram studiose rogamus et in domino exhortamur, vobis omnibus et singulis nihilominus in remissione peccaminum et in virtute sancte obediencie mandamus firmiter injungentes quatinus quocienscumque Willelmus dictus Bell procurator seu nuncius per eosdem priorem et capitulum ad hoc specialiter deputatus cum hiis litteris nostris ad vos venerit[40] fidelium elemosinas ad tam sumptuosi operis fabricam petiturus, ipsum in hoc pio negocio omnibus aliis negociis quousque predictum ecclesie nostre negocium[41] expeditum fuerit interim cessantibus sine impedimento quolibet cum favore[42] benevolo admittatis, vestrosque parochianos et subditos dei et gloriose virginis Marie matris ejus in cujus honore dicta ecclesia est constructa ac nostri intuitu in ecclesiis vestris et capellis ac aliis locis ubi et quando expedire videritis per vos et alios inducatis ut ad prefati chori [fabricam][43] ejusdem ecclesie nostre larga conferant subsidia caritatis illaque fideliter colligi faciatis. Et quicquid collectum

---

[38] MS. repeats *cum*
[39] **599** (of 1357) here inserts *cum ad tanti operis consummacionem dictorum prioris et capituli proprie non suppetant facultates*
[40] **599**: *venerint seu aliquis eorum venerit*
[41] **599** here inserts *quod non sine causa racionabili omnibus aliis negociis volumus et petimus anteferri*
[42] **599** substitutes *spiritu*
[43] Supplied from **599**.

fuerit in hac parte, sine diminucione seu retencione quibuslibet eidem procuratori seu nuncio liberetis sub pena excommunicacionis majoris quam contravenientes poterunt non immerito formidare; inhibicione[44] nostra de non admittendo questores alios [Fo.55; p. 109] pridem vobis facta predicto Willelmo seu deputato per ipsum specialiter in hac parte nullatenus obsistente. Et nos de dei omnipotentis misericordia et prefate virginis gloriose ac beatorum apostolorum Petri et Pauli omniumque sanctorum meritis et intercessionibus confidentes, omnibus parochianis nostris et aliis quorum diocesani hanc nostram indulgenciam ratam habuerint de peccatis suis vere contritis penitentibus et confessis, qui juxta exhortacionem nostram predictam de bonis sibi a deo collatis ad fabricam ejusdem chori grata contulerint subsidia caritatis[45] vel manus suas porrexerint quomodolibet adjutrices, quadraginta dies de injuncta sibi penitencia deo propicio misericorditer relaxamus. In cujus rei testimonium sigillum nostrum presentibus est appensum per unum annum datam presencium proximo tantummodo duraturis. Datum apud manerium nostrum de Rosa xxi° die mensis Aprilis anno domini Millesimo CCC^{mo} quinquagesimo quarto, et nostre consecracionis primo.

543

[Fo.56; p. 111] COMMISSIO AD ABSOLVENDUM EXCOMMUNICATUM PRO SANGUINIS EFFUSIONE INFRA CIMITERIUM. G. suppriori ecclesie nostre Karlii' salutem [*etc*]. Quia Willelmus de Hakeneshowe a sentencia excommunicacionis majoris contracta propter violacionem libertatis ecclesiastice sanguinisque effusionem infra cimiterium ecclesie nostre Karlii' involutus extiterat, injuncta sibi pro excessu hujusmodi penitencia salutari, videlicet quod idem Willelmus hac instanti die dominica et eciam die dominica sequenti discalciatus distinctus et absque[46] capucio more penitentis processionem in dicta ecclesia nostra faciendam precedat, unum cereum saltim mediatatis unius libre cere in manu sua gestans dictis diebus dominicis successive, absolvimus in forma juris; vobis mandamus quatinus ipsum Willelmum ad hujusmodi penitenciam diebus dominicis supradictis evocetis, et ipsum Willelmum sic absolutum fuisse et esse publice et solempniter nuncietis et per alios faciatis nunciari. Et nos de omni eo quod feceritis in premissis post lapsum dictorum dierum certificetis etc. Datum etc.

555

[Fo.58; p. 115] MONICIO CONTRA CHRISTOFORUM DE LANCASTRE QUOD ADHEREAT UXORI SUE. G. etc. dilecto filio decano nostro Westmerl' salutem [*etc.*]. Licet nuper Christoforum de Lancastre coram nobis in capella manerii nostri de Rosa presencialiter constitutum quod Johanne uxori sue legitime adhereret ac ipsam

---

[44] **300** (of 1360) omits from here to *obsistente*.
[45] **300** here inserts *seu ad id alios induxerint*
[46] Interlined over *sine* (cancelled).

in thoro et in mensa juxta legem conjugii pertractaret,[47] idem tamen Christoforus spretis monicionibus hujusmodi ex causis frivolis et confictis a dicta Johanna uxore sua sine causa racionabili temere se divertit, eidem adherere conjugio maritali ut deberet penitus recusando, in anime sue periculum exemplumque pessimum aliorum. Quocirca tibi in virtute obediencie mandamus firmiter injungentes quatinus dictum Christoforum iterato moneas vice nostra quod infra duodecim dierum spacium a tempore monicionis hujusmodi eidem Johanne uxori sue legitime adhereat, ipsamque maritali affeccione pertractet in thoro et in mensa juxta legem conjugii ut tenetur, sub pena excommunicacionis majoris quam in personam suam lapso termino hujusmodi si monitis tuis quin verius nostris non paruerit cum effectu ipsius culpa mora et offensa precedentibus et id merito exigentibus ferimus in hiis scriptis; quam eciam lapso termino hujusmodi si ejus protervitas exigerit contra personam suam per te mandamus et volumus diebus et locis quibus magis expedire videbitur solempniter publicari, nisi causam racionabilem habuerit quare ipsum ad id compellere minime debeamus, ad quam ostendendam proponendam allegandam et prout juris fuerit probandam cites ipsum peremptorio quod compareat coram nobis vel commissariis nostris pluribus aut uno in capella manerii nostri de Rosa proximo die juridico post festum sancte Scolastice virginis proximo futurum causam hujusmodi ostensurus propositurus allegaturus et probaturus ulteriusque facturus et recepturus quod justum fuerit in hoc casu. Et ad premissa omnia et singula facienda tibi tenore presencium committimus vices nostras, certificans nos citra dictum festum de omni eo quod feceris et inveneris in premissis ac qualiter idem Christoforus monitis hujusmodi curaverit obedire per litteras tuas patentes harum seriem continentes. Datum [Rose, 20 Jan. 1355].

572

[Fo.59ᵛ; p. 118] LICENCIA CONCESSA WILLELMO DE BOLTON UT MATRIMONIUM INTER IPSUM ET ELENAM FILIAM DOMINI ALLEXANDRI DE MOUBRAY POSSIT FACERE CELEBRARI, BANNIS PRIUS CORAM OCTO VEL SEX ETC. EDITIS INTER EOS. Noverint universi quod nos .. Gilbertus [*etc.*] consideratis quibusdam per Willelmum de Bolton parochianum nostrum coram nobis allegatis, concessimus eidem de nostra gracia speciali ut ipse matrimonium inter ipsum et Elenam filiam domini Allexandri de Moubray militis in quacumque ecclesia parochiali et per quemcumque capellanum quos infra nostram diocesim duxerit eligendos possit licite facere celebrari, bannis prius trina vice saltem coram octo vel sex viris diebus dominicis vel festivis per dictum Willelmum ad hoc electis editis inter eos. In cujus rei testimonium sigillum nostrum presentibus est appensum. Datum [Rose, 14 Nov. 1355].

---

[47] At least one word (e.g. *monuerimus*) is missing from the preceding clause.

582

[Fo.60; p. 119] LITTERA COMMINATORIA CONTRA DETENTORES BONORUM PONTI DE EDEN LEGATORUM ET DONATORUM. G. permissione divina etc. dilectis filiis decanis nostris rectoribus vicariis ac capellanis parochialibus per nostram diocesim ubilibet constitutis salutem [*etc.*]. Quia diversa bona et pecuniarum summe fabrice pontis de Eden inter civitatem nostram Karlii' et Staynewygges nostre diocesis diruti et prostrati legata sunt ut recepimus et donata, que nonnulli sue salutis immemores detinent occupant et concelant in animarum suarum[48] periculum, civitatis nostre Karl' civium incolarum ac villarum conjacencium et aliorum Christi fidelium jacturam impedimentum periculum non modicum et gravamen; quocirca vobis et vestrum cuilibet in virtute sancte obediencie mandamus firmiter injungentes quatinus omnes et singulos hujusmodi bonorum et pecuniarum summarum detentores occupatores et concelatores moneatis et quilibet vestrum moneat qui per dominum Henricum Martyn rectorem ecclesie de Stapilton' latorem presencium, quem bonorum hujusmodi et pecuniarum summarum sic ut premittitur legatarum ac eciam donatarum deputavimus receptorem, securitate ab eodem sufficienti[49] recepta quod fidele de sic collectis et perceptis reddet raciocinium cum exactum fuerit in eventum, fueritis seu aliquis vestrum fuerit congrue requisitus quod de hujusmodi bonis et pecuniarum summis infra quindecim dies a tempore monicionis vestre seu alicujus vestrum eis facte continue numerandas prefato domino Henrico satisfaciant integraliter ut tenentur, sub excommunicacionis majoris [sentencia] quam in omnes et singulos monicionibus vestris in hac parte non parentes lapso termino hujusmodi, servato processu legitimo in hoc casu requisito, mandamus et volumus adhibita solempnitate qua decet solempniter publicari; inquirentes nichilominus et quilibet vestrum inquirens de nominibus hujusmodi bona et percuniarum summas detencium occupancium et concelancium de quibus cum vobis seu alicui vestrum constiterit nobis constare faciatis et quilibet vestrum faciat de eisdem. Datum [Rose, 12 May 1356].

587

[Fo.60ᵛ; p. 120] PROCLAMACIO SI QUIS VOLUERIT OPPONERE SE CONTRA PURGACIONEM RICARDI DE RAGARTH. Gilbertus [*etc.*] dilectis decano nostro Karli' et presbiteris parochialibus beate Marie et sancti Cudberti Karlii' salutem [*etc.*]. Ex parte Ricardi de Ragarth clerici in foro seculari coram domino Thoma de Seton et sociis suis justiciariis domini nostri regis apud Karlm' assignatis super eo quod idem Ricardus depredavit unum bovettum precii quattuor solidorum sterlingorum de Ricardo Doste de Midilscugh apud Midilscugh die Mercurii proximo ante festum sancti Martini anno regni regis Edwardi tercii post conquestum xxviiᵒ defamati nostreque carcerali custodie juxta consuetudinem ecclesie Angl' mancipati nobis est humiliter supplicatum, quod cum ipso a dicto crimine ut asserit sit immunis et de ipso coram nobis cupiat canonice se

---

[48] MS. repeats *suarum*
[49] MS. *sufficiente*

purgare, purgacionem suam hujusmodi admittere et sibi justiciam exhibere juxta qualitatem negocii dignaremur; de cujus vita conversacione et moribus ac qualis nominis et opinionis in suis partibus extitit et existit et an super dicto crimine culpabilis existeret inquiri fecimus diligenter. Quocirca nos premissorum qualitatem considerantes ac volentes omnibus justiciam exhibere ut tenemur, vobis et cuilibet vestrum mandamus firmiter injungentes quatinus tam in ecclesiis beate Marie et sancti Cudberti predictis de Dalston ac foro Karli' tam aliis locis de[50] quibus magis videritis expedire proclametis et eciam publicetis, denunciando solempniter quod si quis vel qui quicquam juste proponere voluerit vel voluerint quominus ad admissionem purgacionis predicte procedere debeamus die Sabbati in vigilia Pentecostes proximo futura in ecclesia parochiali de Dalston coram nobis vel commissariis nostris pluribus aut uno compareat vel compareant canonicum quod si habuerint vel habuerit proposituri et cum plenitudine justicie audietur et eciam audientur juxta canonicas sanctiones. Et nos seu dictos commissarios nostros plures aut unum super presentis execucione mandati ac omni eo quod feceritis et inveneritis in premissis dictis die et loco tempestive per vestras litteras[51] patentes et clausas harum seriem continentes reddatis et reddat quilibet vestrum plenarie cerciores. Datum [Rose, 15 May 1356].

604

[Fo.62ᵛ; p. 124] DIMISSIO CONCERNENS RECTOREM DE BOUNES. Noverint universi quod cum dominus Willelmus atte Hall rector ecclesie de Bounes nostre diocesis nuper rector ecclesie de Kirconnyle Glasgcuen' diocesis fuisset coram nobis Gilberto etc. Karlii' episcopo super eo quod idem dominus Willelmus priusquam in eadem ecclesia de Kirconnyle institutus fuerat canonice et inductus, fructus et proventus ejusdem ecclesie de Kirconnyle ut dicebatur usurpavit percepit et diucius occupavit contra canonicas sancciones judicialiter impetitus, idem dominus Willelmus ad certos diem et locum sibi in hac parte assignatos coram nobis personaliter comparens diffitebatur se fructus aliquos vel proventus qui ad dictam ecclesiam de Kirconnyle pertinebant usurpasse percepisse seu quomodolibet occupasse priusquam institutus et inductus canonice fuerat in eadem, super quo tam per testes quam per alias informaciones legitimas nos in hac parte sufficienter et plenius informavit. Et quia per testes et informaciones hujusmodi nobis constabat predictum dominum Willelmum immunem fuisse et esse in hac parte, ipsum ab ulteriori impeticione officii nostri quoad premissa dimisimus per presentes, quibus sigillum nostrum apposuimus in fidem et testimonium premissorum. Datum [Rose, 8 Aug. 1357].

---

[50] MS. *locis publicetis de*
[51] Interlined.

INDEX OF PERSONS AND PLACES

References in arabic numerals are to the numbered entries and their footnotes; those in Roman numerals to the Introduction. Asterisks with the Roman numerals indicate that there are also full texts of these entries in the Appendix. The word 'WILL' is given in capital letters when transcripts of these documents occur in the register.

Placenames are followed by examples of their original spellings, and next by their pre-1974 counties; the abbreviations YER, YNR and YWR denote the Yorkshire ridings. Compound placenames are shown under their names of substance.

It should be remembered that a second chronological sequence begins from entry number 518, and a third from number 605.

Haryngton, Isabel wife of Thomas de, 233
Hatfield, Haytefeld, John de, OCF of Appleby,
    554
  Thomas, bishop of Durham (1345–81),
    110–12, 296n., 490, 561
Haukesgarth, Thomes de, abbot of Whitby,
    54
Haulay (*or* Hanley), Robert, 388
  William, chaplain, 336
Hauville, John de, vicar of Bampton, 226
Hawan, Richard, OFM of Carlisle, 592
Hawksdale, Haukesdale, in Dalston, Cumb.,
    294, 389, 403
Haytefeld, *see* Hatfield
Haythwayt, Simon de, WILL of, 272
  William de, 272
Hayton, Cumb., church, 97
Hayton, Hugh de, vicar of Burgh by Sands,
    174n.
  John de, vicar of Brampton, 405
  Thomas de, clerk, 374
Helton, Isabel wife of William de, 350
  Robert de, rector of Dufton, xx n.73
  Thomas de, of Burton, 463
  Thomas son of Hugh de, clerk, 473
  M. Walter de, skilled in law, 79, 609–11
  Walter de, vicar of Addingham, 470
Henrey, John, of Broughton, priest, 195
Hepp', Robert de, chaplain, 226
Heriz, M. John de, advocate of York, 584,
    602
Hermythwayt, Lady Agnes de, 144
Heversham, Westm., church, 313
Hexham, Hextildesham, Northumb., Aug.
    priory, 119, 250–1, 515
  priors of (named), 119, 251
Hextildesham, John de, canon of Lanercost,
    622
  Thomas de, prior of Lanercost, 69, 70, 72, 100,
    102
Heynes, M. Henry de, *alias* Rosse, rector of
    Cliburn, xviii, 254, 373
Heyning', Richard del, of Bothel, 169
Highhead, Heyheved, in Dalston, Cumb.,
    castle, 246
Hill, John del, 216
  John del (of Doncaster?), 336
  William del, 336
Hiltoft', John de, 388
Hilton, in Appleby St. Michael, Westm., 429
Hirde, Thomas, and sons, of Hawksdale, 403
Hobsone, William, 91
Hogg, Hogge, Thomas, 17
  Thomas, vicar of Stanwix, 220n.
  Thomas, of Carlisle, questor, 230, 300, 358,
    413, 482
Hoghton, John de, of Arthuret, WILL of,
    401
Holborn, Midd., churchyard, 414
Holgill, John de, 549, 580

Holm Cultram, Holmcoltram, Cumb., Cist.
    abbey, 97, 103–4, 107, 168, 297, 509
  abbots of, 6, 388; *and see* Suthayk, Robert
  bequests to, 231, 233, 467, 481
  monks of, xxii, xxiii; *and see* Langrig', Richard;
    Midelham, Alan; Neuton, Henry
Holme, John de, deacon, 605, 609
Horncastle, Horncastre, Lincs., church, xiv,
    517
  manor, 520n.
Horncastre, John de, prior of Carlisle, bishop-
    elect, ix–xii, 1–5; as prior, xxiv, 261, 265,
    297, 509; *and see* Carlisle, prior of
Hothwayt', Agnes de, 398
  Gilbert de, 139, 251, 327, WILL of, 371
Hoton, Adam de, rector of Kirkby Thore, xviii
    n.55, 49, 479; WILL of, xxiii, 480
  Christine wife of Richard de, 55
  John brother of Adam de, 480
  Richard de, 55–6
  William de, 480
  William de, of Ambrose Holm, xxiv n.84
Hoton in Foresta, Thomas de, 231n., 390–1
Hoton Jon, William de, 390
Hoton Roef, Hoton, Richard de, rector of
    Greystoke, 196, 233, 614–18
Houlotsone, Adam, of Triermain, 117
  Thomas, of Triermain, will of, 118
Hoveden, Hugh de, canon of Shap, vicar of
    Warcop, 279
Howgill (castle), Holgill, in Milburn, Westm.,
    150, 293
Hubrightby, John de, 482
  Margaret de, 482
Huetson, Ellen daughter of William, of
    Blennerhasset, will of, 506
Hull, Robert de, questor, 556
Hund, Henry, vicar of Dalston, 134
Hunter, Adam, 434
  John, 231
  Richard, 344
Hurne, John atte, *alias* Thornton, rector of
    mediety of Kirkbampton, 2, 3, 387
Hurworth, Thomas de, rector of Lowther, xxiii,
    507
Hutton in the Forest, Hoton, church, 97
  chantry in, xxi, 390–1
  rectors of, 231, 390–1
Hyneson, Adam, 280

Ingelby, Henry de, canon of York, 571
Inglewood Forest, Cumb., 231, 246n., 499, 594
Inne (*or* June?), Thomas, vicar of Crosthwaite,
    86, 195, 321n.
Innocent IV, pope (1243–54), 213
Innocent VI, pope (1352–62), 15, 195
  mandate of, *see* Visitations in Index of Subjects
  nuncios of, *see* Index of Subjects
  penitentiaries of, *see* Albornoz, Giles; Aptis,
    Francis

INDEX OF SUBJECTS

Many of the subjects occurring in wills are shown under the headings 'Agriculture', 'Burial', 'Food', 'Garments amd fabrics', 'Household Utensils' and 'Mortuary'.

Cross-references to persons and places are to those names in the preceding index.

Abbeys and priories, in Carlisle diocese, *see*
    Armathwaite; Carlisle; Holm Cultram;
    Lanercost; Shap; Wetheral
  exempt by papal grant, 168
  outside diocese, *see* Calder; Cockersand;
    Conishead; Dundrennan; Felley;
    Fountains; Furness; Guisborough;
    Hexham; Jedburgh; Kirkham; Kirklees;
    Lambley; Marrick; Monk Bretton;
    Rosedale; Selby; Sempringham; Warter;
    Watton; Whalley; Wilberfoss; York, St.
    Andrew's *and* St. Mary's
Absence of clergy licensed, xvii, xviii, 8, 10, 75,
    141, 278, 381, 383–4, 458, 559–60
  for 2 years, 94, 373
  for 3 years, 425
  payments for, 302
  to visit Curia, 62
  while in a suitable place, 141, 179, 258–9, 238,
    337, 372, 471
    for 3 years, 98
  while in service, 29, 67, 113, 124, 127, 166, 239,
    249
    for 2 years, 151, 164, 330, 370
    for 3 years, 302
  See also Non-residence; Study
Absolution, by nuncios' commission, 189,
    193
  See also Excommunication
Adultery, purgation for, 350*
Advowson, bought, 232*n.*
Age, of presentee, 42*
  old, of rector, 431
Agriculture:
  barley, 17, 280, 476, 481
  cattle, 17, 28, 88, 91, 144, 216, 272, 313, 399,
    403, 406, 410, 434, 410, 434, 445–6, 468,
    472, 474–5. 481, 486, 501–2, 504, 514
    stolen, 284–5, 587–8, 591
  crops, 502
  corn, 313, 481
    stored in church, 53
    See also Tithes
  grain, 502

horses, *see* Mortuary
oatmeal, 17, 88, 216, 504
oats, 272, 280, 403, 481
oxen, *see* cattle
pigs, 403
ploughs, 504
rye, 280, 481
sheep, 272, 313, 406, 410, 467–8, 472, 501
wagons, 216, 434, 504
wool, 17, 216, 231, 452, 472, 481, 501
Alien clergy, 431*n.*
Anchorites of Doncaster, 336
Apostate monk, 430
Apparitor, dean's, 247*
Appeals, *see* York, court of
Appeal by bishop, 301*
Appropriations of churches, xxii, 158, 517
  causes about, xix, 86, 291*, 509
  confirmed, 97, 103–4, 106–7, 122, 205, 222,
    234, 240, 250, 253, 276–7, 283*
  revised, 544–5
Archdeacon of Carlisle, xii, xiii, xvii, 14, 69, 102,
    247, 487
  called to convocations, 125, (167,) 296–7
    to parliaments, 155, (199, 311, 494,) 531,
    569
  in remotis, 220, 255
  inductions by, *passim*
  rights of, 316*, 361*
  visitations by, 120, 136, 159, 227
    procurations in, 93*, 177, 228
  See also Routhbury, William
Archives of bishop, 16, 185, 190, 194, 206
Arms, armour, 181, 265*, 452, 453
Arrest, escape from, 549
Ash Wednesday, 87*, 577
Attorneys of bishop, *see* Proctors
Audience of bishop, xix, xx
  citation to, 130, 350*, 509
  commissaries-general for, 77*
  suits, causes in, *see* Appropriations; Churches;
    Concubinage; Incontinence;
    Matrimonial Causes; Pensions
Auditors of bishop, 316*

Constitutions:
  Cum ex eo, see Study
  Siquis suadente diabolo, 429*
  Super cathedram, 568
  legatine, 17, 84*
Convocations, councils, of York province:
  archbishop's mandates for, 125*, 167, 296
    bishop's certificates to, 167, 297
    copied to his official, 296
  grants by, *see* Taxation
  proctors of bishop in, xv, xvi, 584, 602
  writs of king ordering, 167n., 296
  See also Clergy
Council of West March, 420
Court (secular?) of bishop, 600
Courts, *see* Gaol Delivery; King's Bench; Writs
Cross (crucifix?), 434
Curia, Roman, x, xi, 62, 429n.
  appeal to, 301
  licence to visit, 62
  suits at, 103, 195

Deans, accounts of, 316, 352
  appointments of, 11, 105
  in chapters, 361
  mandates to all, 32, 74, 120, 159, 227, 344, 582;
    and see Allerdale; Carlisle; Cumberland;
    Westmorland
  of York diocese, *see* Copeland; Kendal
Debts, listed, 388
  remitted, 336, 434
Deprivation of rector (?), 493n.
Dilapidations, *see* Churches
Dispensations for illegitimate birth, 21–2, 78,
    197, 202, 248, 257, 304, 377, 392, 564
Divorce, *see* Matrimonial Causes
Dogs in priory, 70

Elections, of bishops, ix, xi
  of prioress, 487*
  See also Priors
English, to be spoken, 90
Escheators, 520; *and see* Cumberland;
    Westmorland
Exchanges of benefices, xvii, xxii, 10n.
  abortive, 49n.
  by commission of another bishop, 111–12,
    262, 450, 561, 563
  by papal provision, 226n.
  in diocese, 133, 271, 303, 305
Exchequer, 200, 319, 601
  baron of, *see* Greystoke, Henry
  fine for queen's gold at, 388
  sheriff's account at, 598
Excommunication, absolution from, 90, 115*,
    116*, 163, 279, 543*
  appeal against, 429*, 436
  penalty for debt, 331
  published, 247*, 266, 284*, 285, 332, 348,
    428

signified to king, xix, 92, 146–7, 160, 310, 334,
    424
  writ ensuing not executed, 163
  threatened, 47*, 53*, 99, 252, 298, 344, 349,
    354, 582*
Exemplification of deeds, 103

Fabrics of buildings, *see* Churches; Quests
Falcon, 354
Familiar clerks, *see* Household
Farms of churches, 10, 94, 128, 164, 178, 236,
    442, 559, 560
Food:
  bread, 472
  flour, 17, 410, 468, 502
  malt, 472, 501
  meat, 216
  salt, 410
  See also Agriculture
French, texts in, 123, 287, 417–19, 422, 594, 596,
    598
Friars, acting like questors, 201
  admitted as penitentiaries, 574–5
    as preachers, 554, 568, 574, 592
  licensed to serve chapel, 329
  Austin, *see* Penrith; Thornton, Thomas
  Carmelite, *see* Appleby; Doncaster
  Minor, *see* Carlisle; Doncaster
  Preachers, *see* Carlisle; Doncaster
Funerals, *see* Burial

Gaol delivery, *see* Appleby; Carlisle
Garments and fabrics:
  cloth, 233, 406
    linen, 486
  furs, 514
  gowns, 336
    of livery, 434, 455, 501
  shoes, 233, 468
  tabards, 181, 467, 501–2
  tunics, 216, 467
Graduates:
  doctor of canon law, *see* Rodolphi, Luke
  doctor of civil law, *see* Northburgh, Michael
  doctor of laws, *see* Appelby, John Thomas
  doctor of theology, *see* Deyncourt, Robert
  master of theology, *see* Thornton, Thomas

Hermits, 446, 547, 605–6
Horses, 17, 28, 91, 139, 233, 313, 399, 501
  'Hakyney Dun', 472
  saddles, 434, 453, 455
  share of, 272
Household, familiar clerks, *see* Aslacby,
    Richard; Clave, Gerlac; Piperharowe,
    John; Ragenhill, William; Routhbury,
    William; Salkeld, Thomas; Shupton,
    John; Welton, John; Whiteby, Nicholas
  bishop's livery, 434
  purveyors for, 123, 287, 418–19